BRIDGES

TO

CONSENSUS

IN CONGREGATIONS

Margaret E. Anderson

ISBN: 1453793011
ISBN-13: 9781453793015
LCCN: 2011903309

ACKNOWLEDGEMENTS

First and foremost, my heartfelt thanks to the Rev. Paul Beedle for his excellent critique of the first draft of this book, and to Chris Rogers, the Rev. James Liberatore, Patricia Dwyer Kolodney, and Amy Sharp for their feedback on later drafts.

Thanks also to the clergy who graciously granted me interviews—in alphabetical order, the Reverends Becky Edmiston-Lange, Russell Elleven, Claudia Frost, David Keys, Phil Lloyd, Eric Posa, Matthew Tittle, and Robert Tucker.

Last but not least, thanks to Bill A., Alice, Bill N., Marshall, Brian, Chris, Amy, Grace, Ann and Bill S. for their encouragement and faith in me.

CONTENTS

TABLE OF SAMPLE DIALOGUES

PREFACE

For years, clients, students and friends have encouraged me to write a book about the bridge-building consensus and communication skills I teach. For years, every summer, I would begin a book, only to abandon the effort with the thought, *This won't quite do.* These false starts grew, in part, out of my reasons for becoming a trainer and consultant in the first place—my personal experience with skills training.

Decades ago, while in a different line of work, I read the negotiation classic *Getting to Yes* as soon as it hit the market. I knew immediately that it would become one of the dozen or so books that have most changed my outlook on life for the better, books I wish everyone would read. I felt relieved to know that I did not have to "play hardball" to succeed. On the contrary, the practices that had been scientifically proven to *work best* were compatible with my moral and ethical standards.

Some years later, I heard that Roger Fisher and William Ury, the authors of *Getting to Yes*, gave summer negotiation skills courses at Harvard University. Of course, I signed up for Fisher's basic course the very next summer. A couple of years later, I returned for advanced training from Bill Ury.

That first summer, after a very long week in which I did several mock negotiations per day and prepared for the next day's negotiations by night, I not only learned much more about how to negotiate, I learned the best way to learn—at least when it comes to a skill, like negotiation, as opposed to a body of information, like medieval history.

My earlier efforts to apply the principles from Fisher and Ury's book alone had worked for me—worked much better than my old wing-it approach. But after training that included plenty of hands-on practice sessions, followed by facilitated debriefing, those early book-based efforts seemed a bit clumsy and inefficient by comparison. It was as if I'd first tried to drive a car after reading up on the subject, then later taken a hands-on driving course that prepared me to pass the licensing test with flying colors.

Another advantage of hands-on training is pacing. Reading a book straight through can leave you feeling overwhelmed if you try to remember and practice the whole package. In contrast, hands-on training paces the learning experience. I was able to solidify my assimilation of a skill or two before moving on to the next one.

The entire experience sparked my interest in learning more about dealing with people. What makes us alike? What makes us different? What makes us tick? And how do these things affect the best ways to build bridges between us? After several more years of study, part-time teaching and real-life practice, I decided to begin sharing what I had learned full-time.

Though I dearly loved writing, my personal learning experiences inspired me to share by developing my own hands-on skills training courses. I wanted my clients not only to know consensus skills, but to master them. This perfectionism—both blessing and curse—led me to abandon many a summer book-writing project.

Eventually, and fortunately, the desire to share with as many people as possible, along with an epiphany about how to make my own book unique, won out over misplaced perfectionism. After all, not everyone can attend a training course. And even if I had never attended those Harvard courses, I would still be much better for having read *Getting to Yes* and its sequels, just as I am better for having read many other books, even though I have not taken classes in all of their subjects. Moreover, when I have read a book before taking a related course, I get exponentially more from the classes. This, I have come to realize, accounts for part of the power of my experience with the Harvard courses.

My epiphany on uniqueness came from the calling I felt to extend my services to faith communities and other non-profits. Once I began doing so, I saw through these clients' eyes how people who are trying to do good in this world can, with the right skills, do so with greater ease and efficiency, and with better, more satisfying results for all concerned. Applying better skills to congregational life can even enhance spirituality.

Thus I focused this book on applications of the skills to a particular environment—congregational life. I peppered the text with detailed examples of realistic conversations, "sample dialogues," featuring characters and situations that clergy, lay leaders, and members alike can identify with.

The result follows. I hope you enjoy reading and learning from it as much as I enjoyed writing it.

Margaret Anderson

PART I: CONCEPTS TO BUILD ON

CHAPTER 1
BRIDGES—WHAT, WHY, AND HOW

I think, at a child's birth, if a mother could ask a fairy godmother to endow it with the most useful gift, that gift should be curiosity.

- Eleanor Roosevelt

Everyone involved in congregational life—clergy, staff, lay leaders and other members—needs and wants things from others. They need information, co-operation, goods and services, money, respect, compassion, or perhaps just an open ear. Since *thinking people think differently from one another,* their needs and wants sometimes collide. What one person wants sometimes seems difficult or impossible for the other to give. Such *collisions signify the mental and emotional health of these people* in that they feel secure in expressing their thoughts.

Reactions to this healthy diversity, however, can leave something to be desired. We've all seen, for example, people trying to pull together a plan for an event, or a solution to a problem, from several different visions of what that event or solution should look like. We've also seen them adopt a luke-warm compromise that offends no one, but also fails to engage and excite anyone. We've seen one person hurt another's feelings, then one or both refuse to discuss the matter because they don't know how. And we've seen—often too late—people who repeatedly stifled their needs until, one not so fine day, they gave up, or even blew up.

The question is not *whether* congregants will try to get what they need from others. The question is not *whether* they will sometimes have difficulties with others' needs. The question is not *whether* they will try to change one another's minds. Rather, the question is *how* they will go about it.

Will they waste time trying to execute ill-conceived decisions? Will they tax their patience to the max? Will they burn bridges, and thus lose difficult but possibly valuable relationships? Or will they build bridges of consensus? *This book is about the how.* It presents concrete practices for building consensus.

Even in commercial environments, consensus skills motivate people better that the old "command and control" paradigm. Because faith communities and other non-profits depend heavily on volunteers, rather than paid workforces, consensus skills are even more important for these groups.

Neither Doormat nor Bulldozer nor Compromiser

Good-hearted, church-going people often assume that zealously advocating for their own needs requires taking advantage of others. They may feel that values such as compassion mean lying down like a doormat and sacrificing their needs in favor of others. All too often, these people burn out and drop out.

Others can't see past their needs to the effects of their speech and behavior on the rest of the congregation. Even one such person can create repeated strife, and often seems to live outside basic communal values, running over others like a bulldozer, crushing bridges as they go.

Neither the doormat nor the bulldozer gets her own needs met as well as she might have. Fortunately, we don't have to choose between these two ineffective ways of dealing with others.

Nor do we have to settle for lukewarm compromise. By stepping away from the scale that ranges from doormat to compromiser to bulldozer, and embracing a different paradigm, each of us can get *more* of our own needs met while building bridges, not burning them. We not only avoid the two extremes of that tired old scale, but also its ho-hum middle—compromise. We create breakthrough solutions that address the true interests of all concerned.

Skills and Values

The consensus skills in this book are compatible with spiritual values and high ethical standards. Indeed, when properly applied, these practices not only utilize such values, but also help us to develop them. Three in particular deserve comment—compassion, calmness and curiosity.

- I like to think of *compassion* as empathy plus caring. Using consensus skills makes it easier to deal compassionately with others because we learn that compassion need not mean compromise. On the contrary, we can gain more of what we need, while also doing better by other people, when we practice enlightened consensus skills.

- Knowing that you have effective consensus skills instills *calmness* and boosts your courage and confidence. Calmness, in turn, helps us practice the skills one thoughtful, manageable step at a time.

- Consensus skills also promote *curiosity*, for the better we understand others, the easier it is to address our own needs while also building bridges.

We build better bridges when compassion, calmness and curiosity underlie our efforts.

Getting the Most from This Book

I think of the skills I teach as a system. No doubt there are prodigies out there who can read this book in the space of one week, assimilate all the skills, then go out and use the entire system. For most of us, however, learning a system of skills works best if we take it a step at a time. Some readers may feel overwhelmed if they operate on the assumption that they will simply read it all then do it all.

Fortunately, while these skills work best as an integrated system, most of the skills can be used independently of the others and to good effect. You don't have to do everything at once in order to start reaping the benefits of easier, more satisfying and efficient dealings with others.

Some people may prefer to read a chapter, then take a break to reflect on and try out what they've learned before going on to the next chapter. I've even built in short activities to help you experience some of the concepts.

About "Try-This" Segments

Throughout this book, you will notice a number of short passages labeled, "Try This." Each of these segments of the text presents a few questions that are fun to answer and can help ease you into new ways of thinking about how you deal with others.

Try-This Segments also help with another common problem. You can't learn a skill set, such as driving a car, by simply reading about it. Sooner or later, you must get into the car and practice. Yet there is a natural human tendency to defer trying consensus skills until you want to discuss an important matter on which you and another disagree. But that's like making your first attempt to drive a car on a busy freeway. Working through the Try-This Segments is like getting ready to drive by shifting into gear.

There is no one correct solution to any of these questions. However, sample solutions are given in Appendix B.

About Sample Dialogues

In designing my training courses, I build in two types of practical application: classroom exercises and expert demonstrations. In a classroom exercise, I divide the group into pairs who assume opposite sides of a detailed hypothetical situation and practice full-out use of consensus skills by resolving the problem. These hypotheticals are carefully crafted to provide opportunities to use whichever skills we are currently studying. Challenges appropriate to the trainees' current skill level are balanced with opportunities for success and fun. Much like practicing steering and braking in an empty parking lot, hypothetical situations offer the safest way to practice.

Often, these exercises work so well with both partners using the skills that trainees suspect it's too good to be true. They wonder, *How will the skills work when I'm the only one using them?* Thus, my *second* form of practical application—expert demonstration—is designed to show them that consensus skills can work for an individual even when the other party either doesn't know or doesn't use them. In this second form of classroom application, I perform an improvisational role-play demonstration with an actor who either hasn't studied the skills or is instructed not to use them. For the trainees, watching a demonstration is rather like riding along in the passenger seat while the instructor drives and explains what he's doing and why.

No book can replace the first form of practical application. A book can't partner you in an exercise or debrief and coach you afterward as I do with my trainees and clients. However, I have approximated the *second* form of practical application with the sample dialogues in this book. These dialogues simulate the experience of watching an expert role-play demonstration.

The fact that I don't script my classroom demonstrations lends credibility for the trainees observing them. I aimed to capture this unscripted quality when writing the sample dialogues in this book. To begin a dialogue, I placed myself in the shoes of the lead character and began with a skill-based opening statement he might make. I followed with a probable response from the second character, assuming she does not know the skills in question. Back in the shoes of the lead character, I wrote a skill-based reply to the second character's statement, and so on.

Rather than directing the dialogue toward a particular end, I allowed the dialogue to lead the way. Often, I was surprised at the resolution my characters reached. The main progress points and the end result evolved from the dialogue, not vice versa. This method of composition assured me that each dialogue was realistic. I hope that, likewise, it gives the dialogues greater credibility for the reader.

A Note on Character Gender

In writing the sample dialogues, I wished to distribute skill usage more or less evenly among characters of different genders. I also wished to illustrate each skill with a dialogue based on whichever fact scenario best lent itself to efficient illustration of that particular skill. As it turned out, one scenario, involving issues between a minister (Spencer) and a volunteer (Fran), seemed best for illustrating a great many of the skills. Since the skill user in that scenario was usually (though not always) the minister, who happened to be male, I balanced that by making the skill user in most of the remaining dialogues female. Elsewhere in the text, I endeavored to use gender-specific pronouns randomly. Any apparent imbalance between genders is unintentional.

The What-Ifs

Skill sets must be presented and learned one manageable step at a time. With mechanical skills, such as driving, we have a pretty good idea of what's ahead. When you first teach a teenager how to turn on the engine and put the car in gear, he's unlikely to ask, "But what if I'm driving on ice and I go into a skid?" He knows you'll cover that after he's got the basics.

Not so with interpersonal skills. In a typical training class, after learning the first skill or two, people begin to ask the what-if questions—"What if the other person just won't listen?" "What if I can't think fast enough?" and so on. Being with trainees in person, I can easily assure them that we will cover the question more fully in a future class and give them a small taste of the answer to tide them over.

While I can't interact directly with you as you read this book, I can make a suggestion. If, as you read about a skill, you find yourself wondering, *But what if...?* or if you read a dialogue and ask yourself, *Couldn't the character also have said...?* read on. You'll probably find the answer in the material that follows.

Likewise, it's impossible to write a realistic and effective dialogue using only the skill currently under discussion in a given section of the book. As you read about additional skills, you'll find it helpful to go back and reread the preceding dialogues with the newer skills in mind. A table of sample dialogues is provided for your convenience on page vii.

What You Will Learn

I have divided the book into five parts:

- **Part I: Concepts to Build On** focuses on some of the factors that underlie human differences and our reactions to those differences. Knowing these factors will help you understand and appreciate the skills presented in the rest of the book. You will learn why basic principles such as love and respect aren't always enough to build sustainable consensus, and how various well-meaning individuals can interpret such principles very differently. We'll explore the ways that diversity in temperament, culture and other factors underpins different interpretations of good principles and causes misjudgment and conflict. And you will learn the single most important concept for consensus success.

- **Part II: The Basic Skill Set—What to Talk About** presents alternatives to lukewarm compromise. You'll learn how to ask what I've dubbed "The Three Magic Questions" to discover and address the underlying interests that really drive our positions.

You'll learn skills for discussing those interests instead of arguing, and see them applied to sample dialogues based on realistic congregational situations. You'll also gain inspiration for crafting one of my "Solution Smorgasbords" of mutually satisfying consensus content.

- **Part III: The Basic Skill Set—How to Talk About It** offers a number of communication tools you can choose from to draw people together in a cooperative and collaborative frame of mind. Learn how to get people to listen to you, how to make progress by using questions rather than statements, the value of validation, how to deal with verbal attacks, and more.

- **Part IV: Introduction to Advanced Applications** touches on additional skills for dealing with difficult behavior such as bullying, dishonesty and triangulation. You'll learn what to do when your best efforts fail. In this section, you will also gain some of the most important techniques for creating consensus in larger groups.

- **Part V: Where It All Comes Together** demonstrates how well the skills work when both parties know and use them, and offers ideas for moving forward.

Skills for One or Many

Whether you're discussing a difference of opinion about programming for a fundraiser or dealing with a hostile person who feels unfairly treated, consensus skills can bridge the gap—easier, faster, better.

Those who plan and regulate our traffic systems *must* understand how to drive well, but the systems work best if *everyone* knows how to drive well. The same holds true for building the bridges of consensus. While skills are especially important for clergy and other leaders, the more congregation members who possess these skills, the better the group functions. The more skilled the congregants, the less they need leaders to facilitate difficult conversations. When they do choose to involve a facilitator, or even a mediator, the whole group works faster and better with a common set of skills and the common vocabulary to enlist those skills efficiently.

Thus, best conclusions come quickest and easiest if everyone in your group uses the consensus skills described in this book. But even if you are the only one who learns and uses them, your own interactions will be more effective, efficient and satisfying, not only in congregational life, but also at home, at work and in society at large. You can model the skills for others. If someone compliments you on the way you handled a challenging dialogue, take the opportunity to encourage him to learn the skills for himself.

There's something here for everyone. If you are an intuitively skilled leader who has enjoyed success in dealing with others, this book will help you more clearly identify the things that have worked for you so that you can duplicate your successes more often. If the very thought of discussing a difference of opinion makes you queasy, the book will start you off with a dose of confidence tonic.

Whether you are an intuitive leader, a shrinking violet, or somewhere in between, you have no doubt observed that the principles you share with others in your congregation aren't enough to build the best consensus. We all need something more. The next few chapters provide the underpinnings for that something more.

Key Points from Chapter 1

- Thinking people think differently from one another, so collisions between their wants and needs are normal and healthy
- Those in your congregation *will* try to get what they need from others. Sometimes they will resist others' demands on them. The only issue is *how* they go about it
- People do not have to choose between lying down like a doormat or running over others like a bulldozer. Nor do they have to settle for lukewarm compromise
- You can learn to get what you need from others while building bridges, not burning them
- Not only are consensus skills compatible with spiritual values, practicing them helps us develop traits such as compassion, calmness and curiosity

- To get the most from this book:
    - Try out the skills a little at a time; don't try to use them all at once
    - Use Try-This Segments to begin getting a feel for some of the concepts
    - Read and reread the sample dialogues to see how the skills look in use
- Practicing consensus skills will improve your interactions with others, whether or not the others know or use the skills

CHAPTER 2
PRINCIPLES PLUS

Whenever two good people argue about principles, both are always right.
- Marie von Ebner-Eschenbach

Imagine hiring a driving instructor for your teenage triplets—Winken, Blinken and Nod. She tells the kids that they should follow three principles:

- Drive carefully
- Drive defensively
- Stay alert

She has the students memorize these three principles and then quizzes them. They answer correctly, so she graduates them with passing grades.

Of course you agree that they should drive carefully, defensively and alertly, but that's not enough. They need to know how. So you send them back for more detailed instruction. When the kids return, they tell you they've now learned three instructions for changing lanes carefully: flip the turn indicator switch, check the adjacent lanes, then steer into the next lane.

You decide to see for yourself. You take the kids to a safe, quiet street, let Winken behind the wheel, and ask him to change lanes. He flips on the turn indicator. *So far so good.* He checks the inside rearview mirror, but not the wing mirrors, then moves over. *Not so good.* Now it's Blinken's turn. He turns on the indicator light, checks the two wing mirrors, but not the inside mirror, then moves over. *Uh oh.* Finally, you give Nod a chance. He turns on the indicator, looks back over his shoulder then changes lanes without checking any of the mirrors. *Ouch!*

Each of the triplets had a different interpretation of the instruction to "check the adjacent lanes." Each could legitimately claim he followed that instruction. Each could also claim the other two did not follow the first basic principle to "drive carefully." Each knows the basic principles and instructions, but none performed the task as well as he might have.

Why the Golden Rule Isn't Always Enough

Just as we all agree that we should drive carefully, defensively and alertly, we embrace basic principles of how to deal with one another. Many religious leaders, philosophers and sages have pronounced a Golden Rule of Love—we should treat others as we ourselves would like to be treated.

- Judaism teaches, "[L]ove your neighbor as yourself."[1]

- Jesus is described as honoring this teaching and illustrating it with the parable of The Good Samaritan, suggesting a broad view of who our neighbors are.[2]

- One of the teachings attributed to Muhammad is that a Muslim owes six duties to a Muslim, one of which is, "He should love for him what he loves for himself."[3]

- Buddha said, "A generous heart, kind speech, and a life of service and compassion are the things which renew humanity."

- The Hindu scriptures teach: "What is the value of eyes in which there is no kindness? Kindness is the real wealth."[4]

- A Unitarian Universalist affirmation, called the Williams Covenant, states: "Love is the doctrine of this church; the quest for truth is its sacrament; and service is its prayer."

You might say that the Golden Rule is the moral equivalent of "Drive carefully." Yet people, even people of the same faith, differ about what love looks like in various situations. They differ about how they themselves would like to be treated. Many of these differences pertain to how we speak to one another.

Take Charlie, the chair of a congregational committee on ministering to the homeless. He's a great organizer and works hard but frequently mispronounces words such as "indigent" and "philanthropy." He will soon attend an inter-denominational meeting where he is likely to use these terms in front of people from other congregations.

---

1 Lev. 19:18.

2 Luke 10:25-37.

3 Tirmidhi Hadith 24:1.

4 Cural.

One member of his committee, Abby, feels it's most loving to ignore the gaffs. Bert favors waiting until Charlie hasn't said "in-DYE-gent" for awhile, then working the word, properly pronounced, into his conversation. Darlene thinks it's more loving to gently call the error to Charlie's attention in a private moment. Ethan feels a private talk would be more embarrassing, making too big a deal of the mistake; he favors correcting Charlie in a matter-of-fact way the next time he mispronounces a word during a meeting. Nell wants to consult with one or two other members before deciding what, if anything, to do. If she talks about Charlie with third parties, or if they conclude that it would be better for Charlie's close friend, Hunter, to discuss pronunciation with him, Gary accuses Nell of "triangulation."

Why Second Tier Guidelines Aren't Enough

In addition to a Golden Rule, most congregations also have a second, more specific, tier of guidelines elaborating what loving behavior looks like. These may be as casual as a theme reiterated in a series of sermons or as formal as a written congregational covenant, handbook, statement of right relations, or other document. However, like the three-step lane changing instruction, these are general guidelines only. They, too, are subject to different interpretations.

Consider a sample covenant that reads as follows:

We build our church on a foundation of *love* and covenant with one another,

To *freely explore our values* and honor our diversity as a source of communal strength,

To *accept responsibility* for our individual acts and promote *justice* and peace,

To celebrate the joys of discovery, embracing the fullest measure of our humanity,

To communicate with *kindness* and *support*,

To serve with *compassion* and *commitment*,

To *openly share* our laughter and tears and,

To show *reverence* for *the divine* in all that it is.[5] [Emphasis added]

---

5 This covenant, from All Souls Church Unitarian Universalist, Battleboro, VT, is cited as a sample on the website of the Unitarian Universalist Association, http://www.uua.org.

Let's look at some questions that could arise when Charlie's committee members try to address specific situations using those sample guidelines:

- All the above questions about the "loving" way to respond to the committee chair's errors also apply to the "kind" way and the "compassionate" way.
- Suppose Darlene is so offended and upset by Ethan's blunt manner of correcting Charlie that she walks out of the meeting. Is she acting against Ethan's right to "freely explore (or even express) his values"? Is it OK for Darlene to keep her opinion to herself, rather than "freely exploring" it? What if Darlene walked out to prevent herself from blowing a gasket?
- Suppose Ethan upsets and hurts Charlie. Does "accepting responsibility" mean privately apologizing to Charlie? Apologizing to the whole committee? What if Ethan's action was one of several reasonable options in a situation with no clear "right" choice?
- Laurel accidentally breaks a window. Others usually pay for accidental damage they cause. But Laurel contributes an exceptional amount of volunteer time and money to the church. Is it more "just" to ask Laurel to pay for the window or to let it slide?
- Ethan insults Abby during a committee meeting, and Bert rushes in to defend her. Is Bert "supportive" or patronizing?
- Peggy asks to bow out of a task she agreed to perform for the committee. What, if any, reasons justify breaking her "commitment"? Only major illness, financial difficulty, or family emergency? What if the task prevents her from getting as much exercise as she should have? What if every committee meeting prevents her from getting a full night's sleep?

Similar questions could be raised about terms such as "openly sharing" and showing "reverence for the divine" when different individuals try to apply them to specific situations. Even in a congregation that adopted this exemplary covenant (or any other set of principles), members would differ on how it should play out in practice. Like the teenage triplets, each member of Charlie's committee might know and accept the principle of love and the seven guidelines in the covenant, but each could accuse others of breaking them when their interpretations differ.

When Two Worthy Guidelines Conflict

The questions above arose when people applied different interpretations to one and the same principle, "support," for example. Other questions stem from apparent conflicts between two worthy principles. In addition to love, for example, many religions espouse principles of fairness or justice. When Laurel, a major contributor and volunteer, broke a classroom window, and minimally involved Mike backed over a church sign, how would we balance the principle of love with the principle of justice in determining who pays for what? What if Laurel broke the window trying to grab a child who was running with a pair of scissors in hand, while Mike just made an ordinary mistake? Mike might say justice requires a set rule apply to all: "You break it, you buy it." Laurel might say love requires factoring in all her contributions and/or the fact that she broke the window trying to prevent a worse accident. And both of them make plausible points.

Like "Drive carefully" or even "Check the adjacent lanes," *neither principles nor general guidelines suffice. They tell people what, but not how.* Hands-on driving skills make the broad, general principle, "Drive carefully," meaningful. Beginning a child's instruction with principles, like "Drive carefully," provides a grounding foundation for her to build the skills to control the car and assimilate the rules of the road before we send her out in traffic. Once she acquires that knowledge and skill, a reminder to "Drive carefully" efficiently calls all of it to the forefront of her attention when she takes the wheel.

Likewise, covenants and statements of principles, such as love, can provide a framework and touchstones for the ideals to which we aspire. Ideals offer us hope and a sense of direction for spiritual growth. *The consensus skills in Parts II and III of this book can show you how to live those ideals in dealing with others.*

But have you ever wondered *why* things like love look so different to other people? Have you asked yourself why you just can't get through to certain folks? The next chapter will give you some answers, not only about those folks, but about yourself as well.

Key Points from Chapter 2

- In any given situation, two well-meaning people can disagree about how the Golden Rule should apply
- More specific guidelines, such as covenants and handbooks, may help, but even they do not eliminate such disagreements
- Principles and guidelines tell us what; consensus skills show us how

CHAPTER 3
THE LENSES OF LOVE

What people often mean by getting rid of conflict is getting rid of diversity, and it is of the utmost importance that these should not be considered the same.

- Mary Parker Follett

Before trying to drive a car, it helps to know some basics about how cars work. If someone plans to earn extra money by delivering used cars from one sales facility to another, he should know about differences between cars, such as: automatic transmissions versus manual transmissions; ABS brakes versus conventional brakes; and the way high- and low-profile vehicles, respectively, react under different driving conditions.

Since we use our consensus skills with many different people, it helps to know how different minds work.

Why do various well-meaning people, including clergy, see love, respect, compassion and fairness so differently when actually applied to a given situation? In the case of Charlie, our pronunciation-challenged committee chair, different committee members saw the loving, respectful, compassionate way of dealing with his errors through different lenses. Any of them, trying to do unto Charlie as they'd like Charlie to do unto them, might have offended him if he viewed the situation through a different type of lens. And other members might have judged the offender as unkind, as acting outside the group's principles or covenant, as not being "in right relationship," or the like.

Many factors can affect the lenses through which we see love and other worthy principles. A few of the more common factors are:

- Temperament or personality
- Culture, which can include, among other factors
    - Nationality
    - Regionality
    - Ancestral nationality

- o Generation
- o Religion
- o Family life
- o Type of schooling (public, private, home, large school, small school)
- o Types of employment (corporate, military, retail sales, self-employment, administrative, consulting, etc.)
- o Exposure to different types of literature and entertainment
- Gender[6]
- Individual package of life experience
- Learning style

By way of example, I will briefly introduce a few of these factors which my students and clients find most interesting and helpful. As you'll see, sometimes one factor reinforces another. At other times, one factor moderates another.

Temperamental Lenses

Temperament or personality shapes our perceptions from early childhood, probably even from birth.[7] For example, *some temperaments resonate to structure, rules and regulations*. This type might be the most inclined to feel embarrassed or irritated by Charlie's mistakes and to try to correct them in one way or another. *Other temperaments are more free-spirited and pragmatic. So what if Charlie says, "in-DYE-gent"?* they think. *We all know what he means, and we get our job done.*

Some temperaments are grounded in the here and now. What harm does it do for Charlie to mispronounce things here among those who know and respect him? Others think more abstractly, projecting possible future consequences of current choices. *If Charlie doesn't learn proper pronunciation, he might say "in-DYE-gent" at the interdenominational meeting. People might not realize how smart he is. They could discount his suggestions or even judge our entire congregation poorly.*

6 As explained more fully later in this chapter, gender is, at least in part, a subset of culture.

7 Experts have developed a number of temperament tests and typing systems. The newest and most detailed of these may work best for professionals counseling others about career choices, for example. However for a general understanding of temperament diversity, I recommend: David Kiersey, *Please Understand Me II* (Prometheus Nemesis Book Co., 1998).

Some people are natural diplomats. The morale of everyone in the group is all-important to them. Being an intuitive peacemaker, a committee member with this temperament might seek to assuage the discomfort of members who object to Charlie's gaffs without embarrassing Charlie. She might speak to Charlie privately, first giving careful thought to how to phrase her suggestion in as upbeat a way as possible, and choosing her moment carefully.

Others tend to communicate spontaneously and directly and to use language literally. They believe that, if put in Charlie's shoes, they would feel more respected if someone corrected them directly, without "making a big deal out of it." When Charlie says "in-DYE-gent," a person with this temperament might immediately remark, "That's 'IN-di-jent.'"

Temperament drives differences in response time. Some people have a talent for thinking on their feet; they're good tacticians in an unexpected crisis. In a committee meeting, they tend to respond quickly to any issue or question that comes up. Others enjoy the mental staying power to excel at long-range planning and strategy. This can cause them to respond more slowly.

Similarly, introverts may take longer to respond, but not because they are shy. Whereas extroverts seek external stimulation to get their mental gears turning, introverts have a higher level of brain activity even when resting.[8] During a lively meeting, they may go on sensory overload. They do their best thinking quietly, on their own, often returning with excellent ideas at a follow-up meeting.

As with other temperament-driven differences in communication style, differences in response time can cause mutual aggravation. Worse, the fast talker may misjudge those who respond more slowly as disinterested, or even unintelligent. Conversely, those who gravitate to quiet reflection might think others' spur of the moment comments could not possibly be well thought out or worth listening to.

Groups benefit from including a variety of personality types. For example, they need both quick and reflective thinkers. They need sound, well-thought-out plans, and they also need people who can respond quickly when unpredictable circumstances upset those plans.

---

8 Laurie Helgoe, "Revenge of the Introvert," *Psychology Today* 43 no. 5 (2010): 54.

However, quick and reflective thinkers, respectively, often find it difficult to tolerate each other's styles. If quick thinkers dominate a committee, they may press the reflective member to answer before he has formulated important thoughts that would benefit the group. Even worse, they may assume silence means consent and fail to include a valuable opinion that would have completed a half-baked plan. On the other hand, in an emergency, the reflective thinker might not react quickly enough. He needs a quick thinker by his side.

These are only a few examples of diversity in outlook, and therefore, in communication style, stemming from temperament. We might think of them as lenses of different colors—the red, green, blue or yellow sunglasses people wear while driving the communication car.

Cultural Lenses

However, lenses differ in other ways as well. If temperament colors our lenses, cultural background deepens or lightens them. Let's say a naturally regulatory temperament colors a person's lenses reddish. If that person also grew up in a highly structured family or a school with strictly enforced rules, her lenses may be very deep red. She will be especially sensitive to Charlie's mistakes. The mispronunciation might speak so loud she can't hear what Charlie says; "in-DYE-gent" is just too distracting for her. But, if she was raised by free-spirited, pragmatic parents and teachers, her naturally red lenses may be lightened to pale pink. She takes a more moderate view of the mispronunciation. Ideally, she'd like Charlie to change, but it's not crucial to her.

We all have many cultural elements, such as nationality, generation, etc., deepening and lightening the natural colors of our lenses. They enhance or diminish all of our instinctive preferences—rules or spontaneity, focus on the present or projection into the future, and so on. We only have to compare a typical native of New York City to someone from Maine or the Deep South to hear culture affecting response time and overall pace of speech.

Cultural differences determine many speech patterns, such as more or less direct expressions. A person from one region, generation, family background, or the like might express requests as orders, "Give me the folder." Others find this too blunt, jarring or offensive. They would prefer, "May I have that folder?" or "Would you please hand me the folder?" Some might even say, "I'd like to have a look at that folder," without literally requesting another to hand it over. They intend to be polite or tactful, but more direct speakers may feel uncomfortable with such indirectness. To them, it may even seem manipulative or sneaky.

These and many other cultural differences in communication style are thoroughly discussed in Deborah Tannen's *That's Not What I Meant!: How Conversational Style Makes or Breaks Relationships.*[9] I recommend this book because, rather than presenting the reader with a huge laundry list of dos and don'ts specific to respective cultures, she presents a common denominator for most cultural differences in linguistic style. Tannen relates them to whether a given cultural element is more hierarchical or more egalitarian in orientation.

In the above example, the more direct speaker, one who expresses a request in the imperative, "Give me the folder," could be manifesting hierarchical aspects of his culture. The one who suggests, "I'd like to have a look at that folder," manifests egalitarian norms.

Gender Lenses

Dr. Tannen treats gender as a specific example of cultural differences in communication style.[10] Though very important as a frequent cause of misunderstandings, gender differences in communication style often go unrecognized. A different nationality, or even a different regionality, might inspire us to cut someone a little extra slack before judging him by the way he speaks. *That just must be the way they do it up (or down or over) there*, we think. But we expect people from our own place and time to share our standards of "polite" speech. Many people simply don't realize that, for example, both the "arrogant" man and the "manipulative" woman are trying their best to speak properly in terms of the unwritten rules of their respective intra-gender cultural systems.

---

9 (Harper Paperbacks, 2001).

10 See *You Just Don't Understand* (Harper Paperbacks, 2001) and *Talking from 9 to 5* (Harper Paperbacks, 1995). Others contend there is a biological factor behind at least some of these differences. A growing body of research indicates that both culture and biology contribute and actually influence each other. See Theresa L. Crenshaw, M.D., *The Alchemy of Love and Lust*, (G. P. Putnam's Sons, 1996); Judith Newman, "I Thought I Could Trust Him…," *The Oprah Magazine* 10 no. 3 (2009); Rev. Dr. Becky Edmiston-Lange,"The Brain that Changes Itself, Part I," "The Brain that Changes Itself, Part II," http://www.emersonhouston.org/who/selSermons.html.

When I teach a complete consensus system, my trainees often find the session on gender one of the most helpful. They are relieved to learn that they aren't "crazy" or "wrong," and neither are their coworkers, friends and relatives of the opposite gender. They're just looking at things in two different, but equally plausible, ways.

Gender also makes a good instructional illustration of how relatively hierarchical or egalitarian cultural backgrounds can inspire preferences for different speech styles. After all, we can't all relate to an example about Japanese-American differences. Some westerners may not know a single Japanese person, and vice versa. But we are all acquainted with a statistically significant sample of people of the opposite gender.

For all of these reasons, I'll spend a little more time on the gender factor.

Lens-wise, we might think of gender as changing the magnification. *Like other cultural differences, many gender-based differences boil down to backgrounds in relatively hierarchical or egalitarian social systems.* Most people need both some hierarchy and some level-field relations in their lives, yet lean more or less toward one or the other. *Although there are many exceptions, on average, men are usually exposed to more hierarchical social structures than women of the same nationality, regionality, etc. Among themselves, women generally experience more egalitarian social systems than demographically similar males.*

History shows how hierarchical orientation can go hand-in-hand with, for example, regulation. During the industrial revolution in England, poor, male factory workers organized themselves into mutual aid societies with hierarchies of leaders and specific rules on what each member had to do in order to receive certain benefits. For example, a man might have to pay in a certain amount of money every week in order to draw out a given amount in event of emergency.

Female groups tend to be more egalitarian and less regulated. Poor, working women also banded together during the industrial revolution. Their groups involved little or no hierarchy, rules, etc. At a typical meeting, one woman (not necessarily "the leader," if the group even had a leader) might have pointed out, "Bess is expecting a baby soon. Who can work which of her shifts while she recuperates so she doesn't lose her job?" (No medical leave back then.) Various women volunteered for various days and times until all Bess's shifts were covered.

If these people were anything like we are, the women probably thought the men wasted a lot of time with all their regulatory rigamarole, and the men couldn't believe the women managed to get anything accomplished without knowing who was in charge and what the rules were. Yet each group did function reasonably well and achieved their objectives. Perhaps the men's groups could have done even better with a little more flexibility, and the women's groups could have done better with a little more structure, but contrary to what they probably thought of each other, they both did OK.

Preferences for hierarchy or egalitarianism spill over into our outlooks and speech styles. Consequently, if the relative status of the people involved in a conversation is ambiguous, many (but not all) men, being more accustomed to hierarchical systems, are more sensitive to any possible interpretation that sets one person in a higher status position, such as being stronger or the one in control. Many (but not all) women prefer to see the two people on a level field, and do tend to see them that way. However, when these women do see a hierarchical interpretation, in particular when they believe that someone who ought to be their equal is trying to establish higher status, they may be highly offended.

Hierarchical or egalitarian viewpoints manifest themselves in many ways that can either intensify or diminish our temperamental differences. For example, when one person tells another about a problem, a man may see that as "revealing" or "admitting" the problem. He senses, often below his conscious radar screen, that the one with the problem has lower status. Therefore, he may tend not to reveal a problem except for a given purpose, typically to get the other person to help or advise him. So, when people reveal their problems, he assumes they want the listener's help.

For many women, talking about a problem means "sharing" the problem. For them, discussing problems is a way of connecting with another person on a level field. Below their mental radar screens flies the assumption that we all have problems; that's one of the things that makes us alike. When one woman tells another about a problem, hearing her friend reciprocate with empathy, perhaps by relating a similar experience of her own, reinforces the sense that she's not alone. She does not necessarily want help, but if she does, she may seek collaboration and consensus, rather than action or directives from the other woman. In fact, stress in women triggers not only impulses to fight or flee, but also impulses to reach out and connect.

If Nell tells Gary she feels frazzled, trying to juggle her job, family and church volunteer work, Gary may reply, "So drop the volunteer work." He assumes she wants advice, but Nell, wanting connection and understanding, feels offended. Where does Gary get off bossing her around when she tried to reach out to him? In addition, she might feel Gary is demeaning volunteer work that is very important to her as a source of fulfillment.

If Gary tells Nell his volunteer work is becoming too much for him, she might say, "I know just what you mean. I often feel that way too." She offers understanding when he wants help. Gary thinks, *Thanks for nothing. If you don't want to help me, just say so.*

When Nell confabs with others about Charlie's pronunciation problems, and they decide among them that his closest friend, Hunter, should be the one to approach him, Gary accuses Nell of triangulation. From his point of view, Nell wanted Charlie to change, and finagled Hunter into doing her dirty work for her.

From Nell's point of view, she first spoke to others about Charlie to reality check her desire that he change his pronunciation. She wouldn't act on her opinion alone, but rather would look for a common interest in change. Then, if there were consensus, she wanted to collaborate about how to handle the situation with a view to Charlie's comfort. If the others had thought she, rather than Hunter, would be the best one to speak to him, she would have been perfectly willing to do so.

Like other cultural factors, such as nationality or regionality, gender can also trigger more direct or less direct speech. Men often (but not always) use oppositional or imperative linguistic styles, as in, "Hey, Charlie, that's 'IN-di-jent.'" Many women, sensing the teacher-like (higher) status of one who corrects another, feel uncomfortable using such language among peers. As little girls, they learned the hard way that the fastest road to becoming a social pariah was to "boss" other girls around. This doesn't end in childhood. In most, though not all, societies, women who speak too directly are judged negatively. Other women as well as men may accuse them of being too blunt, pushy, strident or even bitchy.[11]

---

11 Note, however, that, like all indirect speakers, for example those from the Deep South, women who speak in more typical female style may be judged manipulative by direct speakers. Thus women sometimes feel they are in a no-win situation when it comes to seeking what they need from others.

Thus a woman's gender can magnify the view through naturally diplomatic temperamental lenses. A woman with the diplomatic temperament would take utmost care in approaching Charlie, choosing words that ameliorate his sense of being corrected. But even a woman with a regulatory temperament may learn to use less oppositional language to influence people to follow the rules. She might try casually pronouncing the word properly in a sentence of her own. Her gender reduces the magnification of her red lenses.

Men are often *expected* to speak in oppositional styles. The same tone that earns a woman the "bitch" label seems "confident" when used by a man. Anything less and other men might doubt that he means what he says. To the mystification of many women, men may see oppositional styles as more respectful of the other person. The man who also has a naturally direct temperament might be the most likely to simply blurt out a correction in the course of a meeting. The temperamentally diplomatic man might take Charlie aside, but broach the issue in direct terms. "By the way, I thought you'd want to know that it's 'IN-di-jent,' not 'in-DYE-gent.'"

Similarly, some men tend to speak in absolutes. They might make a generic statement even though they know there are exceptions, "Kids are mean and irresponsible." Or such a man might state an opinion or belief as if he were stating a fact. For example, if such a person believes that the congregation's bylaws do not, or should not, require background checks on prospective staff, he might state, "We don't have to do background checks." When they hear qualifiers such as "some," "often," "in my opinion," and "maybe," some men assume the speaker doesn't feel strongly about the statement or isn't sure of herself, or they may judge the speaker and/or the statement as "weak" or lacking confidence.

Some women find such absolute statements offensive. They may, for example, assume a speaker knows a statement, such as the example about background checks, to be true, else he would have qualified it. If such a woman later learns that the speaker wasn't sure, she feels unfairly misled. Similarly, a generic statement, such as the one about kids, may feel offensive to a woman who knows there are exceptions. Such generic statements seem to judge all persons of a given category, and therefore, to unfairly misjudge some. Women may, therefore, qualify their statements to avoid seeming "dishonest," "arrogant," or "pushy."

Some women, and a few men, will even qualify a statement they know to be true so as to temper any indication of higher status (knowing more than the other person), "Charlie, *I think* that *might* be 'IN-di-jent.'" Some are most likely to qualify a statement when they feel most strongly about it; they don't want the strength of their feelings to show through lest they cause offense.

The tendency to qualify or not can also relate to other cultural factors, such as certain professions, or to personality. Kiersey describes a temperament type he dubs "the Rational," who sees shades of gray, rather than black and white, and therefore, tends to qualify statements so as to make them technically accurate. Kiersey also describes "the Idealist," who takes absolutes all the way to feast-or-famine level. A charming Idealist friend of mine, when she developed her first middle-age health issue, said, "My life is over," even though the condition was not life threatening. But when times are good, this Idealist is just as quick to categorize life as "nirvana."

Cultural and temperamental factors can intensify or temper gender-related tendencies regarding the use of qualifiers, and vice versa. I happen to have a lot of the relatively uncommon "Rational" temperament in me, and am also female, so you'll find a lot of qualified statements in this text even though I feel quite confident of those statements.

The above are only a few of many many ways female and male viewpoints can differ, and like other cultural differences, either intensify or diminish our temperamental preferences. There are, of course, many exceptions to "typical" gender preferences in communication style. Such exceptions arise from the different temperaments and the other cultural factors mentioned above.

"Different" doesn't have to mean better or worse. Disbelief in gender-based speech and behavior patterns can itself be gender-based. While many of my students and trainees consider my classes on temperament and gender their favorites, I've observed that some people shy away from any discussion of non-physical differences between women and men, often dismissing the subject before true discussion can begin. Interestingly, part of their very aversion to

the concept of gender-related speech patterns may be due to their preferences for either the level field or the hierarchical structure.

Some people, mostly women but some men, may have such an egalitarian orientation that they need to believe that different demographic groups are not only equal but the same. Because speech and behavior patterns are so often and so strongly associated with correctness, these egalitarians fear that, if two groups' typical behaviors are different, one of them is being put down as behaving incorrectly. So they refuse to accept or discuss the matter.

Other people, mostly men but some women, are so inclined to see status differences as between any two people or two groups, that, to their minds, discussing difference must mean discussing which is better. They don't want to hear why their way of speaking on a given occasion with a given individual didn't work for them. They assume that will mean hearing that the other person's way of speaking is better than theirs. Ergo, people who speak in that other way are better than they are.

Still others object, "That's wrong. I know a woman who's so hierarchical she always has to be the boss," or "I know a man who's very open about sharing his day-to-day problems." They assume statements about trends refer to *all* women or *all* men. Qualifying words such as, "Mostly men but some women," or "with many exceptions," don't even register with these folks. But this dichotomous, all or nothing, way of thinking is itself more characteristic of men than of women (with many exceptions).

Once you understand a typical dynamic, you can apply it to the exceptions. If we can hear the qualifications, if we can understand the principles without prejudging the people, we can better understand all people, whether their behaviors are typical or atypical for their respective groups, whether their speech patterns arise from gender or some other factor.

For example, there have been occasions when, wanting only an empathetic ear, I expressed a problem to a woman, and she began to tell me, "Well, you've just got to..." I felt hurt and offended. However, having learned how this dynamic more typically works between men and women, I was able to see her words through another lens. She didn't mean to brush me off or put me down (as my gut said). She thought I needed or wanted help and was trying to give it. I terminated the phone call, because it wasn't what I needed at the time, but I didn't terminate the friendship.

Conversely, there have been other occasions when a woman I care deeply about told me a problem, and eager to help, I began to make suggestions. Then, sensing that she was hurt by my response, I knew why and shifted gears. I stopped advising and started empathizing.

In other words, knowing about a common, but not universal, dynamic between opposite genders, I was better able to handle myself when that same dynamic occurred in atypical same-gender conversations.

Communication Diversity

These and other lens characteristics, such as one's preferred learning style(s) (visual, aural, linguistic, kinesthetic, logical, social, solitary)[12] and one's own particular package of life experiences, lead to what I call "communication diversity." *Some of the most inclusive people in the world*, people who would never deliberately discriminate against a person on the basis of gender, race, nationality, sexual orientation, or the like, *unknowingly discriminate against those with different lenses*.

These people aren't mean-spirited. They've simply always viewed the world through lenses of a particular color, say red. They aren't aware of their red lenses. They think the world *is* red. No one's ever shown them how it might look in blue or green or yellow.

Even when we become aware of lenses of different color, darkness and magnification, *we still tend to feel the way we see the world is "right,"* and many of us feel it very strongly indeed. In some of my classes trainees argue vehemently over whether it is more polite to say, "Would you change the printer cartridge," or "Could you change the printer cartridge," even after I have explained the rationale behind each of those perspectives.

Compassion in the presence of communication diversity means accepting the mutual difficulty of changing the way we see the world and its effect on the way we speak. It's just as hard for Bert to say, "Hey, Charlie, that's

---

12 http://www.learning-styles-online.com/overview/.

IN-di-jent," as it is for Ethan to bide his time and wait for an opportunity to pronounce the word properly, and vice versa. It's just as hard for the here-and-now-grounded person to get motivated by what might happen next year as it is for the abstract thinker to ignore potential future ramifications; just as hard for the free-spirited person to accept rules as it is for the regulatory person to live without them. It's every bit as difficult for the Southerner to become, in her view, "brash" as it would be for the New Yorker to hint at what he wants without stating it directly.

Peppy finds it agonizing to wait for Pokey to get the words together and spit them out, but doesn't realize that Pokey can't follow her rapid-fire delivery; he loses half of what Peppy says. Pokey, on the other hand, fails to see that, by the time he gets to the end of his thought, Peppy has lost sight of the beginning. Neither of them understands why they just can't get through to the other.

A good practical tool for understanding this type of diversity is to imagine how it would feel to speak like the person whose style offends you. Say you're Charlie, and during a meeting, Ethan blurts out, "Hey, that's 'IN-di-jent,' not 'in-DYE-gent.'" You feel highly indignant. *Ethan didn't need to embarrass me in front of everyone*, you think. Visualize yourself saying what Ethan said in the same tone and in a similar setting. Feel the discomfort of behaving in a way that seems disrespectful and unkind by *your* standards. Then tell yourself, that's probably how hard it would be for Ethan to bide his time and look for a natural opportunity to pronounce the word properly.

This doesn't mean Charlie has to adopt Ethan's style. It doesn't mean Charlie can't tell Ethan he felt embarrassed and put down. It doesn't mean he shouldn't ask Ethan to correct him privately if a similar situation should arise in the future. But this imaginary exercise will help Charlie to:

- Let go of assumptions about Ethan's intentions
- Understand how hard it is for Ethan to modify his style, and
- Match his manner of inspiring change to that level of difficulty, as by using the skills presented later in this book

In short, the practice develops the compassion and curiosity that boost consensus skills.

Try This: Observing Lenses

Review the various committee members' ideas of the best way to correct Charlie's mispronunciations on pages 14 and 15. If you were Charlie, which approach would you prefer that someone take with you?

For each of the other approaches, the ones you did not prefer, try to think of someone you know who has taken that approach in a similar situation.

What to Do?

This book offers many practices for improving conversations, especially consensus-seeking conversations. Some of the practices come easier to one temperament than to another. Some feel more natural to people of certain cultures. Some skills are easier for typical women, and others easier for typical men. Does this cut against my bid for compassionate understanding of communication diversity?

The short answer is "No." The practices recommended in this book simply work better than others when seeking consensus with the vast majority of people—people of various temperaments, cultures, genders, generations, life experiences, etc. The point is not that these practices (and people who use them) are right and others wrong, but that the practices generally *serve the speaker* better. Though they are tools, not rules, they tend to earn us more of what we need from people, while building bridges, not burning them. They make the difficult conversations easier, more effective, more efficient, and more comfortable.

You will likely find some of the skills in this book easier than others. But almost anyone can master them all with practice. Once you try them and see for yourself how well they work, you'll consider it well worth the effort of having learned them, even if you had to buck some of your natural preferences. You'll also want others to use them with you.

So far, we've covered quite a bit of the theory that underlies consensus skills. If you're eager for a practical way to use this knowledge, the next chapter is for you. It explains the single most important rule for building consensus. Follow this one rule, and you will start to enjoy more consensus success.

Key Points from Chapter 3

- Several types of personal difference affect the way we see the situations in which we find ourselves and what we consider the loving or polite way to speak:
    - o Temperament
    - o Culture
    - o Gender
    - o And others
- Though different thinking and speaking styles can aggravate us, the fact is that groups benefit from diversity

CHAPTER 4
THE SILVER RULE

There is nothing so bad or so good that you will not find Englishmen doing it; but you will never find an Englishman in the wrong.

- George Bernard Shaw

The most challenging conversations, the ones that call for consensus skills, arise from differences—differences of opinion, belief, or behavior—that can grow into disagreements or conflicts. We want or need something from another—information, cooperation, help, money, a change of mind or action—but we know, or suspect, they will disagree, resist, or feel so offended that their attitude takes a downturn. Or perhaps they want something from us that we can't give, or don't want to. Sometimes the difference resides in their lenses. Each person wants the other to see the world their way, and to speak and behave accordingly.

Scenarios for Our Sample Dialogues

Here are a few examples of how different needs can collide in a congregational setting. These fact scenarios will form the basis for skill use examples peppered throughout the remainder of this book, including the sample dialogues:

- *Charlie's committee* members want him to improve his pronunciation, but they also want him to remain enthusiastically on board. How to call his errors to his attention without alienating him?
- *Fran*, a hard-working volunteer, has organized an annual fundraiser banquet and auction for the last fifteen years and takes great pride in getting prestigious speakers at a discounted price. The caliber of the speakers has more than made up for

the honoraria by attracting many visitors from outside the congregation to the event. For the last couple of years, however, some of the younger adults haven't attended. After speaking to Yolanda, a member in her early twenties, *Spencer*, the minister, concluded that some young people might find a speaker boring and prefer to have games instead. How can Spencer persuade Fran to consider a change without hurting and possibly alienating such a devoted volunteer?

- *Mike*, who is asked to pay for the church sign he backed over, makes snide remarks to *Laurel*, implying that she should have paid for the window she accidentally broke a few weeks before. Laurel feels insulted. Does all the time and money she has contributed to their church count for nothing? Doesn't it matter that she broke the window trying to prevent a worse accident? Why should her accident be treated the same as Mike's carelessness, especially when he only makes a minimal pledge and never volunteers for anything?

- *Brandon* is an enthusiastic, but often clumsy, volunteer who has borrowed things from *Molly* in the past, and returned them late and damaged, if at all. Now he wants to use Molly's dollhouse in a children's program he's directing. Molly treasures the dollhouse, which her grandfather made for her when she was a child. She's worried about what could happen to it, not only because of Brandon's history, but also because it will be used by a large group of rambunctious kids. Though reluctant to "make waves" with a fellow congregant, Molly had decided to turn Brandon down. Then she heard that he had already told the children about the dollhouse. They, their parents, and the Director of Religious Education are all excited about the dollhouse and the program they've planned around it. Molly is angry with Brandon for speaking out of turn. He has set her up in a no-win situation with three poor choices: disappoint everyone without explanation; embarrass Brandon by explaining her decision; or give in and risk the dollhouse.

- Some members feel strongly that their congregation should dismiss their full-time music director, **Kayla**. They say eliminating that one salary would allow them to expand more important outreach ministries. Others rally behind Kayla, claiming the church's music program attracts people; dismissing her would not only reduce growth, but could reduce current membership. The debate becomes heated. How to resolve the matter?[13]

So many problems! Nobody likes to think about all these things happening in their congregation. Yet, we know that such things do happen (rarely all at once). But they don't have to grow into major conflicts. As you watch these scenarios play out in Chapters 5 through 13, you'll learn how you can nip such situations in the bud and resolve them to everyone's satisfaction.

And that's good news because it's not always easy to ignore or avoid troublesome people and situations in a congregational setting. Consider Laurel's situation, for example. Unless her congregation is very large, it might be impossible to avoid Mike and his snide comments. Yet, she might think those comments aren't enough to make it worth her while to uproot herself from a community that, aside from Mike, "feels like family." She may be wise enough to realize that, even if she did change churches, at her new congregation, she might well encounter a new Mike. While some people switch churches the way they might change cell phone providers, most would rather not.

Likewise, if Brandon and Molly were not members of the same faith community, and Molly refused to lend Brandon the dollhouse, Brandon would be the only person Molly knows who would resent her. But if she refuses to lend it within her own congregation, she will encounter children who know her and will now consider her mean. Even some parents might resent her.

Some relationships are just worth a little more effort. *Yet our intuitive efforts are often inadequate, or even counterproductive.* As you'll see, using consensus skills eases those efforts while boosting their potential for success.

Some readers might think it would be easier for them to simply walk away from one of the above scenarios, or to give in to the other person. They

---

13 As seasoned leaders know, positions and behaviors like these can involve an element of significant pathology warranting referral of a congregant to a mental health professional. Although we will touch on such situations in Chapters 13 and 14, we'll generally assume that the characters in our scenarios do not fall into this category.

might feel they would be content with the results. That's OK too. Each of us learns how to apply the consensus practices from reading the sample dialogues, then applies them to whatever situations we see fit.

People Resist Being Made Wrong

While some people actually gravitate toward conflict, most of us dread it, and with good reason. It can hurt, and hurt people hurt other people. Hence the Golden Rule.

But the Golden Rule is not the only force that repels us from conflict. People instinctively resist being "made wrong." I use terms like "made wrong" and "wrong making" to mean overtly telling someone they are wrong, as by contradicting, arguing or reprimanding, or indirectly implying that someone is wrong, for example by a should statement like "you should put in more volunteer time." Wrong making can even be non-verbal, heaving a sigh, rolling one's eyes, or directing a disapproving glare at another.

I don't mean to suggest that no one ever *is* wrong, objectively speaking. The point is that, when we make people wrong in the ways just mentioned, we should expect resistance.

When we feel others are trying to cast us as wrong, we tend to push back. The more important my opinion, statement or behavior is to me, the more likely I am to resist when someone makes it wrong, and the harder I push back.

We actually react physiologically when our important concepts are contradicted. In *Power with People*,[14] Dr. Gregory W. Lester describes Victor Frankl's accounts of relatively healthy prisoners in Nazi camps suddenly dying when their expectations about liberation proved wrong.

Feeling wrong is physically weakening. In my classes, I often do an impromptu demonstration in which a trainee holds her arm out, and I try to push it down. Her ability to resist my pushing weakens visibly after I instruct her to engage in a bit of self-critical head talk. Conversely, re-focusing on a legitimate self-compliment boosts her strength back up.

The effect is so strong that even an indirect suggestion that a person is wrong can be weakening. The arm strength demonstration works just as well

---

14 (Ashcroft Press, 1995).

when the subject replaces the self-criticism by a "have to" statement, such as "I must start exercising more" or even "I have to go grocery shopping."

Terms such as "have to," "must," "should," and "need to" suggest that we should do something different, in other words, that what we're doing now is wrong. These terms become so closely associated with wrong in our minds, that they automatically trigger the same dragged-down mood and physical weakness as criticism, even when logic tells us that no criticism is intended, as in "I have to go to a meeting tomorrow."

This is why, to my mind, some of the best covenants are couched in terms of values which we aspire to live and which offer us hope for personal growth, rather than as rules; energizing want-tos, rather than weakening have-tos. I find myself more motivated to live such a statement, and more successful in doing so.

Three Ways We Resist

Beginning in childhood, when someone is made wrong, they typically push back in three ways. You're walking past the door of the family room, and hear the *boings* and *crashes* of a video game. "Dandelion," you call to your daughter, "I told you to do your homework." She calls back, "I am doing it." **Denial** is the first way of resisting wrong making.

The next day, you walk past the room and hear the television. "Dandie, I told you to do your homework, and you're watching TV." "But, Mom, I'm watching PBS. It's educational." This second form of resistance is *rationalization*.

Third day, same scenario, worst form of resistance: "Dandie, you aren't doing your homework." "Well, I was doing it till a few minutes ago, but brother's been out riding his bike ever since we got home from school." In this form of resistance, *projection*, little Dandelion alleviates the discomfort of being made wrong, by making someone else (brother) even more wrong than she is, so she feels right by comparison. However, the person adults usually project onto is the one who made them wrong. Projection and counter-projection can easily spin out of control in a series of escalating accusations.

The urge to resist being wrong is a strong one. In prehistoric societies, wrong concepts could be life threatening. If one member of a hunting group got the signals wrong, one or more of them could be maimed or killed by the prey animal. If a member of the tribe got the rules of behavior wrong, she could be ostracized and would not likely survive alone. To our instincts, being wrong reads as a threat, and we react accordingly.

The more essential a concept, and the more it guides our day-to-day actions and decisions, the more we tend to resist changing it. Consider this example from an online article about a disease known as "childbed fever":

> In the late 1840's, Dr. Ignaz Semmelweis was an assistant in the maternity wards of a Vienna hospital. There he observed that the mortality rate in a delivery room staffed by medical students was up to three times higher than in a second delivery room staffed by midwives. In fact, women were terrified of the room staffed by the medical students. Semmelweis observed that the students were coming straight from their lessons in the autopsy room to the delivery room. He postulated that the students might be carrying the infection from their dissections to birthing mothers. He ordered doctors and medical students to wash their hands with a chlorinated solution before examining women in labor. The mortality rate in his maternity wards eventually dropped to less than one percent.
>
> Despite the remarkable results, Semmelweis's colleagues greeted his findings with hostility. He eventually resigned his position. Later, he had similar dramatic results with handwashing in another maternity clinic, but to no avail. Ironically Semmelweis died in 1865 of *Streptococcus pyogenes*, with his views still largely ridiculed.[15]

For Semmelweis's colleagues, accepting the simple measure of hand washing would be tantamount to admitting that their dirty paws had killed many people. That would make them very wrong indeed. So they went into denial and kept up their current practice, taking even more lives.

---

15 Christine L. Case, Ed.D, "Handwashing," http://www.accessexcellence.org/AE/AEC/CC/hand_background.php.

Try This: Recognizing Resistance

Think of a statement you made that the listener resisted. Don't start with an example involving an important figure in your life, such as a relative or boss, but rather a more casual acquaintance.

What form did the resistance take? Was it denial? Rationalization? Projection?

Can you imagine a way the person might have felt your statement made them wrong?

Our instinctive distaste for talking about matters on which we differ or disagree often stems from the prospect of injecting the discomfort of wrong making into an important relationship, even though we might not consciously analyze a situation this way. We don't want to inflict such discomfort on someone we value, nor do we want it inflicted on us in the form of projection.

Dr. Lester tells us that the more mature a person is, the more likely that, in time, he can move past the initial visceral resistance to being made wrong, can refrain from offensive counter-accusations, and can self-assess.[16] Some people do this better than others, but no one does it every time. The harder the disagreement pokes at our most closely held concepts, the more likely we are to fall back on our instinctive resistance to the threat we sense. At the very least, it delays our progress toward a new perspective, and sometimes it blocks progress altogether.

Yet the very problem with many difficult conversations is that rightness and wrongness seem implicit in the situation. Seeking a change of someone's mind or behavior suggests wrongness of that person's current beliefs or actions. Rev. Spencer wants Fran to consider changing her long-standing fundraiser programming. This implies that what she's been lovingly doing all these years is wrong, thus the difficulty in the conversation. Fran might trivialize or insult the young people's taste, thus making them wrong, and/

---

16 Lester, *Power with People.*

or she might accuse Spencer, the minister who broaches the subject with her, of ingratitude.

Some readers might think, *Wait a minute. Our Fran wouldn't call Spencer an ingrate.* And these readers might well be correct. **People often suppress such negative statements in congregational dealings** even more than they might in other contexts, such as family or work life, especially when clergy are involved or present.

This may or may not be good news. One congregation's Fran truly gets over the sting of feeling made wrong and the urge to project. Another's Fran never regains her warm, fuzzy enthusiasm. She may quit the congregation or simply fade from view. If she does remain in the fold, she may harbor negative attitudes toward certain people, attitudes that emerge in future dealings, sometimes in very subtle ways. Indeed, Fran herself may be unaware of how past wrong making influences new issues and situations.

Let's say Spencer speaks to Fran about changing the programming for this year's fundraiser. Fran recognizes his tactful choice of words and kind tone of voice. Although she feels hurt, Fran's rational brain accepts the need for change. She decides she will not hold this against Spencer, resolves to "get back to normal," and believes she succeeds in doing so.

Spencer, however, begins to notice a change in Fran's facial expression and body language. He senses a new reserve when he speaks to her. In various meetings, it seems Fran more often questions his suggestions and opinions. She always presents reasonable arguments, often persuasive even to him. Still, the number of those reasonable arguments represents a change.

Subconscious Decision Drivers

Could Fran's attitude and behavior toward Spencer change without her realizing it? Scientists are learning more and more about how many of our brains' driving forces fly below our conscious radar screens. In one experiment, a professor offered students the opportunity to bid on a bottle of wine using a four-part questionnaire. Question 1 asked for their names, Question 2 for the last two digits of their social security numbers. Question 3 asked them to think about the number represented by their answer to Question 2 and indicate whether or not they would be willing to pay a corresponding number of dollars for the wine. Question 4 requested their actual bids.

When asked whether considering paying the amount suggested by their social security numbers had influenced their bids, participants said, "No." However, tabulating the results showed that, although they did not bid the exact amounts considered in Question 3, those whose social security number digits suggested low numbers, such as 15, bid lower amounts than those whose social security numbers suggested higher amounts, such as 84. In other words, their bids were roughly proportional to the amounts they contemplated in Question 3.[17]

In another study, summarized by Robert Cialdini in *Influence: The Psychology of Persuasion*,[18] homeowners were asked to display an unsightly "Drive Carefully" sign in their front yards. The sign, as shown to the homeowners in a sample photo, was poorly lettered and so large it would significantly obscure the view of the house. In a control group, 83% of the residents refused to display the sign. The test group, however, had been primed two weeks earlier when asked to display a three-inch square sticker reading, "Be a safe driver." Of those who had accepted and displayed the window sticker, 76% agreed to display the big, ugly sign.

Cialdini explains that, when a person commits to an idea or position, especially if he publicly goes on record, as by displaying the window sticker, his psychological need to act consistently with that position is virtually irresistible. One of his most chilling examples comes from the Korean War. Whereas the North Koreans tried to coerce captives to cooperate through cruelty and punishment, the Chinese took a different, and much more successful tack, their "lenient policy." Post-war psychological studies revealed that, unlike World War II prisoners, almost all American prisoners in Chinese camps had collaborated with the enemy in some way or other.

The lenient policy began by asking the prisoner to make a seemingly inconsequential statement like, "The United States is not perfect." Once the prisoner made the statement (went on record), the interrogator could usually get him to build on it, as by listing problems with America and signing the list. Later, he agreed to discuss his list with other prisoners or write a more complete essay, which was then aired on radio broadcasts to many POW camps.

---

17 Dan Ariely, *Predictably Irrational* (Harper Collins, 2008).

18 (Quill, William Morrow, 1995).

"Aware that he had written the essay without any strong threats or coercion, many times a man would change his image of himself to be consistent with the deed and with the new 'collaborator' label." When an American escaped from a camp, at least one such "collaborator" was willing to inform on him for as little as a bag of rice. The Chinese had a near perfect record on recapture.[19]

The drive for consistency is so irresistible that people can use it to manipulate others into making decisions that are clearly against their better interests. Sales people build on a small sale to procure a bigger one. Cult leaders use people's public commitments to a belief or cause to draw them into suicide pacts such as the Heaven's Gate tragedy.

Not all the subtle influences on our attitudes and behavior arise from overt suggestions by others. In college, I took an instinctive dislike to a fellow who sat next to me in class. Later, I became friends with his sister, which motivated me to take a second look at my classmate. Eventually, I figured out that my initial dislike of him stemmed from the fact that he wore the same fragrance as the first teenage boyfriend to break up with me.

These are just a few of many, many examples of subtle influences that affect our actions, decisions, opinions, indeed our very concepts of reality, without our conscious awareness. They operate below our mental radar screens, and our responses to them proceed on autopilot.

Our assumptions about speech styles, such as those discussed in the preceding chapter, also run on autopilot. Nell doesn't think, *Ethan's style felt rude to me because he spoke more directly than I would.* Gary doesn't think, *Nell's confab seemed like triangulation to me because I assumed she wanted someone else to speak to Charlie for her.* Each of them simply "knows" the other is rude, disrespectful, manipulative or otherwise wrong.

If merely considering paying an amount suggested by one's social security number subconsciously affects a subsequent bid, imagine what feeling made wrong can do to a person's attitude.

Moreover, such autopilot behaviors masquerade as conscious decisions. In what, to me, is the most amazing example of this, a researcher could stimulate the part of the brain that caused subjects to raise their arms. When asked why they had raised their arms, you would think most would say something like, "I don't know. It just flew up on its own." However, most subjects gave

---

19 Cialdini, *Influence.*

answers like, "I just decided to." Our brains are fast and silent computers. They can rationalize any autopilot reaction so quickly we believe the rationalization is our original and only reason for our action.

So, yes, Fran's attitude toward Spencer could change without her knowing it. This could negatively affect her reactions to the opinions he airs at meetings. And Fran could honestly believe that the rational arguments she states are the only reasons for her objections to Spencer's opinions.

On the other side of the fence, Spencer may sense that Fran thinks he did something wrong. Depending on how hostile Fran seems, he may counter project, thinking Fran is wrong (unfair, vindictive, or the like). He might believe that he isn't acting out, that he treats her just the same as he always did. Yet his attitude can take a downturn that reveals itself to Fran in ways neither of them is overtly aware of.

Well-meaning people can get sucked into the spiral of wrong making even when projections and counter projections remain unspoken, perhaps not even fully identified in those people's own minds.

If wrong making sucks us into such downward spirals, education and awareness can boost us up. When Spencer recognizes the threat of wrongness that precipitated Fran's attitude change, he awakens his compassion for her. He also realizes that his own discomfort with her new attitude arose from his feeling that she made him wrong. While these realizations might not wipe his feelings off the slate, they help him to rein in any instinctive counter projection. He can tell himself, *It's not about me; it's about her discomfort.* He can take proactive measures to validate Fran and help her feel right. For example, when her well-reasoned arguments against his positions at committee meetings persuade him, he can tell her so.

Education and awareness are not just for clergy and other leaders. If Fran and other members of her congregation learn about the dynamics of wrong making, the entire group will function better.

If they understand the basic human tendency to deny, rationalize and project, they are more likely to check their own denials, rationalizations and projections. They realize that everyone has these tendencies, so they are no more wrong than anyone else for feeling them. And they also realize that they don't have to act on them. When they recognize their own resistance, they can then choose to rein it in, especially when it takes the form of projection. And when they try checking their projection, they learn, not only in theory, but also through experience, that their discussions with others run more smoothly and effectively. They get *more* of what they need easier and faster, and they get it in ways that build bridges rather than burning them.

Developing awareness of communication diversity also helps. One person, who can't bring herself to do more than hint at what she wants, and another, whose request takes the form of an order, can learn not to judge each other wrong (manipulative or rude, respectively). Ditto the free spirit and the organizer, the quick thinker and the contemplative, etc.

Introducing the Silver Rule

Still, we can't count on knowledge alone to always boost others (and ourselves, for that matter) past the urge to resist and project. And even when knowledge does the trick, conquering that urge takes time and energy. Why put those extra hurdles in our way?

If love is golden, I call *"Minimize wrong making" silver—the Silver Rule of Consensus.* The rule serves you well because it draws others to your side, and it makes you feel right because it's compassion in action.

Again, the focus here is not on whether people are or are not wrong. Of course we are all wrong at times. Sometimes it is necessary to overtly make someone wrong, as in teaching a small child to avoid doing harmful things, or in some of the situations explored in Part IV of this book.

There are also many situations in which the wrong does not carry enough emotional weight for resistance to be a significant problem. If I say we've got thirty minutes to set up for a meeting, I'm not likely to resist significantly when someone tells me, "Your watch must have stopped. It's six forty-five." I'll even be glad he corrected me.

But if Spencer wants to facilitate consensus on a fundraiser program plan—a plan that actually excites congregants Fran and Yolanda, rather than a ho-hum compromise that simply avoids offending either—he'll do well to avoid making either Fran or Yolanda wrong as much as he can.

If Laurel not only wants Mike to stop sniping at her, but wishes to proactively build a comfortable relationship with him, she, too, is well-advised to avoid making him wrong.

The point of the Silver Rule, therefore, is that, when what you seek is consensus, when people feel strongly about their respective opinions, it's best to avoid, or at least minimize, wrong making.

Beginning in the next chapter, we'll see how specific consensus skills support the Silver Rule by addressing your interests while minimizing the need to overtly contradict or make others wrong. Once you learn these skills, you'll find that wrong making is easier to avoid than you ever thought possible.

Key Points from Chapter 4

- People naturally resist being made wrong in one or more of these three ways
  - o Denial
  - o Rationalization
  - o Projection
- Such resistance is one reason we avoid difficult conversations
- People often suppress hurt feelings and the like in congregational settings
- Such suppression can make matters worse
- Many of the influences that drive our decisions and behaviors fly below our conscious radar screens, yet these decisions and behaviors feel rational
- If merely considering paying an amount suggested by one's social security number subconsciously affects a subsequent bid, imagine what feeling made wrong can do to a person's attitude
- "Minimize wrong making" is the Silver Rule of consensus
- Specific consensus skills in the chapters that follow help us follow the Silver Rule to get our needs met

PART II: THE BASIC SKILL SET—WHAT TO TALK ABOUT

CHAPTER 5
THE THREE MAGIC QUESTIONS—PREPARATION

Measure Twice, Cut Once

- (Book title) Norm Abram

Your most satisfying resolution of a difference, disagreement or conflict is the discovery that the true, ultimate objectives or interests of the people involved were not at odds after all, or at least not so far apart as they thought. Such resolutions tend to take judgments of right and wrong off the table.

This chapter focuses on skills for zeroing in on what it is you really want, your true interests. Toward the end of the chapter, we'll see how you can even begin to anticipate what another individual really wants, her true interests, before you speak with her. When we discuss our true interests, we arrive at more satisfying solutions for all involved.

But why learn skills for homing in on our own interests? Surely we know what we want, don't we? Well, not exactly.

The human brain is a fast and silent computer. A need or want can propel it through a series of steps—from objective to solution—so seamlessly that the brain's owner temporarily loses sight of the original objective. It's as if a driver decides to take the Interstate from the suburbs to his job downtown, then proceeds as if being on the Interstate were his objective. The traffic grows heavier and heavier, moves slower and slower. He's running late, might not have time to check his email before his first meeting. He might even run late for the meeting itself. Yet he continues on autopilot, never trying a different route (if, in fact, he even knows another route).

Few, if any, of us would prefer to drive this way. Yet, when it comes to getting what we need from others, one of many possible solutions assumes the appearance of our objective.

The Inadequacy of Compromise

In such situations, people often try to compromise, but compromise might not satisfy the true interests of either party. Before turning to our congregational scenarios, let's look at a simpler example of how compromise often works in general.

A Simple Example

The basics of compromise are easiest to see in a buy-sell transaction. Salvador the Sailor wants to sell his boat. He lists it for $40,000. A prospective buyer, Trudy, offers him $10,000. After inching away from their opening positions, the two agree on a price of $25,000. Did Salvador make a good deal?

Not if Sal's reason for selling the boat is that he wants to buy a recreational vehicle that costs $35,000. He will have to come up with another $10,000 to purchase the RV.

If it were a child's tricycle Sal wanted to sell, numerical compromise might represent a good choice because it saves time and no one is likely to be seriously hurt or to harbor ill feelings afterward. But with high stakes, as in the sale of the boat, it pays to seek a better solution.

If Sal tells Trudy his reason for selling the boat is to buy an RV, and it turns out that Trudy just happens to own an RV she wants to sell, one that suits Sal's needs, Sal could make a better deal with an even trade, no money at all changing hands. Both parties would fully satisfy their true interests. Better yet, judgments about which party offered a fair or "right" price would fade from view.

Maybe Trudy doesn't have an RV, but Sal tells her that the reason he wants the RV is so that he can travel overland and see the sights at low cost. What if Trudy owns some timeshares in condominiums in various locations around the country?

Perhaps Trudy owns neither an RV nor timeshares. If Sal can discover her reason for offering $10,000 is that the rest of her money is tied up in bonds that don't mature for another year. Sal could consider accepting a $10,000 down payment plus a promissory note for $25,000 secured by the bonds, or alternatively, an assignment of the bonds themselves.

In a best-case scenario, Trudy has an RV, timeshares, and bonds and is equally willing to trade any of them for the boat. This gives her and Sal several options for meeting Sal's interests. The more options they have, the more likely the two can agree on one—not only agree, but optimize the deal for both. Sal would be like the driver who has a mental map, with various routes, in the back of his mind. He could choose the one that works best.

But Sal is unlikely to discover these options unless he maintains a view of his ultimate interests, discusses them with Trudy, and seeks information on her interests. Before looking at ways to do this, let's consider compromise in a little more depth.

Congregational Examples

Dichotomous (either-or) thinking gives rise to attempts at compromise. Should Fran hire a prestigious speaker or have games? Should Laurel pay for the broken window or not? Should Molly lend Brandon the dollhouse or not? Should the conflicted congregation dismiss music director Kayla or not?

In these cases, a quantitative compromise might be even less satisfying than in the case of the boat sale. For Fran's fundraiser, quantitative compromise could mean a short guest speech plus a short game period. This approach would leave everyone underwhelmed and could actually minimize overall enthusiasm for the event. Similarly, if Laurel pays a portion of the cost of fixing the window, both she and Mike might well remain dissatisfied and resentful. In Molly's situation, how is quantitative compromise even possible? She can't lend Brandon part of the dollhouse.

As for the music director, quantitative compromise is theoretically possible. The church could cut Kayla to part-time work—a fairly obvious option. However, this would still diminish a successful music program, yet might not free up enough funds to expand the other ministries as desired. Thus, at best, it would represent only a lukewarm solution to either objective, and probably the worst solution when both objectives are considered. Moreover, part-time work might not be enough for Kayla. What if she resigns, and the congregation can't find someone else willing to work for her modest salary?

The morale and goodwill of valuable members like Fran, Mike, Laurel, Brandon and Molly may hang on the way these matters are resolved. The argument over the music director threatens to rip an entire congregation apart.

A close cousin of compromise is default. People avoid doing anything that anyone objects to. This often amounts to doing nothing at all. People think they are avoiding a difficult decision, but choosing inaction, or the status quo, *is* a decision. Clergy tell me they have to be careful not to fuel this tendency because, while they may not have the power to *make* something happen, they can *stop* almost anything.

It's worth the time and effort to aim for a solution that serves the true interests of all concerned as well as possible.

The Three Magic Questions

How do we home in on ultimate interests? My clients like a tool I call "The Three Magic Questions." They help us shift from an either-or perspective to a both-and point of view. They guide us to optimum results. They give us the courage and confidence to take proactive consensus-building action rather than choosing avoidance. The Three Magic Questions are:
1. "Why?"
2. "What else?" and
3. "How do I want to feel?"

We'll learn how to use these questions while preparing for a consensus-seeking conversation in this chapter. An ounce of preparation eliminates a pound of unfocused rambling and struggling in the conversation itself. In Chapters 6 and 7, we'll apply the Magic Questions in conversation.

The First Magic Question—Why?

Remember how Salvador arrived at better solutions? He turned his mind back to his original reasons for selling the boat and told Trudy about them. He also asked Trudy about her reasons for offering $10,000. In other words, he asked "Why?" our first magic question.

What does your two-year-old do when you answer her question?

Toddler:	Why is the grass green?
You:	Because it has chlorophyll.
Toddler:	Why?
You:	To make food for the grass.
Toddler:	But why?
You:	So the grass can grow bigger.
Toddler:	But why, Mommy, why?

This is how you should ask yourself the first magic question. Keep asking why to each answer till you can't go any further, till you reach the silly point—the point where you think, *Duh. Anybody knows that*, or the point where answers begin to repeat themselves. Some whys have multiple answers. Be sure you consider them all.

Bear in mind that, even when you think you've reached that silly point, you will often find, later in the process, that you can expand your answers further. Don't consider your answers static, but rather stay alert to even broader (more ultimate) interests. A significant part of the value of making an initial list lies in the curious, interest-oriented frame of mind it inspires. This should also be your frame of mind when you enter dialogue with the other person.

In formulating your first why questions, you can begin with what you currently think you want. Realizing that your position represents only one route to a broader interest, you ask and answer the question "Why?" to uncover the broader objectives or interests behind the position.

When Sal broadened out from one way to satisfy his interest, selling the boat for a given price, and re-defined his objective broadly as "travel overland and see the sights at low cost," he opened up other possibilities for reaching his true goal. He might trade the boat for Trudy's RV, or for her timeshares, or for a lesser amount of cash plus an assignment of her bonds.

Why does Spencer want Fran to consider changing the fundraiser programming? Why does Fran resist? Why does Mike want Laurel to pay for the broken window? Why does she resist? Why does Brandon want to borrow the dollhouse? Why does Molly not want to lend it? Why does one member of a congregation want to dismiss the music director? Why does someone else insist on keeping her? Each of these people can benefit from asking themselves, "Why?"

Don't worry that preparation focused on your own interests will lead to a selfish attitude that violates the Golden Rule. Remember that, when Sal focused on his broad interest in traveling overland, he not only opened new options for obtaining the means to travel, he also opened up options for Trudy to get a boat she wanted without spending money she didn't have or couldn't afford to spend.

Interest-based consensus building works best when we work with both parties' interests, but working with one party's interests works better, for both of them, than arguing positions.

I strongly recommend preparing in writing. Many times, when facing an interaction the next day, I would begin the Magic Questions in my mind while driving home from work. By the time I arrived, I thought, *I've got it. No need to write this down.* But having learned by experience how much the writing helps, I would sit down and make notes. Without fail, the writing provided me with fresh and valuable insights about my interests. Now, I never assume I've got it all in my head. I prepare in writing.

Tips for Preparation Notes:
- *Suspend judgment.* Don't censor yourself. These notes are for your eyes only. You need to address the interests you have, not those you think you should have.
- *Don't over-intellectualize.* You can take time later to go back over the list in a more studious manner.
- *Let your thoughts flow.* Use whatever medium allows them to flow fast and free, whether writing by hand on a tablet or typing on your computer. If you write by hand (as I like to do), be sure to leave plenty of space around entries so that you can go back and further develop various threads.
- *Take a break.* Then reread and tweak your notes.

Spencer Asks "Why?" To Define His Interests

In considering the following example of Spencer's preparation, it's important to realize that any two people, in Spencer's shoes, will list different interests, different answers to the question "Why?" The example is not about *what* Spencer's interests should be. Rather, it's about *how* Spencer can go about developing his own individual list. In Spencer's situation, or any other, you can go about enlightening your interests in the same manner even though the end result might look different from that of another person in the same situation.

Spencer could begin with what he currently thinks he wants:
1. Fran to consider games instead of speaker
2. To keep Fran happy

Next, he asks *why* he wants Fran to consider games. He asks why about each of his answers, and keeps asking till he can't go any further. Then he identifies the broad interests he really wants to satisfy. If Spencer takes my advice and makes notes, this portion of his notes might look like this:

My Interests:

First Magic Question—Why do I want the following?

  1. I want Fran to consider games instead of speaker—*Why?*
   - More young people attend fundraiser—*Why do I want that?*
     o Maximize attendance—*Why?*
       ▪ <u>Maximize fundraiser income</u>
       ▪ Maximize member involvement—*Why?*
         • <u>High energy level of congregation as a whole</u>
   - Reduce overhead for fundraiser—*Why?*
     o <u>Maximize fundraiser income</u>

Can you see how the broader interests Spencer has underlined could inspire less contentious, less wrong-making discussion points than, "Consider switching to games"? Maximum fundraiser income and high congregational energy are likely interests that Fran will share, whereas "Consider switching to games" is a suggestion she will likely resist. As with Sal, Spencer's clarity about his own interests benefits both him and Fran.

Can you also see how grounding a discussion on these upbeat interests could save more time than Spencer spent preparing? Don't worry if you can't visualize how the whole conversation would play out. We'll cover that in Chapter 7. For now, just note how these broader interests give Spencer possible directions to follow.

Returning to Spencer's preparation, he repeats the process for his second want, asking why he wants to keep Fran happy, and so forth. A complete set of interest notes for Spencer is given in Appendix A along with a brief explanation of a recommended format.

Asking "Why?" Opens Up More Options

The answers to such questions might seem obvious, but when you articulate them, you'll be surprised at the insights you receive. In this example, Spencer realizes that the broader reasons why he wanted Fran to consider games were to maximize income and inspire a high energy level of the congregation as a whole.

As shown in Appendix A, the broader interests behind his desire to keep Fran happy include feeling good in his own skin, retaining Fran's large pledge, reaping the benefits of her knowledge and experience in optimizing the current fundraiser and in educating back-up volunteers and future leaders, and sincere care for Fran's sense of identity and purpose (she was recently laid off). His interests in maximizing income and inspiring high energy reappear at the ends of several chains. Both their end-chain positions and the fact that they repeat are signs that these are particularly important interests.

Even if Spencer already knew these broad interests at some level, making a list keeps him focused on what's really important. Otherwise, with so many interests and potential solutions to this complex situation, he could temporarily lose sight of broad objectives such as high congregational energy, his sincere caring about Fran's welfare, or the value of back-ups for Fran and smooth future transitions in leadership. Staying clear on his broad interests is important because:

- *The more broadly Spencer defines his objectives*, the more ways there are to reach them.
- *The more ways there are to reach those objectives*, the more likely it is that Spencer can find at least one that satisfies both him and Fran.

For example, games aren't the only way to promote high energy in the congregation as a whole. In fact, if games are off-putting to as many mature adults as speakers are to the younger ones, games will not improve the overall energy level at all. And if games reduce overhead, but don't draw visitors as Fran's speakers do, their net effect on income is questionable. Perhaps a third programming option, like musical entertainment, or a mystery dinner, would interest all generations, boosting income and congregational energy better than either a speaker or games.

Looking at the situation even more broadly, a free social, educational or entertainment event, plus a large gift from a single wealthy individual could, at least in theory, satisfy Spencer's interests as well as a fundraiser.

As mentioned above, many readers, putting themselves in Spencer's shoes, will come up with different initial wants, and will answer some of the whys differently. This is perfectly all right. The example does not represent "the right" answers. Again, *the example shows how Spencer can focus on his broadest interests, not what those interests should be.*

Try This: Asking Yourself Why

Reread the description of the scenario involving Laurel and Mike on page 36.

Put yourself in Laurel's shoes. Start with the statement, "I want Mike to stop his snide remarks."

Now ask, "Why do I want Mike to stop the remarks?" Then ask why to each answer until you can't go any further. Any two people will do this at least slightly differently, so don't be concerned if your answer differs from the sample in Appendix B.

What ways of approaching or speaking to Mike do your answers inspire?

Clergy and other leaders should be particularly careful not to confuse a congregation's interests with their own. If Spencer knows that a majority of his congregation wants to expand their prison ministry, and sees it as his job to help them do that, then expanding the ministry is one of his interests in that sense.

But if a number of people want this expansion to include setting up a lending library, and Spencer thinks that would duplicate existing resources, then a library is not one of *his* interests. Later, he can ask "Why?" about the library option, but that's about others' interests, not his.

On the other hand, what if Spencer has an interest that does not parallel the interests of the congregation in general? Let's say that, while using the Why tool on his second want, keeping Fran happy, Spencer sees that he really likes (or dislikes) dealing with Fran.

Suppose she's a real beauty, and all other things being equal, he'd rather face her in a meeting than someone off-putting. Spencer might tell himself this is not an interest that should influence his approach to the fundraiser programming decision. He might be tempted to leave "I like looking at Fran" off the list because he thinks it "shouldn't" influence him.

But omitting the eye candy interest would be self-defeating. This list is for Spencer's use only, and the best way to keep subtle psychological factors from unduly affecting his decisions is to be aware of them.

Recall the experiment in which people who had been primed by accepting a small window sticker found it extremely difficult to resist accepting large, unsightly signs in their front yards. Their best defense is awareness of the brain-wired urge to remain consistent with positions on which they've previously taken a public stand. When they see the offers of sticker and sign as what they really are—attempts to manipulate them by taking advantage of their brain's autopilot responses, they can overcome that hard-wired drive. They can accept the sticker and refuse the sign.

Likewise, when Spencer lists his hard-wired pleasure in looking at pretty people, keeping it visible on the radar screen of his awareness, he stands a better chance of separating his substantive decisions about the fundraiser from that natural, hard-wired urge. He can continue to enjoy the eye candy and also make more objective decisions about the fundraiser program.

There's even a spiritual bonus for Spencer in listing the eye candy interest. It might inspire an additional interest related to his personal growth. *Do I give short shrift to less pleasant congregants?* he asks himself. This inspires him to work harder at treating all members of the congregation, and their concerns, equally. But unless he can undo eons of human evolution and re-wire his brain, the influence of attractiveness should remain on his list.

Asking "Why?" Can Lead to Breakthroughs

In the above example, the value of the Why tool lay mostly in focusing and grounding Spencer in interests he might temporarily lose sight of when considering the issue of games. In other cases, asking why can lead to surprising breakthroughs. For example, by asking why, Mike, who accidentally backed over the sign in the church parking lot, might come to realize that one of the things he really wants is a sense of equality with Laurel, even though she is wealthier and has more free time for volunteering.

Preparation Saves You Time in the Long Run

Once you become familiar with this type of analysis, you'll find you can do it much more quickly than you'd imagine. Even for important or challenging conversations, I usually find this part of my preparation takes less than an hour, and often only a few minutes. Better yet, it saves me time in the long run. Once I have my ideas down in writing, I can stop stewing over the prospective dialogue and move on to other work (or fun!). Plus, I can refer to these notes before, or even during, that future dialogue. It can also help to review and amend such notes after the conversation, especially if, as is often the case, I made progress but follow-up dialogue is needed.

Suppose it takes Spencer a little longer to ask and answer his whys. That's a small price to pay compared with the value of achieving his important objectives, such as high energy level in the congregation, maximum fund-raiser income and Fran's enthusiasm and cooperation.

Try This: Appreciating Time Investment

About how long did it take you to work through ASKING YOURSELF WHY on page 59?

If you were Laurel, would you rather converse with Mike before or after you did the work?

The Second Magic Question—What Else?

In driving, periodically noticing one's peripheral vision, or broad field view, produces better performance. From behind the wheel, a broad field view enhances safety. But it can also enhance other aspects of a road trip. The occasional glance at distant scenery makes driving more pleasant. Sometimes you notice an interesting little town, park or historical site and take a detour that becomes one of your most vivid memories.

When dealing with challenging differences, it's only natural to focus on the issues at hand, but as in driving, a broader view can actually help you reach agreement. In consensus building, field view means keeping an eye out for additional interests that may seem unrelated to the matter at hand, but can help you to:

- *Pull consensus out of a seemingly hopeless situation* by providing extra bargaining chips, or
- *Improve a lukewarm agreement* so that it serves more interests and serves them better

We develop peripheral vision by asking the second magic question, "What else do we want?" to actively seek a few extraneous interests.

Spencer Asks "What Else Do I Want?"

Let's say something else Spencer wants is relief from overwork. His congregation has grown to a point that he has less and less time for his own spiritual and personal life, but it's not yet large enough to hire more staff. If he can get volunteers to assist, something else he'd want is for each of them, and himself, to engage in tasks they find personally fulfilling.

To further refine these two answers to the question "What else do I want?" he applies the first question "Why" to his answers, developing broader concepts of his "What Else" interests. As shown in Appendix A, these include: his and his congregants' personal enjoyment, health and well-being, and opportunities to use their best gifts.

Of course there are any number of other things Spencer might want, and each of us might want different things if we were Spencer. For example, he might want his work, and that of each volunteer, to be aligned with the congregation's mission. The most important thing, at this point, is for Spencer to exercise his mental muscles and poke a few holes in the blinders that focus him on the fundraiser.

How What-Else Interests Can Help

What do these extraneous interests have to do with Fran or the fundraiser? Perhaps nothing. But when Spencer speaks with Fran, his broad frame of mind will make him alert to anything that might serve extraneous interests, whether listed or not. It may be a long shot, but what if he should learn that Fran is tired of doing the same volunteer job every year? What if she could take over some of his duties instead of running the fundraiser? This might take care of a lot of the fundraiser program issues and serve both Fran and Spencer better than any agreement they might have reached about programming per se.

It is a long shot. Spencer knows Fran well. Chances are his perception—that Fran loves doing the fundraiser and wants to continue—is correct. Again, the real value of asking "What else?" is developing curiosity for the broad field view. Thus, he need not spend more than a few minutes on the question "What else?"

If you need any more incentive to try the second Magic Question to develop a broad field view, studies have shown that people who are considered lucky maintain broad flexible views. Dr. Richard Wiseman, author of *The Luck Factor*,[20] performed an experiment in which two forms of "luck" were placed in the paths of subjects—cash lying on the sidewalk and a well-connected businessman at the coffee shop to which the subjects were headed. The subject who considered himself lucky noticed and pocketed the cash and later began a conversation with the businessman. A self-described "unlucky" subject walked right past the money without noticing it and never spoke to the businessman in the shop.[21] In short, a little less focus can be a good thing.

Flexible behavior can steer you toward flexible thinking. If you are a creature of habit, make a point of breaking your routine once or twice a week. Choose habits that have no apparent relation to any issues or problems in your life. If you have a regular coffee hole, try someplace new. Sit in a different place in church or in a class. Trade chores with your spouse. Do something on a different day of the week or different time of day than usual. You may find yourself becoming more creative when you face issues or problems.

The Third Magic Question—How Do I Want To Feel?

This third magic question, though frequently ignored, can be the most important of all. People often make the mistake of addressing only the material issues. But ill feelings can cause us to resist coming to agreement even when both parties' material interests have been addressed. Conversely, enabling

---

20 (Miramax, 2004).

21 Rebecca Webber, "Make Your Own Luck," *Psychology Today,* June 2010; this article also reports that lucky people think in the way our first Magic Question, "Why?" inspires, realizing that there are many ways to reach their broadly defined objectives.

good feelings, the ways people want to feel, can keep them working toward breakthrough agreements even under seemingly impossible circumstances.

Sometimes our minds go directly to the ways we want to feel, in other words, to our positive feeling interests. As I write this book, I know I want to feel proud of it when it's published. At other times, when unpleasant feelings drive disagreement, *we can use the current bad feelings as clues to the opposite feelings that represent our interests*. If someone feels anxious or panicky, he might like to feel calm. If threatened, secure. If insulted, respected.

Sometimes we are simply unaware of how we feel or how it affects our attitude on a subject. Curiosity can help us slow down and take a good look at what's really going on. Calmness, and compassion for ourselves, help us honestly name those feelings.

People sometimes believe, quite correctly, that certain feelings should not affect a decision. For example, music director Kayla may have assigned a number of children's choir solos to Alma's son instead of Beatrice's son. Beatrice may know that her resentment should not affect how she votes on the issue of whether the congregation really benefits from a full-time director. So Beatrice might not acknowledge her resentment, even to herself.

But denial actually exacerbates the very effects it's intended to avoid. *Feelings we suppress, ignore or deny control us.* But when we accurately identify our feelings, we can control them, if we decide that's best. Or we can use them to guide and motivate us. We get to decide. *When we become fully aware of our feelings, we open up options for what to do with them.* We can even decide whether our feelings indicate additional interests we wish to pursue.

- *We can decide how much weight to give our feelings.* Some feelings should be weighted heavily, others questioned. I once got an offer of referral business from a powerful man in a position to affect my career for better or worse. The offer was tempting, but the vibes between us felt wrong, creepy, vaguely dangerous. I felt relieved when I found an excuse to politely decline the work. Years later, the man pled guilty to charges concerning sexual harassment of a number of women. I shuddered to think what payback he might have wanted for that referral and what retribution he might have taken when I refused to pay back. My intuition to avoid him had been right on the mark.

- But remember the college classmate I disliked instantly? When I realized that my feelings were triggered by his cologne, I was able to set those feelings aside and get to know him for the nice guy he was.[22]
- *We can choose to try to control the expression of our feelings.* Molly, who doesn't wish to lend her dollhouse to Brandon, might sense that Brandon scorns her as a rigid pain in the neck. However, if she approaches him wearing the expectation of scorn on her shirtsleeve, she's likely to get it. People often live down to our negative expectations. This does not mean that Molly should trust Brandon blindly. But she can zealously protect her dollhouse while treating Brandon as if he has only good intentions. If she chooses this tack, she can get what she needs with minimum chance of burning bridges. She might even improve relations. But she can only choose to behave this way if she first clarifies her current feelings in her own mind.
- *We can choose to try to change the feelings themselves.* Suppose Spencer realizes he doesn't want to spend time talking to Fran; he feels a jittery urge to hurry, get it over with and complete his other tasks so he can spend time tonight with a captivating book he's reading. Having identified this feeling, he can ask himself how it will affect the conversation. He can see that an impatient attitude will work against his interest of keeping Fran enthusiastically involved. He can choose to take some deep calming breaths before the conversation, and visualize a great fundraiser, to replace anxieties with pleasant anticipation.
- *We can choose to factor in the effects of our feelings on what seem like rational decisions.* Let's say Yolanda, the young woman who suggested games to Spencer, has made an especially good impression on him. Spencer hopes Yolanda will eventually work her way up into church leadership, and she seems interested. He wants to support her to share her gifts for the benefit of the congregation. Has this subconsciously skewed his enthusiasm

---

22 Malcolm Gladwell, *Blink* (Back Bay Books/Little, Brown and Company, 2005), discusses numerous examples of the accuracy of many intuitions but how they can sometimes lead us astray.

for games? Recognizing this possibility, he can stay alert to the question of whether or not games will actually further his ultimate interests in maximizing income, etc.

If the people involved in the above examples had denied their feelings, those feelings could have controlled them without their awareness. If that fast computer in a person's brain can make him believe he decided to raise an arm that, in fact, was artificially stimulated, imagine what such brains can do with personal feelings their owners would rather not acknowledge.

The people who accepted a big, ugly yard sign after displaying a small sticker with a similar message did so because of *feeling* a great need to remain consistent. So did the POWs who were steered into making anti-American statements. And these are only a few examples. Scientists are discovering more and more ways that feelings override intellect.

Spencer Asks, "How Do I Want to Feel?"

Spencer adds to his interest notes the ways he would like to feel. He notes some feelings peculiar to the fundraiser situation. He would like to feel calm, as if things are under control, and to feel objective in his assessment of the program. He also reminds himself that he wants to feel he's living his core values, whatever they may be.

Try This: Asking How I Want to Feel

Review the scenario involving Mike and Laurel on page 36. If you were Laurel, how would you feel about Mike's remarks, and how would you like to feel after you speak with him?

Preparing with Respect to the Other Person

Understanding the interests of the person with whom you seek consensus is every bit as important as clarifying your own interests. *The* way you inspire others to address your interests is by showing them how you might address theirs in turn. If another person does not ask himself the Magic Questions, it's up to you to draw him out, and the next chapter explains how to do that.

I find it immensely helpful to get a jump on the process by asking the Magic Questions about the other person as part of my preparation. There is a catch, however. My answers might be wrong, and they are almost certainly incomplete. I want to be poised to learn more interests and different interests than those I imagined for the other person, rather than lock into my preliminary answers. When we interact with another person, it is important that we address those things *he* sees as his interests, not things we think he should see.

Therefore, when I answer the Magic Questions from the perspective of the other person, I find it helps to think of my answers not as his interests, but rather as hypotheses to be tested in conversation. The value of asking yourself in advance about the other person's interests lies largely in

- Preparing your mind to see things empathetically from his point of view when you converse, and
- Helping you find the right questions to ask him

But if the other person can't or won't express his interests to you, even though you actively welcome them, your own empathetic imaginings may be all you have to go on. They make better starting points for discussion than groping in the dark, provided you remember that your aim is to confirm or correct them, not to take them as facts or to impose them on the other person. I find it useful to begin these imaginings in advance, when I can reflect without distraction or pressure.

To help myself remember that I don't know for sure, I like to put question marks before my hypotheses, as I've done for Spencer's notes.

You may find that this aspect of preparation works well for you. But if you find it too difficult to later hold your hypotheses in suspension and open your mind to what the other person's words, expressions and body language say about his interests, you might decide to skip this step in preparation.

Spencer Asks the Magic Questions about Fran

Returning to Spencer's preparation for his upcoming dialogue with Fran, he decides to ask the Magic Questions about her in advance. ***He asks the first Magic Question, why, about her possible interests.*** He can't guess them all, and he may be wrong about those he does envision. To remind himself of this, he puts question marks before the items he is not absolutely sure of, but might wish to explore when he speaks with Fran.

Spencer begins with two things he thinks Fran might want:

1. ? To keep running the fundraiser
2. ? To have speaker/not games

Next he asks "Why?" and develops chains of increasingly broad interests as he did for himself. One possible broader interest behind Fran's desire to keep running the fundraiser is an outlet for her unique personal gifts, an outlet that values and utilizes what makes her who she is. This interest may also underlie her possible desire to have a speaker. Other possibilities are shown in the complete notes in Appendix A.

Spencer also spends a few minutes on what else Fran might possibly want. What else is happening in her life? He knows she has an anniversary coming up. Maybe she'd like to buy her spouse a special gift, but wants inspiration. If Spencer's hobby is digital photography, he'd enjoy nothing better than suggesting a few suitable cameras.

If Spencer and Fran can reach any mutually beneficial agreement on anything, albeit a what-else interest unrelated to the fundraiser, their attitudes toward each other will improve. They'll build, or strengthen, a bridge between them. The tendency to make each other wrong will diminish. They will be more likely to come to consensus on the fundraiser.

Finally, Spencer asks himself how Fran might want to feel. Advance consideration of this question is especially helpful because feeling interests are the ones people find most difficult to express. Some probable feeling interests naturally arose from Spencer's earlier use of the Magic Questions. Most people want to feel valued for who they are, and so, in all likelihood, does Fran. Considering further, if the suggestion of a programming change might make her feel threatened, she probably wants to feel reassured that a fulfilling role remains for her.

How Preparation Pulls Things Together

Spencer now reviews his entire list for the interests and objectives he wishes to focus on in dialogue. Notice how, even before speaking to Fran, Spencer has shifted the focus of the fundraiser issue from a limited either-or, games-or-speaker perspective to a more expansive view, optimize-the-fundraiser and keep the congregation healthy. He has developed a broader definition of what he wants. This not only opens up more options for achieving his and Fran's objectives, but also increases the chances of finding the best solution, rather than a mediocre one. Spencer has included in his vision the other interests, such as Fran's feeling valued, which can make the outcome truly satisfying for both parties.

I like to keep my preparation notes handy when I'm dealing with another person. If the conversation takes a turn that leaves me temporarily stumped, a glance at the notes can re-focus me. If, for any reason, I don't want the other person to see the notes, I take a little break. Ironically, knowing I have the notes often removes the need to refer to them. In addition, in important or complex matters, it's always best to review my notes to be sure that all my interests are satisfied before finalizing an agreement.

Such notes make you more aware of interests and objectives, but you should never consider them static. Once in this expansive frame of mind, you'll often find that you glean additional interest insights as the conversation proceeds. Consider your notes a work in progress.

In the next chapter, we turn from personal exploration of interests to skills for discussing them, skills you can use whether you have time to prepare or whether someone blindsides you with a matter you didn't anticipate.

Key Points from Chapter 5

- Compromise is often inadequate
- Both parties often get their needs met better if they discuss the true interests that underlie the things they think they want and say they want
- The more broadly you define your interests, the more ways you will find to satisfy them
- The more ways you find to satisfy your interests, the more likely it is that at least one satisfies the other person as well, thus leading to consensus
- It helps to develop notes on your interests before you seek

consensus with someone
- o Preparation saves you time in the long run
- To uncover underlying interests, ask the Three Magic Questions
  - o Why do I want what I think I want?
    - Ask "Why?" about each answer till you can't go any further, developing chains or threads of increasingly broad definitions of your interests
  - o What else do I want?
    - Explore interests that are unrelated to the matter at hand
    - These can
      - Pull consensus out of a seemingly hopeless situation by providing extra bargaining chips, or
      - Improve a lukewarm agreement so that it serves more interests and serves them better
  - o How do I want to feel?
    - If you feel bad, identify the bad feeling; how you want to feel is the opposite
    - Feelings we don't recognize control us
    - When we identify our feelings, we can decide what to do with them
- Some people find it also helps to ask the Three Magic Questions about the other person as part of their preparation
  - o Don't lock into your answers
    - They are not facts, but rather hypotheses to be explored
    - They help us decide what questions to ask the other person

Chapter 6
The Three Magic Questions—Interactive Skills

We want people to feel with us more than to act for us.

- George Eliot

You will find that your most successful consensus-building conversations focus on options for meeting the interests revealed by the Three Magic Questions. They begin with discussing what those interests and objectives are, maximizing fundraiser income, for example, *instead of* offering, accepting, rejecting or debating specific positions or proposals, such as switching the fundraiser programming from speaker to games.

This bears repeating: *we discuss interests and various ways we might meet them, rather than debating or deciding on a given solution, in the early phases of the dialogue.*

- If someone tries to draw you into debating or deciding prematurely on a specific request or proposal, then unless you wholeheartedly like that proposal, don't accept it. Interest talk may well produce an even better option.
- Even if you consider the proposal completely unacceptable, don't reject it, at least not yet; that will lead to positional haggling, wrong making and resistance. Instead, refocus the discussion on ultimate objectives or interests. If this interest talk produces an alternative that satisfies your interests, then there's no need to voice your rejection of the first proposal, no need to make someone else, or his ideas, wrong.
- If you know a way to meet your interests, but you doubt the other person will like it, don't begin by asking them if they will accept your idea. Don't even mention the idea at that point. Instead, begin by discussing the interests that idea would satisfy.

What's the difference between interest talk, on the one hand, and debating positions, on the other? Interest talk may discuss one's concerns about an idea, but does not seek to dismiss the idea. Likewise, interest talk may discuss reasons you like a given idea, but does not push the other person to agree to it. Interest talk defers judgments and decisions until after such discussion.

Compare:

Debate/Judgment	Interest Talk
No way.	I have some concerns about that. They are...
I can't do that.	Here's how doing that would affect me.
It'll never work.	...could happen. How might we prevent that?
That will cost too much.	What about the cost?
I must insist that you...	How can we satisfy my interest in...?
No. We've tried that before.	How would this be different from the time we...
We have to do it this way. It's a tradition.	What would we give up if we break from tradition?

This chapter describes ways to use the Magic Questions during interactions with others. The next chapter will demonstrate the skills in sample dialogues. These skills give us the confidence to state our interests and explore others' interests with an open mind. Knowing how to ask others the Three Magic Questions is particularly important. As we saw in the last chapter, we can analyze our own interests thoroughly before a dialogue, but for the most part, have to rely on educated guesses about the other's interests until we speak to them.

How to Begin a Dialogue

Many people struggle most with starting a difficult conversation. When in doubt, start with an interest.

Spencer could begin with something he believes is a mutual interest, such as maximum fundraiser income. "Fran, I know we both want to maximize income from the fundraiser. It seems to me that attendance has dropped a bit the last couple of years. What's your take on that?"

Alternatively, he could begin by appealing to something he believes is one of Fran's interests and/or seeking to learn more about her interests. "It's hard for me to find words to express how much I appreciate your work on the fundraiser every year." This opener appeals to her interest in being valued for her gifts. After Fran answers, he can learn more about her interests by asking questions such as, "What are your goals for this year's fundraiser?" or "What would help you achieve your goals?"

Or he might begin by mentioning one of his own interests, even a what-else interest. Ordinary pleasantries can offer graceful lead-ins. "How are you, Fran?" he asks. Fran replies, "Fine, how are you?" Spencer says, "I'm well, but a little frazzled. My work load's increased as the congregation has grown, and I often wish I had more help."

Finally, but very importantly, don't lock into any one way to begin. If the other person speaks first, consider that a gift and listen carefully. The gift is information that leads to a better understanding of her interests. It eliminates some of the question marks in your preparation notes, thus helping you refine your ideas of what to say.

No matter how you begin, look for graceful ways to include the Three Magic Questions, and your current answers, in the natural flow of the conversation. *Expect surprises.* As the conversation develops, you will often find that the other person has interests you never dreamed of. You may even find that you have interests that hadn't occurred to you before. Amend your list as you go.

Why?

Telling Others About Your Interests

Whether at the outset, or during the course of a dialogue, you can tell the other person one of your broad interests and solicit their ideas on how to address it. "I'd like to increase our congregation's net income and member involvement. How can we mesh those objectives with the fundraiser?"

Interest talk often means explaining your reasoning. Reasons are exactly what the question "Why?" uncovers. Some people instinctively recoil from stating their reasons. Mike might think, *Laurel isn't my boss. I don't owe her any explanations for why she should pay for the window.* Mike may be right; he may not owe Laurel an explanation, but he may owe it to himself.

Understanding the power of reasons gives us the confidence to offer them to others. Influence, the Psychology of Persuasion[23] describes a set of experiments in which a researcher sent assistants out to try different scripts for getting people to let them cut ahead in lines of people waiting to make photocopies. Using the script, "Excuse me. I have five pages. May I use the Xerox machine?" the assistant was allowed to skip ahead 60% of the time. But using the script, "Excuse me, I have five pages. May I use the Xerox machine because I'm in a rush?" the assistant was allowed to go ahead 94% of the time. Even more amazingly, "Excuse me, I have five pages. May I use the Xerox machine because I have to make some copies," worked almost as well as "because I'm in a rush," 93% of the time, even though the "reason" given simply stated the obvious. Apparently, the word "because" followed by almost any other words triggers a favorable response, at least when the issue is relatively minor.

Cialdini tells us the human mind dislikes arbitrariness. Reasons are powerful, and conversely, concealing them can hurt you. If you don't supply reasons for your requests, the other person will imagine some. Your actual reason or interest is rarely as bad as what they imagine and react to. It may even be quite benign.

Once I declined a neighbor's offer of a bumper sticker for a candidate we both planned to vote for, saying, "I don't do bumper stickers." Sometime later, another neighbor told me he had heard I was a member of the candidate's

---

23 Robert Cialdini (Quill, William Morrow, 1995).

party but that I didn't want anyone to know it. He was wrong on both counts. I considered myself independent, but was open about my plans to vote for the candidate in question. My reason for declining bumper stickers was that I didn't like removing them after an election. In retrospect, I would rather have explained this reason, and been thought lazy, than to be judged as afraid to express my opinion.

Of course you should be prudent. Of course you should think through the way you phrase a reason or explanation. And of course there are times when explaining certain interests can backfire on you. If you want a volunteer to switch from greeter to set-up crew on Sundays because he has a heavy accent visitors can't understand, that might be a good one to keep to yourself, if possible. In my experience, however, people who tend to reveal a bit too much achieve better results, across significant numbers of interactions, than those who keep too much hidden.

We need not habitually conceal our interests. In a given situation, ask yourself, *What's the worst that could happen if I open up about this interest?* and, *What's the worst that could happen if we don't achieve a mutually satisfying consensus?* Put yourself in the other person's likely frame of mind then honestly answer, *If I were in his shoes, would I work with me if I didn't know the reason?* Your answers help you make a considered decision whether or not to reveal interests. In a congregational setting, the answer is usually yes.

If, due to temperament, culture or gender, this idea is a bit scary, if you feel a vague sense that giving reasons makes you seem weak or vulnerable, you can start with small matters. In a household debate over which movie to attend or whether to order Chinese or pizza, explain your interests, and notice the results. Your courage, confidence and comfort will rise with your skill and success rate.

Asking Others About Their Interests

To broaden the definition of another person's objectives, we ask them the question "Why?" This helps us confirm or correct any interests we may have guessed at during our preparation. And of course, it uncovers additional interests. However, if we literally say "Why?" over and over, we can become as tiresome as a two-year-old. Some people even take offense at being asked "Why?" They see it as a challenge.

Fortunately, there are many other ways to phrase a why question. Any question that solicits reasons or interests can work:

- What are the benefits of having a speaker at the fundraiser?
- What would be the downsides of having games?
- How would having games affect your end of things?
- Help me understand your hesitation about games.
- Because…?

Simply adding additional words to the "why" softens it. "Could you elaborate on why you prefer a speaker?" feels less confrontational than "Why?"

Non-verbal cues, such as tone of voice, facial expression and body language, of course, strongly affect the impression you project. Genuine curiosity helps you project sincere interest rather than challenge.

Try This: Converting to Interest Talk

Referring to the scenarios on pages 35 and 36, replace each of the following positional statements with an interest-oriented statement or question:

1. Molly to Brandon: "No, I won't lend you my dollhouse."
2. Brandon to Molly: "Aw, come on, lend me the dollhouse. I'll take good care of it."
3. Mike to Laurel: "You fat cats get special treatment around here."
4. Fran to Spencer: "Yolanda [the younger woman who suggested games] doesn't know what she's talking about. I'm the one who's been doing this for fifteen years."

What Else?

As mentioned above, Spencer could use one of his "what-else" interests, more help with his workload, as an opener. That works well in his situation because there's an outside chance it ties in with the matter at hand. Fran might be the one to give him the help he wants. He can bring it up casually early on and later ask about her interest in doing a different type of volunteer work instead of the fundraiser.

In most situations, however, our extraneous objectives prove helpful later in a conversation, when thorough exploration of the interests around the main subject matter has failed to lead to consensus. The parties have made progress, but their interests aren't completely satisfied. *An extraneous interest can provide another bargaining chip that bridges that last little gap.*

To understand how this might work, let's return to our simple buy-sell dialogue between Sal and Trudy. Suppose Sal wants Trudy to assign a bond to him as payment for the boat, but they've agreed the boat is worth less than the bond, and Sal doesn't have the cash to pay Trudy the difference. However, Trudy has an extraneous interest in getting a new roof on her house, and Sal happens to be a roofer. He could install her roof, discounting the price by the difference between the bond value and the boat value. Trudy's extraneous interest provides an additional bargaining chip to help them reach a final and mutually agreeable consensus.

An underutilized value of extraneous interests lies in boosting an adequate agreement to the next level, optimizing the parties' satisfaction. Let's say Fran and Spencer agree that she will take on some new task and turn the fundraiser over to a committee that includes members of various ages— a perfectly adequate solution. But, in the course of the conversation, Fran reveals a what-else interest—she loves looking at the photo albums she's kept from high school to present. This inspires Spencer to suggest a slideshow of past fundraiser photos, silently running in the background at this year's dinner. The slideshow not only enhances the event, but also shows appreciation for Fran's past work. Working from an "extraneous" interest yields a better result for both of them.

How to Ask

Those unfamiliar with the Three Magic Questions often stumble when asked bluntly, "What else do you want?" People have trouble stretching their minds beyond the primary issue at hand. So they reply, "Nothing," or "I can't think of anything." Try asking "What else?" in the form of a fanciful hypothetical. "If the good fairy granted you three wishes, what would you wish for?" "What would you do if you won $50,000 to spend for the congregation?"

How Do We Want to Feel?

Feeling interests challenge us more than why interests and what-else interests. Talking about them discomfits many people. Yet feelings ignored can thwart our efforts to reach consensus.

Even if we reach an agreement of sorts without addressing the feeling interests, that agreement has less chance of working out in practice, and future disagreements between the two parties are more likely.

People may tell themselves they are "respecting each other's feelings" by failing to explore or discuss them. Too often, the real motivator is not respect, but still another feeling—the discomfort of admitting to others how we really feel and/or listening to expressions of their feelings that may anger or offend us.

But if people stifle the feelings that drive their attitudes and behavior, they make decisions on the substantive issues for the wrong reasons. Those decisions are not sustainable, and in time, the unresolved feelings erupt into higher-level conflicts that may require significant investment in de-escalation measures before people can re-enter a problem-solving frame of mind.

Some Reasons People Avoid Discussing Feelings

Sometimes people deny they have feelings, or that those feelings influence their positions and decisions. To them, such feelings aren't the right stuff. In fact, *they feel that feelings aren't the right stuff,* rather than think it. So their very resistance to discussing them *is* a feeling, and it controls their ability to reach consensus. This is particularly common in congregations because people erroneously assume that, if we are in the right place spiritually, we won't experience such unseemly emotions as anger, resentment or envy. Thus, discussing such feelings seems like admitting that we are in the wrong place spiritually or accusing someone else of being in the wrong place.

We may also find it difficult to explore and talk about feelings because we *can't find words for them*. We know we feel bad and we have an interest in feeling better, but can't say much more. We might *give an analogy*, as opposed to a name or definition.

For example, suppose Leo, a choir member, envies the music director, Kayla, because she was hired from among the rank and file choristers; Kayla moved up. It is very difficult for people to discuss their own envy. As a practical matter, it's often impossible, either because the person can't see his own envy, or can't tolerate the intense discomfort of making himself wrong by owning it.

However, if Leo tried to think of an analogy for his feelings, he might say, "OK, it's like Kayla and I started off as equally talented singers. Now she's the shining star on the top of the church Christmas tree, and I'm the tinsel." Everyone would get the idea without the need for him to don the label "envious."

Or let's say Fran tells Spencer, "I feel like a recording of Beverly Sills singing a beautiful aria that nobody listens to anymore." Spencer gets a clearer picture of her feelings than if Fran had articulated the name of the emotion.

Some Reasons To Discuss Feelings

But must we always reveal our feeling interests in order to reach consensus? "Must"? "Always"? Maybe not, but realistically, if strong feelings play a significant role in a disagreement or conflict, *the chances of building sustainable consensus are very small without addressing those feeling interests* in some way. Conversely, when we do address them with compassion, calmness and curiosity, we can build bridges that support us when future issues arise.

People can't defuse their feelings by simply telling themselves that they don't, or shouldn't, harbor them. In fact, concentrating on those feelings with thoughts like *I don't resent Kayla*, or *I shouldn't envy Kayla*, keep you focused on the envy and resentment.

Try this simple experiment: Don't think of a hamburger. What did you picture in your mind's eye? A burger, right? What happens if you go on a diet and keep telling yourself, "No desserts"? You crave desserts. You feel deprived of them. There's an autopilot aspect of the brain that doesn't hear the "no" or the "not." It only registers "burger" and "dessert."

Feelings we tell ourselves not to harbor tend to grow below the surface. Nor does the mere passage of time always eliminate these feelings. It can even root them more firmly in the brain and give them more power each time your mind goes there unexpectedly and unbidden.

Unilaterally defusing feelings that aren't serving you requires work that can be more time-consuming and difficult than talking about them with the other person. This work is often counterintuitive, and thus, requires education. You might need counseling and/or well-designed visualizations or written cognitive exercises. Entire books, such as *The Art of Forgiving*[24] and *How to Heal a Broken Heart in 30 Days*,[25] have been written about such mental and emotional work.

Expressing your feelings to the person who inspired them may take courage, but it can serve as a powerful tool.

Suppose Spencer had been a bit tactless, as ministers go, and previously tried a blunt, "I hear some of the young folks find speakers boring. How about you try games this year instead?" Now it seems Fran avoids him.

He decides to speak to Fran again and try to clear the air. He sits down with Fran and says, "It could be my imagination, but things don't seem the same since I brought up the fundraiser programming. *I've felt ashamed* of what I said. I wasn't thinking. I'm sorry if I hurt you, and I feel hurt, too, like I'm shut out. What can we do to get back on an even keel?"

Fran would be hard-nosed indeed not to soften to this approach. When Spencer admits he has felt hurt, Fran finds it so much easier to admit that she was hurt too. And if Spencer wants to clear the air, they will probably need to discuss Fran's hurt.

In many situations, feeling interests *must* be expressed to the other in order to fully resolve matters. Solo work, even if you're up to it, isn't enough.

Feeling Interests Call for Feeling Solutions

People often make the mistake of trying to eradicate feeling interests by over addressing material issues. This doesn't work, at least not for long. One of the interests driving Mike's antagonism toward Laurel is that he felt devalued by the original decisions to make him pay for the sign, but to let Laurel off the hook for the window.

Suppose the decision maker now reverses herself and makes Laurel pay for the window. To Mike, the original decisions still show how she really feels about him and Laurel, respectively. Those decisions seem to connote his and

---

24 Lewis B. Smedes (Ballantine Books, 1996).
25 Howard Bronson and Mike Riley (Broadway Books, 2000).

Laurel's relative values. He knows the decision maker only reversed herself to keep the peace. Worse, Mike may see the situation as reflecting not only the decision maker's values, but also the values of "the leadership" in general or "the church."

Paying money or other material consideration doesn't fix hurt feelings. Feeling interests must be addressed directly, as such. In settlement negotiations for civil lawsuits, angry plaintiffs often seek exorbitant amounts with a vague sense that enough money will somehow assuage their feelings. Sometimes defendants pay these amounts. The plaintiffs often emerge with as much hostility or more.

In the music director controversy, let's say the director, Kayla, started as an ordinary choir member back when the congregation was lay led. The board decided to hire Kayla as half-time music director. The congregation grew beyond pastoral size, and they hired a minister, Joan. Upon further growth, and at Joan's recommendation, the board promoted Kayla to full-time.

Now some of those among the fire-the-director group, people who knew Kayla as an ordinary member, envy her special collegial relationship with Joan. As fellow staff members, Joan and Kayla hobnob in the church offices on a routine basis, working closely together to plan and deliver services. They go to lunch together once a week or so. Naturally, Joan gets to know Kayla better than most other church members, and vice versa. Kayla can easily talk to Joan about any personal problem at the office or over lunch, while others have to wait for appointments.

The "pro-Kayla" group includes several good singers, recruited into the congregation and its choir by Kayla, who often assigns them solo parts. Believing the "anti-Kayla" group is envious, mean-spirited and ungrateful, they feel angry with them and protective of Kayla.

Yet, the first group bases their move to dismiss Kayla on budgetary considerations. Indeed, there are some among them who don't envy Kayla. They took at face value the budgetary rationale presented by people they didn't realize were envious and were persuaded by their arguments. The envious might believe their motives, too, are strictly financial, like the man who believes he decided to raise his arm, when in fact, it was artificially stimulated.

Meanwhile, Kayla's supporters base their position on the value of the music program in attracting and retaining members and boosting attendance.

Kayla's soloists represent only a portion of this group. Like the experimental arm raiser, they believe membership and attendance are their real motives. And like those whose real driver is envy, these people persuade others with their rationale about membership and attendance.

Solving the budget issue will not put this controversy to rest. If the congregation finds a way to expand the outreach ministries while retaining Kayla, whether full-time or part-time, the envious will raise new complaints. Before you know it, someone accuses Kayla of misusing her portion of the budget. If the records prove this accusation false (make the accusers wrong), their resistance and resentment toward Kayla only grows. Next someone finds fault with her choice of music.

These people swat at one swarming gnat after another while ignoring the big, nasty hornet buzzing around stinging them. Eventually, there is a painful rift.

The best hope of fully resolving the problem, without losing members from one faction or the other, lies in addressing feelings by something other than budget juggling and changes in the choice of music, something directed squarely at the envy of some members and defensiveness of others.

Drawing Out Others' Feelings

If you sense strongly that the other person's unspoken feelings are getting in the way or that they *are* the issue, you have little to lose by trying to draw them out and address them, for you will probably not reach consensus or clear the air, in other words, satisfy your own interests, unless you do. We've seen that you inspire others to satisfy your interests by demonstrating your desire to address theirs. You can't address their feeling interests unless you know how they feel.

But how do you draw out people who don't want to talk about their feelings? A blunt "How do you feel?" can put them off or intimidate them. Instead, try one or more of the following:

Request an Analogy

We've seen above how Leo, the soloist who felt passed up by Kayla, thought of a Christmas tree analogy for his feelings, while Fran likened hers to a beautiful but neglected recording. You can also ask others for analogies. If the person can't think of one, make your request more specific. "Can you recall another time you felt like this?" "If your feeling were an animal, what would it be?" "If your feeling were food, how would it sit on your stomach?"

Make the First Move

We've seen an example of this technique as well, Spencer breaking the ice by telling Fran he feels ashamed, sorry and hurt. If Fran doesn't consider feelings the right stuff, she certainly doesn't want to be the only one to admit them in a conversation. If you open up first, the other person doesn't have to go one-down to follow suit. You can invite them into the pool rather than telling them to dive in first.

If a person doesn't follow your lead, this doesn't mean that your ice-breaker was pointless. Even if he does not reciprocate by telling you his feelings, your statement might inspire him to think about them, and anytime a person becomes more aware of his own ultimate driving interests, you make progress.

Suppose Spencer mentions feeling hurt, and Fran reacts angrily, *"You're hurt?* What about me? You want to toss my fundraiser format out like an old shoe, and *I'm* the villain here?" He chose words about his feelings, rather than Fran's behavior, in an effort not to inflame her with wrong making. Yet Fran still felt made wrong and lashed out with projection, making Spencer more wrong than she was.

This doesn't mean Spencer failed. First, while his words didn't eliminate Fran's feeling made wrong, they minimized it. Contrast, "You hurt me by shutting me out." If Fran had heard this, she might have walked out of the conversation altogether. By airing his feelings, rather than accusing Fran, Spencer at least kept her engaged.

Secondly, Fran has now opened up about her feelings. *"You're* hurt? What about me?" translates as, "I'm *really* hurt!" Now Spencer can address her hurt issue. "I can't blame you if you're angry. I can see you're really hurting. Can we talk about what would help?"

Ask How They Want to Feel Then Follow Up

Sometimes people feel more comfortable talking about potential positive feelings rather than current negative ones. And that's their real interest, feeling better.

Spencer could ask Fran, "How would you like to feel at the end of our conversation?" "How would you like to feel when you're working on the fundraiser?" or "How would you like to feel when the fundraiser's over?"

One of the virtues of asking how people want to feel is that it minimizes wrong making and other negativity. The downside is that some people find it even harder to answer this question than to state how they feel at present. Use it if and when you can. For other times, there are other techniques to choose from.

Guess and Verify

After Spencer airs his feelings, Fran might not reciprocate, not even indirectly. For example, she could say, "Sorry you feel bad," and maintain a stiff, distant attitude.

Often, people who won't volunteer their feelings can't resist reacting to your speculations. Spencer can say, "You seem angry, are you?" He takes a guess at a driving feeling, anger, then seeks verification, "Are you?" Fran might respond in several possible ways, each of which represents progress.

She might feel relieved. It's hard for some people to express anger toward a member of the clergy. But Spencer said it first, showing he wants to know how she feels and that he's willing to discuss it calmly. If Fran feels relieved, she might confirm, "Yes, I have felt angry." Or she might correct Spencer, "Not so much angry as hurt."

The downside of this technique is that, in seeking verification, "Are you [angry]?" he presents Fran with a closed question,[26] one that can be answered yes or no. He makes it easier for her to simply say, "Yes," than to think about her feelings and express them in her own way. If Fran were inclined to reply to a direct, "How do you feel?" or to reciprocate Spencer's ice-breaker, she might say, "I feel like all the fundraisers I've been so proud of in the past weren't any good, and neither was I." This would enlighten Spencer more than, "Yes, I'm angry." It would tell him Fran feels devalued. But "Yes, I'm angry" is a start. It's better than nothing. It's a base to build on.

As we've seen, sometimes people can't find the words to express their feelings, even when they're willing. In many of the situations described in *Nonviolent Communication—A Language of Life*,[27] another person's emotions

---

26 The use of open and closed questions is discussed more extensively in Chapter 10.
27 Marshall Rosenberg (Puddledance Press, 2005).

run so high that they are temporarily incapable of the kind of reflection necessary to identify and describe their feelings. Author Marshall Rosenberg wisely recommends closed questions in such situations. They help us talk an excited person down to a level from which normal conversation can proceed.

Guess and Act

There are times when none of the above techniques draw out the other person's feelings. There are also times when you have a strong sense of their feelings without their describing them. You may sense another's feelings vicariously even if you can't name them. In such cases, you can simply proceed to say or do something that addresses the feelings you believe they have, then observe their reactions.

Fran sits with her arms folded, scowling up at Spencer from beneath her brows. She's angry, and he knows exactly why. "I'd be angry if I were you, and I want to tell you how very sorry I am."

Georgia has worked all afternoon setting up a buffet for a church social, replenishing dishes, etc. Now almost everyone else has disappeared as she begins to clean up the huge mess, and her friend Ernestine helps. Georgia's hands are immersed in soapy water. Dirty dishes cover every inch of counter space. Miss Piggy, the person who always eats the most and helps the least, waddles into the kitchen and asks Georgia, "Got any more of those meatballs left?" Georgia doesn't answer, but Ernestine sees her shoulders rise. Miss Piggy shrugs and leaves. Ernestine doesn't need to ask how Georgia feels. Maybe she can't name the feeling. But she knows a hug would help, and she gives Georgia one.

Try This: Asking about Feelings

Referring to the scenarios on page 36:
- How might Brandon use one of the above skills to learn how Molly feels about lending the dollhouse?
- How might Laurel draw out the feelings behind Mike's snide remarks?

Hearing Feelings Expressed

On the other side of the coin, listening calmly and attentively when someone expresses unpleasant feelings toward you is equally important and equally difficult as expressing your own, sometimes more so. Such expressions usually make us wrong, and we tend to project, as in, *He didn't have to call me selfish,* or *He didn't have to raise his voice. If I had been in his shoes, I could have made the same point more politely.*

And maybe you could have. He may not have your communication skills. But if you want to reach consensus with him, a clumsy or tactless expression of his feeling interests is better than none at all. It may help you curb your projection to think of his words as gifts—gifts of information about interests you can address in order to get what *you* need from him while building or strengthening a bridge.

Now you know the theory of using the Three Magic Questions in conversation. In the next chapter, you'll see them at work as Spencer and Fran engage in dialogues to get what they need while building bridges.

Key Points from Chapter 6

- Interest talk is a good way to begin a consensus-seeking dialogue
    - Express one of your interests or
    - Ask the other person about one of theirs or
    - Appeal to a mutual interest
- Use the Magic Question "Why?"
    - Explaining the reason (why) you do or don't want something can be a powerful force
    - There are many ways to phrase a why question without literally using the word "Why"
- Use the Magic Question "What else do we want?"
    - Discussing extraneous interests can move you forward in many ways
        - One of your own extraneous interests can be a light-hearted way to begin a dialogue
        - When you make progress toward consensus, but need something more to finish bridging a gap, extraneous interests can serve

- Addressing extraneous interests can bump up an acceptable consensus to an outstanding one
- Use the Magic Question "How do we want to feel?"
  - Material considerations don't address feeling interests; feeling interests must be addressed directly
  - Before you can address feeling interests, you must identify them
  - If someone has trouble telling you how he feels, you might be able to draw him out by one of the following
    - Request an analogy
    - Make the first move by expressing your feelings
    - Ask how they feel, then follow up
    - Guess and verify
    - Guess and act
  - Then listen calmly and attentively, even if the other person expresses himself clumsily or tactlessly

CHAPTER 7
THE THREE MAGIC QUESTIONS—IN DIALOGUE

With Mrs. Fairford conversation seemed to be a concert and not a solo.

\- Edith Wharton

If you're like most people, you learn easier when you can observe examples of skills in action. This chapter presents specific examples of how the Three Magic Questions can play out in practice. By following a complete dialogue, with parallel commentary, you will see how our characters employ the Magic Questions, and their answers, in the natural flow of a conversation; how they pick and choose different conversational tools from their toolkits as the moment suggests; and how they regroup and proceed when one effort disappoints or backfires.

We'll start with three examples of dialogue between Spencer and Fran:

- One in which Spencer begins by discussing one of his own interests
- A second in which he begins by asking about one of Fran's interests
- And a third in which Fran, rather than Spencer, uses the skills when he blindsides her with a suggestion for a program change

The left column contains the dialogue. The right column gives comments from the skill-user's point of view. Try first reading across rows to intersperse the comments. Then reread down the left column to better appreciate the flow of the conversation.

Dialogue 1: Rev. Spencer (S) begins by discussing one of his interests with Fran (F)

Spencer's View:	Fran's View:
S: Fran, I know we both want to maximize income from the fundraiser. It seems to me that attendance has dropped a bit the last couple of years. What's your take on that?	Asking himself "Why?" about games led Spencer to an interest broader than considering games. He begins by telling Fran this interest, then soliciting her thoughts.
F: It was a little lower last year. I hadn't realized Oak St. Church moved their fundraiser up to February, like ours. I want to re-think the date this year.	He's glad to know a date change might help. He still wants to explore programming options.
S: Good idea. Who did you see attending ours—what age groups, marital status?	He wants to know if Fran has noticed fewer young adults and whether she shares an interest in boosting their attendance. The impression of the lady who commented might be wrong. He first tries an open question (see Chapter 10) to avoid suggesting an answer.
F: I saw basically the same kind of folks I've always seen.	The question does not elicit any ideas about age groups.
S: I didn't see as many of our younger members.	So he suggests an answer.

F:	We can't gear it to the young folks.	Fran takes a categorical position. Spencer can work from here to uncover the interest(s) behind it.
S:	What are the downsides of that?	A way of asking "Why?"
F:	It's us mature people who can afford to spend the most on the silent auction.	"Us"? Is Fran defensive? She might feel made wrong.
S:	True, and I hear a lot of good feedback from them about how much they enjoy it, thanks to you.	He makes her right with a true statement and a sincere compliment that appeals to her feeling interests.
F:	But...?	Fran senses the other shoe is about to drop. Maybe she thinks Spencer is only stroking her.
S:	(Chuckles) No buts. I have nothing but praise for the fundraiser—and for you. I'm curious to look at anything that might increase income. My workload's so heavy that I was hoping we could earn enough to hire a part-time assistant.	He reinforces his esteem for Fran and elaborates on his income interest by tying it to a what-else interest that fits the context and doesn't threaten her.
F:	Hmm.	She has slowed down and started to think—progress.

S: Planning the fundraiser's the next thing on the agenda, so naturally my mind turned to how we could make a good thing even better.

F: Maybe we could try including a greater number of modestly priced auction items that the young people can afford, but still have the big-ticket items as well.

After hearing a non-threatening reason (why) that makes sense to her, Fran now shares Spencer's interest in fundraiser changes that could increase attendance and participation.

S: Lots of small donations add up. Let's think about modestly priced items people can donate to the auction.

Rather than immediately turn the conversation back to the program issue, Spencer follows up on Fran's suggestion, keeping an open mind.

F: Things like group dinners at people's homes sell well. We could actively solicit younger people to donate those. No actual bidding. First 15, or whatever number, who sign up get seats for $20 or so. And they and their friends would also be more likely to sign up for those events.

S: Good. Good. And young people like game nights.

This could be another way to address any interest in games.

F: They could donate game nights, and they'd only have to provide snacks, not a full meal.

S: What about having games at the fundraiser itself?

Good ideas have developed, but Spencer still wants to explore overall appeal of the programming.

F: When would we have time for them?

S: What would you think about going all games instead of a speaker?

Asking her opinion validates her, whereas suggesting all games might have threatened her.

F: What? You don't want my speaker?

Uh-oh. She still got upset, but probably not as upset as if he had made a direct suggestion.

S: Personally, I'd miss the speaker. I'm just thinking out loud.

Spencer perseveres. Returns to interest talk and explanation.

F: Well, I'd miss the speaker, too, and so would others my age. The caliber of our speakers draws visitors as well. And that boosts income.

Spencer's approach has inspired Fran to begin talking interests.

S: Two different types of fundraisers—summer and winter?

In the spirit of suspended judgment, he puts many options on the table. They can go back and choose later. (See Chapter 8)

F: (Groans)

S: If we could find another person to head the second fundraiser?

F: Auctions at both? Meals at both? Would the two events compete with each other for people's resources? We might end up doing twice the work for the same money.

Fran shares Spencer's interest in maximizing income from a given amount of effort.

S: Yes, we'd want to avoid that. Well, we've given each other a lot to think about. Let's mull it over and talk again, say Thursday at 10:00?

Spencer has achieved his short-term goal of getting Fran to consider new options while keeping her involved. A think break will help them both.

F: OK.

Notice how focusing on the broadly defined interests naturally leads to a joint-problem-solving mindset, as opposed to a right-or-wrong, either-or mindset. Spencer and Fran now have many options to consider. The think break may produce additional options. Then they can pick and choose, mix and match, to develop an optimum fundraiser plan.

Spencer spoke about his own interests, rather than representing (triangulating into) those of Yolanda, who requested games. From among his various interests, he chose to begin with income, a material interest, but one that worked well in this situation.

Suppose that, instead, he had expressed concern for younger people who feel distanced by the program. At first blush, caring (for the young people) seems a compassionate interest, perhaps more seemly for a minister to express than a monetary interest. However, this might have implied that Fran doesn't care and/or that she's the one who made the young people feel distanced. He could make Fran wrong, triggering resistance.

Moreover, chances are Fran has heard through the grapevine that Yolanda is talking up games, so Spencer's "caring" would seem to place him on Yolanda's side. The interest in income was a better opener because Spencer could be virtually certain that he, Fran and Yolanda all share that interest.

Note that Spencer did not over-strategize. He did not try to determine in advance the order in which various interests might come up or to plan ways to steer the conversation toward a particular solution. Rather, he got his primary interests in mind, selected one as a starting point, then focused on learning about Fran's interests and looking for ways to mesh them with his own. With a broad goal of finding a solution that would address his own interests as well as Fran's (whatever those might turn out to be), *he went with the flow of the conversation.* This is what interest talk, as opposed to positional negotiation, looks like.

Not even Spencer's starting point was cast in stone. He might have planned to begin as he did in Dialogue 1 with his interest in maximizing fundraiser income, but when he sat down with Fran, she might have spoken first. If so, Fran was offering him a gift—the opportunity to learn more about her interests before deciding how best to introduce his own.

As mentioned in Chapter 1, in composing this and all the other sample dialogues, I put myself in the shoes of the skill-user (in this case, Spencer) and took the interest-oriented approach. I did not plan the dialogue before drafting it. Nor did I try to steer it toward a given solution while drafting. Rather, I chose a starting point for Spencer and wrote it. Then I shifted myself into Fran's shoes, let myself feel her probable reaction, and wrote it. Back in Spencer's shoes, I decided what to say next based on what Fran had said, not on some predetermined strategy or plan. While I did edit the draft for clarity, I did not change the basic direction the dialogue took.

This go-with-the-flow composition method comes as close as possible to the way my unscripted role-play demonstrations work out in my classes, when I don't know in advance what the improvisational actor will say. I hope this composition method increases your confidence in the effectiveness of interest talk.

Some readers, upon first reviewing such a dialogue, think, *That was too easy. It wouldn't really go like that.* They're right. The above dialogue is compact, so as not to bore the reader with side trips down avenues that don't pan out, and from which Spencer would regroup and try again, in an actual conversation. However, Spencer's statements, their effects on Fran, and the end result are all well within the range of realistic possibilities.

Example 2 shows how Spencer could begin in a very different way and could end up with a different, but equally promising, result.

Dialogue 2: Rev. Spencer begins by exploring Fran's interests

Dialogue:	Spencer's View:
S: Well, it's fundraiser time again.	
F: Yep.	
S: It's hard for me to find words to express how much I appreciate your work every year.	He addresses Fran's near-certain feeling interest, appreciation.
F: Thanks.	Appreciation inspires appreciation.
S: How does it feel, knowing it's time to start planning once again?	He begins to ask about her other feeling interests.
F: Well, there's a little sigh, because I know how much work it is. But there's a lot I enjoy about it.	
S: What do you enjoy the most?	He invites her to elaborate on positive feeling interests.

F: You know, I used to think I wouldn't enjoy selling. But I've learned how to sell good speakers on appearing at a discounted rate. I sell people on making large donations to the auction. I feel proud when I bring somebody on board like that.

S: What do you enjoy the least?

Now he seeks info on negative feeling interests.

F: Details. Keeping track of everything and everyone.

S: What about dealing with all the other volunteers, trying to keep them happy and motivated?

F: Well, it's hard, not like dealing with paid employees. Sometimes I have to walk on eggs, but when I succeed, I feel proud of that too. It's another form of selling.

S: Are there ways we could sell even more people on attending? I've heard a speaker doesn't grab some of the younger folks. They might like a more active program.

After noting above info on her feeling interests, he shifts discussion toward one of his tangible interests, maximizing fundraiser attendance.

F: (Bristling) If "some" means Yolanda, she's just stirring up trouble.

More feeling issues pop up. Also, Spencer detriangulates by letting Fran name Yolanda.

S: I don't want trouble, and I do want to understand. Could you elaborate about what you see going on?

He shifts back to learn more about Fran's feeling interests so he can address them. He also avoids taking sides.

F: I heard she wants to ditch the speaker and change this into a game party. She's probably trying to talk all her friends into it.

S: I wonder how we might go about finding out what the younger people really want?

He ties his interest in attendance to her interest in respect by asking her input and by recognizing the validity of her implication that Yolanda doesn't necessarily speak for all the young people.

F: Well, first off, I wouldn't lose sight of what we mature people want. We're the ones who spend the most at the auction, and we like speakers.

She wants to feel valued.

S: True. We don't want to increase one group only to decrease another. How might we interest both?

He validates her then returns to interest talk, in particular, asking how they can address multiple interests.

F: Oh, I don't know. Maybe I should just turn this over to Yolanda. If games don't work, they didn't happen on my watch. And if they do work, maybe I've lost touch and ought to step down.

More possible feeling interests.

S: Sounds like you're feeling criticized or tired of doing the same job every year. Are you?

He guesses at feeling interests and seeks confirmation.

F: Well, yeah, a little of both.

S: Well if you're feeling criticized, I want you to know that I have nothing but praise for your work. I prefer speakers myself. I guess I'm just the kind of guy who can't resist trying to make a good thing even better.

F: So what do you want me to do?

S: Me? I'd like to see you involved in work that *you* find rewarding. I'd like to draw on those selling skills you mentioned.

He shows her that her feeling interests are one of his interests. He also shows that he values her skills, again addressing her interest in esteem.

F: Which means?

S: That's up to you. If you really are burned out on the fundraiser, we might talk about other ways to use your talents.

He invites creative discussion about their joint interest in rewarding work for her.

F: Like what?

S: We could make a proposal to Interfaith Ministries for an interdenominational lecture series. You volunteer to chair. That's one idea.

Spencer shows that he is really thinking about Fran's interests by making a specific suggestion.

F: Hmm.

S: Another idea is that I need help providing pastoral care. Frankly, I'm overworked.

He suggests another option, which shows her that these are only ideas. The kind of volunteer work she does is her call.

F: What? Are you suggesting I counsel people?

S: What I'm thinking is that we could work together on organizing and training a caring committee—to help people who need a shoulder, or direction to outside resources, more than they need actual counseling. You're a good big-picture planner. And you'd be good at getting professors or local ministers to help train the committee members.

F: So I'd give up the fundraiser?

S: Only if you prefer one of the other jobs. Otherwise, by all means, stick with the fundraiser, and help me think about *if* there's any way to increase our already good turnout. (Smiles) Maybe you should recruit the young people into the kitchen. After working that banquet, they'll be ready to just sit down and listen to a speaker.

Re-emphasizes the idea that her work is her call, and the fact that the fundraiser is excellent as it is. He only wonders *if* it could be made even better.

He offers another suggestion that introduces a light tone.

F: (Smiles) I'd like to think this over.

S: Me too. Let's talk again in a few days.

A break for reflection is a good idea for both of them.

F: OK.

Spencer's focus on Fran's interests—how she feels, how she wants to feel, volunteer work that uses her best gifts and is truly rewarding for her—inspires her to think about options that would mesh with his interests. This is the heart of the Three Magic Questions' role in building consensus. Addressing others' interests—in ways that are positive, or at least neutral, for you—motivates them to address your interests by cooperating and collaborating with you.

Notice how Spencer addresses Fran's feeling interests. In exploring her feelings, he learns that she knew what Yolanda had been saying and was miffed. He wants to clear the air. His genuine respect for Fran comes out in his choice of words. Fran's interest in respect is especially keen at this time because her way of running the fundraiser has been questioned. When the topic of whether she should stick with the fundraiser prompts him to praise her past work and to say that he always likes to make a good thing better, Fran asks him, "What do you want me to do?" It's as if she's verbally throwing up her hands and giving in to "the boss."

Spencer begins, "Me?" This shows respect; he doesn't want to impose a decision on her. Then he mentions his interest in her involvement in rewarding work, and in drawing on her selling skills (one of her best gifts). When she seeks clarification, "Which means?" Spencer begins, "That's up to you," reinforcing his respect.

Neither of the above dialogues represents "the right answer." Our focus is on *how* Spencer goes about the conversations. Notice that *in neither dialogue did Spencer need to discuss every item on his interest list*. He picked and chose the ones that fit in with the flow of the conversation. Before agreeing to a final consensus with Fran, he can review his list to be sure that all his interests have been addressed. When you do this, you'll often find that interests you did not discuss fell into place in the course of interest talk. But if some interests have been overlooked, you can re-enter discussion. Your pre-agreement review of your list and any further discussion indicated can occur on the spot in simple cases. In more complicated situations, including any time you sense that the other person's or your own mental circuits are overloaded, it's best to take a few days break to review and to plan for follow up discussion.[28]

Our first two dialogues happened to assume Spencer used the skills and that Fran didn't know or didn't consciously use them. But these tools aren't just for clergy to use.

Here's a third version of the dialogue in which Fran knows and uses the Magic Questions, but Spencer does not consciously use them. Thus the comments column is written from Fran's point of view.

---

28 More about breaks in Chapter 9. Other skills Spencer used, such as questions and validation, will also be described in subsequent chapters.

Dialogue 3: Fran uses her interest skills

Dialogue:	Fran's View:
S: I'd like to speak with you about the programming for this year's fundraiser.	
F: OK.	
S: I've heard some of the younger members would like to try having games instead of a speaker.	Fran feels a bit stunned.
F: What are their reasons?	Fran did not see this coming, so she hasn't had time to think about her interests and Spencer's. She will do what she can here and now, and ask for a break if/when she feels she needs time for reflection.
	Asking this equivalent for "why?" should gain her more information about what she's dealing with here. In addition, it builds in some time for her feelings to calm down before she expresses any opinions.
S: It seems they would find games more interesting, more active.	
F: And what do you mean by "younger?" Teens? Twenty-somethings?	In this case, Fran needs info on whose interests she has to address in addition to info on what those interests are.

S: The person who mentioned it to me is in her late twenties. I assume she's talking about people her age. Though the teens, and even younger children, might like games, too. We could make the event more family friendly.

Spencer implies another interest—making the event more family friendly.

F: And how many people are we talking about who share this preference for games?

Use of a question avoids overtly suggesting that Yolanda exaggerated. Just as Fran wishes to avoid making Spencer wrong, she avoids making Yolanda wrong to Spencer.

S: That's a good question. I guess we need more information about that.

F: I have the impression that most of the middle-aged and older folks really like the speakers, and they sell tickets to friends outside the congregation. I don't know how they would react to games. They give the most to the fundraiser. They donate the big-ticket items to the auction, and they also spend the most on purchases. I want to be sure they maintain their enthusiasm and involvement in the fundraiser.

Fran describes some of her interests that Spencer likely shares.

S: So do I.

Spencer confirms that these are mutual interests.

F: Truth be told, I've been really proud of my past speakers. The idea that people find them boring has left me feeling rather deflated. Plus, speakers are what I know how to do. I'm not sure how good a job I'd do on games. I'm not saying I wouldn't do it. I guess I just need some time to get my mind and my emotions around this new idea.

Now Fran mentions her feeling interests.

S: It might re-inflate you to remember that, no matter what program we choose, some people will like it, and some won't. Obviously, lots of people do like the speakers, and they do draw visitors.

Notice how naturally Spencer is led to address Fran's interests.

We're not ready to decide because, as you suggested, we don't know how many people actually want games or how much they want them. Take time to collect your thoughts. Meanwhile, I'll try to get a better read on how serious this games suggestion really is. Let's meet again in a week.

F: OK.

Notice that a more typical volunteer, not knowing the Three Magic Questions, but simply winging it, might have done one of two things. First, an assertive or aggressive person might have said something like, "I bet Yolanda's the one who suggested games. Even if she said, 'Some of us,' Yolanda might just be speaking for herself. And if others have jumped on her bandwagon, it's just because she egged them on, and only a few of them. They probably don't even care that much about games."

Put yourself in Spencer's shoes and try this statement on. Can you feel how differently you would be inclined to react? If Fran had made Yolanda wrong to Spencer, she might be the one to come off looking bad to him, especially since, for all she knows, Spencer admires Yolanda and agrees with her. In that case, criticizing her would amount to criticizing Spencer's taste and judgment.

On the other hand, a more timid person might not have challenged Spencer in any way. She'd bite her tongue and slink away to lick her emotional wounds. Spencer might never know how devalued and hurt she felt nor have the opportunity to address those feelings.

Either of these wing-it approaches would chip away at any bridge existing between Spencer and the volunteer. But when Fran used the Magic Questions, she strengthened the bridge so it will better support future dealings. She not only made more headway with Spencer, but the conversation was more pleasant for both of them. Most of us would like every member of our congregation to use these skills with leaders and fellow members alike.

We move next into skills for creating mutually satisfying ways to address our interests.

Key Points from Chapter 7

- There are many excellent ways in which a dialogue on a given subject can begin and play out
- Don't over strategize
- Go with the flow of the conversation, listening for signs of the other person's interests and looking for ways to mesh them with your own
- It isn't always necessary to mention all your interests in order to reach a conclusion that satisfies all of them

CHAPTER 8
CREATING CONSENSUS CONTENT

It's when we're given choice that we sit with the gods and design ourselves.

\- Dorothy Gilman

You've seen how interest talk can steer your dialogues toward mutually satisfying consensus. You can augment that tendency by actively generating creative solution elements or options from which to put together, not just any acceptable consensus, but the best consensus.

The Three Magic Questions move us away from specific positions, requests or demands, such as "replace speaker with games," to broader definitions of ultimate objectives or interests, like "maximize attendance." *To optimize consensus, we look for a number of alternative ways to address both party's interests before deciding which ideas to adopt.*

Think about this process as laying out a buffet I call a *"Solution Smorgasbord."* When you pass through a preview line in the cafeteria before snaking around to the serving line, you get to defer choosing until you've seen all the options. Once you've previewed all the choices, you can select fish, chicken or beef; rice, noodles or potatoes; spinach, broccoli or carrots; and put them together to create your perfect meal. You pick the items that best suit your interests. A runner prepping for a long-distance race can select rice, noodles and potatoes and pass on the meat. A high school football player who wants to muscle up might choose two servings of beef and avoid carbs. An avid vegan may take rice, beans, spinach, broccoli and carrots.

Discussing interests naturally leads to ideas for what to put on the buffet menu. In Dialogue 1 Spencer's Magic Questions generated a spate of ideas for dealing with such interests as maximizing attendance:

- Younger adults donating low-cost auction items such as game nights
- Games instead of speaker

- Games plus speaker
- Two fundraisers, one with speaker, one with games
    o With or without meals
    o With or without auctions

This left Fran with her circuits overloaded and needing a think break. Pausing to reflect was a good thing for Fran and Spencer to do before making a final decision on such an important matter.

Inspiring Questions

We can enhance the creative thinking inspired by interest talk in various ways. It's important to actively solicit the other person's ideas for options to put on the buffet for two reasons:

- First, if she helps to craft the agreement content, she will more likely buy into it with enthusiasm and follow through.
- Second, if you make all, or most, of the suggestions, you often end up contributing more than your fair share to the final plan, and therefore, more than your fair share of the time and effort to implement the decision.

Open questions inspire creative thinking better than yes-or-no questions. Open questions are those that can not be answered "yes" or "no."[29] I have found six types of open questions particularly helpful in developing a Solution Smorgasbord.

What Would Help?

The underused question *"What would help?"* can be applied to any interest, but *is particularly useful in addressing feeling interests*. Sometimes it's hard to come up with even one option for addressing feeling interests. At other times, someone tells us how she feels, and we launch into "the" answer, or at least "an" answer of our own device.

If, instead, you ask, "What would help?" you learn whether she wants practical help, or just an ear. This is important because offering advice when someone wants empathy, or vice versa, can hurt or offend the person. In either

---

29 For more about open questions, see Chapter 10.

case, you not only learn more about her feelings, but you also show that you wish to deal with her like a peer, not a patriarch or matriarch. In addition, this question steers the person into creative thinking about more promising types of solutions.

"What would help?" is a powerful question. On a first date, a woman I know was thinking, *This won't work. What's the kindest way to tell him, "No more."* Then, toward the end of the evening, she mentioned a problem, and he replied, "What would help?" Like magic, her thoughts changed to, *Wow! A man who asks me instead of making my decisions for me? He might be a keeper.*

Sometimes people shy away from "What would help" in the context of disagreement. We may instinctively fear that soliciting others' feedback on ways to address their interests is tantamount to offering to do whatever they say. We may be concerned that others might reply with requests for material things that we know won't really erase their ill feelings. For example, if Laurel asks Mike, "What would help," and he replies, "You pay for the broken window," that will not relieve his feeling that the leaders value him less than Laurel.

We may fear that the other person will ask for something we can't or won't give them. What if Fran tells Spencer that what would help her is for him to tell Yolanda to butt out and mind her own business? Spencer might imagine that, if he then declines to do what Fran suggests, she will be more resentful than if he'd never opened the door to her ideas.

Such fears need not come to pass if you interlace judicious use of "What would help?" with skillful interest talk and additional questions. In fact, showing another that you are willing to fully explore options for meeting her true interests, *while also ensuring that your own interests are met*, can make her more willing to deal reasonably with you.

Here's one way such interlacing could play out:

Dialogue 4: Rev. Spencer asks, "What would help?"

Dialogue:	Spencer's View:
S: I'd like to speak with you about the programming for this year's fundraiser.	
F: (Sighs)	Something's wrong.
S: Is this a bad time?	Spencer makes a guess.
F: I suppose it's as good a time as any.	This suggests the problem may be the subject matter, rather than the timing.
S: Sounds like there's something about this subject you don't look forward to. Is that right?	Another educated guess.
F: Let's just get it over with. I suppose you want to discuss Yolanda's game campaign.	
S: Games are one option we could consider, but I really want to look more broadly at what's working well and whether there's any room for further improvement. Like we do with our congregational vision statement every few years.	He redirects the conversation from debating one suggestion to broader consideration of various options for addressing interests. Stating the assumption that some things are working well, plus reminding her that even the overall congregational vision is periodically reviewed, help to alleviate her sense of threat.

F: OK. Lay it on me.

But she still feels somewhat threatened.

S: I feel uncomfortable laying something on you. **What would help** you feel better?

Spencer advocates for his interest in proceeding only in a better atmosphere, then asks what would help Fran.

F: If I do a good job, then let me get on with it. If not, don't prolong the agony. Turn the event over to Yolanda and let me get on down the road.

She's opening up—good. And her answer indicates her feeling interest—she senses that the quality of her work is questioned, that her special gift for getting good speakers cheap isn't valued. But Spencer knows her knee-jerk solution won't really satisfy her feeling interest.

S: So you feel the excellence of your fundraiser work is about to be questioned?

F: It already has been. Everybody knows Yolanda wants to ditch the speaker program in favor of games.

S: For what it's worth, I think our past fundraisers have been exemplary. I've personally enjoyed the speakers and learned a lot from their talks. The visitors they draw, plus the reduced honoraria you negotiate, net us a lot more profit than, say, the run-of-the-mill talent show.

She might think he's just stroking her, yet this validation should make an inroad.

F: You're kind.

As he anticipated, she isn't completely convinced of his sincerity, but she is relaxing her defensiveness.

S: **What would help** you believe I'm not just being kind, that I really mean it?

F: Just let me do my job.

The same shortsighted answer, but expressed in less emotional terms, represents progress.

S: Suppose I were to say, "OK. Go ahead as usual." How would you feel?

An open question helps her consider the inadequacies of acting on her last suggestion.

F: Fine.

She probably won't feel fine because her suggestion is not a good way to deal with feeling interests.

S: So let's say we do that, and after service next Sunday, you spot Yolanda and me talking. How would that feel?

A follow-up question to inspire another step in the thought process.

F: (Crosses arms and looks away.)

Confirms that her own suggestion will not adequately address her feeling interests.

S: Looks like you'd feel uncomfortable. If you were a screenwriter, what would you have Yolanda and me talking about?

Further follow-up question, and another step.

F: (Voice cracks) How you had to humor me to keep the peace. Let me bring in another boring speaker.

She's beginning to see the inadequacy of Spencer giving in, how it won't really address her feelings.

S: I have no intention of humoring you because you don't need to be humored. You clearly have a gift for fundraising. I want you on the project, and I want you doing it with the same joy and zeal you've had in the past. It sounds like, now that other programming options have been raised, **you won't really feel comfortable until... What?**

Spencer advocates for his interest in her attitude, then asks a question equivalent to another "What would help?"

F: I guess I need to feel that the congregation is behind the program, or else turn it over to someone else.

The aha moment. She sees that her feeling interest must be addressed directly.

S: Before you throw in the towel, why don't we try to agree on a program everyone, including you, can feel good about?

Spencer makes his pitch for his interest in discussion and consensus, tying it to her interest in feeling the congregation is behind her.

F: Well, OK. But getting speakers is what I'm good at. If you really want games, you should get somebody else to chair the event.

Progress. She's ready to talk.

S: Let's look at the interests behind the suggestion of games. As I understand it, the idea is to make sure we have something to appeal to everyone, young, old, and in between. What other options might appeal to a wide range of ages?

He steers the conversation away from either-or (games or speaker) and toward the underlying interests.

F: One speaker I was considering is an astronaut. That was exactly my idea. She would appeal to everyone.

A good idea that Spencer would not have thought of if he hadn't asked for her ideas on options.

S: That's a really good option. Let's generate a few more ideas, then go back and decide.

But he doesn't stop there. He steers the conversation toward creating a large buffet before choosing what to put on the plate.

What Would Spiderman Do?

Have you ever attended a meeting where the leader asked the group to "Think out of the box" or "Go for a win-win" and the whole group just sat there in silence? Leaders may not say how to think out of the box. They may not even know how. Sometimes, all they *know* is that they want a better result than conventional thinking or lukewarm compromise. *Overly broad directives like "Think out of the box" can leave people stymied. A specific question often produces more creative ideas for the Solution Smorgasbord.*

Another problem can occur when the leader calls for a brainstorming session. She may remind the group that one of the rules is "no censoring." No matter how silly your idea may seem, you should share it. Yet our minds still have trouble finding their way out of that box, and when they do, people still hesitate to voice an unconventional idea. They don't want to stand out as the only one who suggested something that others might laugh at or something that clearly won't work without modification.

Yet *creative, out-of-the-box ideas often start with unworkable ideas*. They are out of the box precisely because they are fanciful. Even though we know they won't really work per se, *they usually contain a kernel of goodness*, some aspect that addresses a difficult interest. Once we identify that kernel, *we can often modify the unworkable aspects, while retaining the kernel of goodness*, to develop a feasible option.

The modification is like altering a food preparation method to improve an unpalatable buffet item, say peeled raw cloves of garlic. They're healthy (the kernel of goodness), but too sharp. We can retain garlic's health benefits and turn it into a tasty treat by slow roasting it in terra cotta and serving it with French bread to spread it on.

Consider a Real-Life Example

The first negotiation class I ever taught was for attorneys. I had devised a working hypothetical involving a dispute between two companies that sold ski equipment. I called for silly, unworkable options. If someone mentioned an option that was actually feasible, I would say we could put it on the option list, but not the unworkable list. "Let's build that unworkable list," I urged. Finally, one woman replied, "The two business owners fight a duel." She got it. That was what I meant by unworkable.

Taking off from the duel idea, the class saw that the kernel of goodness lay in a competition that was quicker and less expensive than proceeding with litigation. The unworkable aspects of a duel were danger and illegality. Searching for safe, legal ideas that retained the kernel of less expensive competition, the class came up with the idea of a "Ski-Off" contest between the two business owners. The winner would get the disputed assets. Both would get publicity and exposure from the event, better publicity than either could expect from a lawsuit.

Ask a Specific and Fanciful Question

You can stimulate this kind of creative thinking by asking a specific question like, "What would Spiderman do?" When you inject your specific question with fancy, you solicit fanciful, sometimes even silly, answers. If everybody's talking about what Spiderman would do, everyone's giving off-the-wall answers that won't work in their initial form. The hesitant guy need not fear that his unworkable idea will stand out and embarrass him. Now it's the person who suggests conventional wisdom who stands out.

Of course the fanciful question doesn't have to involve Spiderman. *Take the template, "What would _____ do?" and fill in the name of anyone who is very different from those involved in your dialogue.* You can name fictional characters like Don Quixote or Dora the Explorer; real people, famous or not, who lived in a very different time or place—Thomas Edison, your grandmother or someone from another continent; people who differ from you in abilities or assets, such as deaf teacher Helen Keller, millionaire tycoon Donald Trump or illusionist Chris Angel.

In congregational settings, it may seem tempting to fill in the blank with Jesus, Buddha, or the like. But then you're not asking a fanciful question. Resist this temptation. When creating a Solution Smorgasbord, we want a non-judgmental frame of mind.

To many people, "What would Jesus do?" is not a fanciful question, but a very serious one. It often translates as, "What is the *right* thing to do?" People who differ on what Jesus would do then see each other as "wrong," another mindset we want to avoid. Just asking the question can feel like a reprimand. Can you hear a mother asking, "What would Jesus do?" of a child who doesn't share her toys?

It's sort of like the old rule about avoiding religion and politics in polite social conversation. *When we want people to think openly and creatively, don't refer to anyone who carries heavy emotional weight for those involved in the discussion.*

Other types of fanciful questions revolve around different circumstances, rather than different people. What would we have done in the Middle Ages? What would we do on a space station? What would we do if stranded on a deserted island?

Suppose Mike and Laurel have a productive conversation in which they clear the air and feel connected again. Mike is able to tell Laurel that his paying for the sign he backed over, while she was forgiven for the window she broke, punctuated his feeling that, "There's three categories of people around here—the really poor folks who get all the sympathy and help, you fat cats who donate big bucks and have time to hang around here and work, and us shmucks who get lost in the shuffle." Concerned that other middle-class members might feel this way, Laurel encourages Mike to speak to their minister, Rev. Joan Black, about feeling lost in the shuffle. Let's look at how Laurel's fanciful questions might help Mike plan an approach for speaking to the minister.

Dialogue 5: Laurel asks Mike fanciful questions

Dialogue:	**Laurel's View:**
M: I'm thinking, but can't come up with anything I'd be comfortable saying to Rev. Black.	
L: I've learned a trick to jumpstart my thinking. Seems a little hokey at first, but it works.	Laurel begins to introduce what might seem like a crazy concept to Mike.
M: What's that?	
L: I ask myself an off-the-wall question like, "What would Yoda do if he wanted to talk to his minister about feeling lost in the shuffle?"	
M: You're right. Sounds hokey.	
L: Try it.	
M: Naa.	
L: OK. I'll go first. Yoda says, "Fear leads to anger."	She goes first to show a willingness to take the same risk she's asking him to take.

M: So I tell Rev. Black that fear leads to anger?

Laurel knows this reaction is normal for first-timers at the fanciful question technique. She doesn't let it discourage her, but rather uses additional consensus skills to convince Mike to try it.

L: You're right. That exact thing wouldn't work. But I could start by telling it to myself. I wouldn't want to go in scared and angry, so what's the opposite of fear? Comfort and confidence. So I'd start by finding ways to make myself feel comfortable and confident when I spoke to Rev. Black.

She introduces another aspect of the technique. A little bit at a time often works better than trying to explain the whole process at once.

M: But it doesn't tell me what to say.

More natural skepticism.

L: This trick works best for me if I get a number of ideas down first, then go back and see which ones I want to work with. What do you think Yoda would do?

Another bit of explanation.

She encourages him to try by repeating the fanciful question.

M: I feel silly.

L: Humor me.

M: Oh, OK. He'd take his light saber. But that's a weapon. I'm not going in and threaten the minister.

L: Of course not. Hang in there with me. We'll go back later and see if we can modify the idea to make it workable.

Now it's your turn to ask a question.

M: I can't think of one, and this is taking too long. Just forget it.
(Mike starts to walk away.)

L: Mike, please wait. We talked through the difference in how our accidents with the sign and the window were handled, and that was worth the time we spent. I never realized how many people in this congregation might feel overlooked. What if ten more minutes could show us a good way to improve things for all those people?

Laurel appeals to Mike's interest in not wasting time by pointing out how time invested has already addressed his interests concerning the accidents and by suggesting they need only spend ten more minutes.

She further appeals to his interest in not feeling overlooked by holding out the possibility of a more far-reaching solution than anything the two of them alone can do.

M: (Sighs.) OK, ten minutes. What do you want me to do?

L: Think of somebody who lived in the past.

She makes her request more specific.

M: Uh... Grandma.

L: What would my Grandma do? She'd bake cookies. Now, what would your Grandma do?

M: She was a wiry old thing. She'd just barge in there and tell Rev. Black how the cow ate the cabbage. I'm not sure I can do that.

L: We'll see.   More encouragement.

Now my turn to question. What would Spiderman do if he felt ignored?

M: (Pauses) He'd shoot a web over the rafters, hoist himself up where everybody could see him, and say, "Hey, look at me. I count too."

L: So he'd call attention to   Laurel recognizes the kernel
himself, right?   of goodness.

M: Yeah.

L: OK. We might want to cre-   Now that they've got a few
ate more ideas later, but for ideas to work with, Laurel
now, let's work with what   feels it's time to show Mike
we've got: how to take the next step,
• Fear leads to anger   so he will see the validity of
• Light saber   the technique.
• Cookies
• Tell how the cow
• Hoist yourself up and
  demand attention
Pick one.

M: Light saber.

L: I know you won't really do it, but if you could take a light saber, what would that do for you?

M: Take away my fear.

Good. Mike has taken a step toward a kernel of goodness.

L: Anything else?

M: It would give me some bargaining power.

A second kernel of goodness from the same (light saber) starting point.

L: So what bargaining power can you take?

M: My pledge, my membership. But I'm not going in and threaten to quit.

More reluctance.

L: You don't have to. What if, before speaking with Rev. Black, you just remind yourself how you contribute to this congregation?

Asks a question to steer Mike toward modifying the original idea while retaining the kernel of goodness.

M: I guess it could boost my confidence.

L: That's a great example of how you can start with something unworkable, like light saber, and end up with something you might decide to do.

Encouragement and a bit more explanation.

M: OK, I think I'm starting to get it. Now I'll take one—cookies. Offer Rev. Black a bribe?

L: Maybe just a token of appreciation and good will.	Models modification of idea to make it more feasible.
M: Still looks like a bribe.	
L: How could you show appreciation without seeming to bribe?	Asks an open question that leads him to modify the unworkable part while retaining the kernel of goodness.
M: Oh! Do like *my* grandma and just tell the Rev. what I appreciate, like her sermons.	
L: Great! Part of the answer to your question about what to say. How could we do something with Spiderman's web hoisting thing?	Another open question about reworking a silly idea.
M: *That's* what I need to tell her. We need a better way to make the middle-class majority feel noticed.	Mike's on his way to developing a viable plan for approaching Rev. Black

In the above example, I've made Mike unfamiliar with the fanciful question tool, and fairly resistant. Yet, using other tools from her consensus skill kit, Laurel leads him into asking and answering the questions, then modifying the answers to keep the kernel of goodness and make the unworkable parts feasible. It took a bit of effort on Laurel's part to draw Mike into giving the technique the old college try, but the results were worth it, and as Mike himself realized, he was going nowhere fast before. Of course, the conversation would be easier and more efficient if both Mike and Laurel had learned the technique before they began.

Some readers might wonder, *Why does Laurel have to help Mike figure out what to say to the minister?* The short answer is: She doesn't. As with all the other dialogues in this book, this example is not about what Laurel should do. It's about how to do whatever it is she has decided serves her interests.

Laurel might believe she and all the other members of the congregation benefit if everyone feels recognized. She might think the congregation would function better if more people know the fanciful question method, so she takes this opportunity to introduce it to one more member. Laurel may simply enjoy helping others. Or perhaps she sees the conversation with Mike as an opportunity to practice and hone her consensus-building skills.

But if Laurel weren't interested in collaborating with Mike on better recognition, she could have bowed out after their earlier conversation when she had satisfied her other interests, such as stopping Mike's snide remarks about the window.

Try This: Answering a Fanciful Question

Try asking yourself what your favorite fictional character would do if (s)he were Fran or Spencer. Then look for the kernels of goodness and re-work your fanciful answers to make them feasible.

Distinguish the Smorgasbord Process from Firm Offers

Another reason people hesitate to think out loud is a fear that their suggestions might be taken as firm offers. Here's a type of introduction I sometimes use when facilitating a Smorgasbord segment of a meeting:

> We're going to generate ideas for twenty minutes. During that time, please defer judgment on the ideas. No censoring—not even censoring yourself, no evaluating or criticizing, and no firm offers. There will be time for those things later. All you can offer during this segment are ideas for everyone to think about. And nobody can say, "OK. It's a deal" to someone else's idea.

How Can I...?

To help another individual think from your point of view, appreciate your interests, and contribute ideas for addressing them, you can say, "**How can I...**" then add one of your interests.

- Spencer: "How can I let members of all ages know I'm listening to them?"
- Molly: "How can I be absolutely sure nothing happens to the dollhouse?"

You may be surprised at what good ideas others have for addressing your interests when you invite their ideas in with this open question.

How Else Can You...?

When someone continues to fixate on one way of addressing his own interests, you can say "**How else can you...**" and add the interest in question.

- Fran: "Games are one idea. How else might we interest the younger adults?"
- Molly: "How else can you get the children what they need for their program?"

How Can We Do This and That?

So far, we've concentrated on questions for generating ideas to address one interest at a time. To arrive at a final agreement or consensus, we combine and/or modify these ideas to create a package that addresses as many interests as possible. We're combining food from the buffet menu to create a meal we'll both eat together.

Spencer and Fran might ask this question that seeks to address three interests: "How can we (1) have a speaker and also (2) provide some activity for those who don't enjoy speakers (3) without drawing those who like both speakers and playing games away from the speaker?" One answer might be to let those who aren't interested in the speaker run games for young children who wouldn't attend the speaker anyway.

In the case of the dollhouse, "How can we get Brandon what he needs for the children's program while ensuring that no harm comes to Molly's dollhouse?" Molly could show the dollhouse to the children and give them pictures to help them remember it; then the children build their own dollhouse with guidance from Brandon. As a bonus, this solution provides another activity for the children, one less for Brandon to plan.

This form of question can be expanded to cover as many interests as necessary or desired. How can music director Kayla's congregation (1) balance the budget and (2) eliminate envy while (3) retaining as many members as possible along with (4) those members' goodwill?

If you can't answer the question, go back and generate more options for dealing with the individual interests.

What *if you've placed on the table options that clearly address every interest expressed by the other person, but he still can't or won't agree to any package?* Or maybe you yourself can see that what's on the table would meet all the interests you've listed, yet you feel hesitant.

This usually indicates an interest that has not been identified. Either it hasn't emerged at all, or it has not been broadened enough to reflect the ultimate objective that's driving the hesitation. Simply *return to the Three Magic Questions, and don't forget, "How do we want to feel?"*

How Can We Do More/Better?

This is a great question to ask after you think you've reached consensus. It can come naturally where people started with a common goal, such as planning a retreat or other event. However, when the dialogue arose from a disagreement, or a potential or actual conflict, we may feel so relieved at resolving the bad stuff that we forget to optimize the good. We've put together a meal we're both willing to eat, but can we spice it up?

Quite apart from the direct benefits of an even better consensus, the experience of an optimized plan, one that really grabs people, one they feel proud of, sells them on the value of using consensus skills in the future. That experience sells them better than any book could ever do. It builds a mentality of interest-driven, right-making, bridge-building communication.

A Solution Smorgasbord Example

The Solution Smorgasbord is the place to list any specific ideas, such as "games instead of speaker," that the Magic Questions broadened into true interests, along with all your other creative ideas.

Spencer and Fran's solution Smorgasbord might look like this:

Fundraiser Options:
- Speaker only
- Games only
- Games & speaker
- Astronaut
- Free program + one huge single-donor gift
- Young adults running games for small children
- Young adults working kitchen
- Performance by Fran and Spencer
- "This is your life, Fran"
- Murder mystery dinner
- Talent contest, open to members and outsiders
    - Prizes
    - Different categories – singing, dancing, etc.
- Athletic contest(s)
- Costumes
    - Contest
    - Guessing-who game
- Cook off
    - Categories—cookies, chili, salads, etc.
    - Prepared ahead and brought in to serve as dinner
- Silent slide show in background
- Professional storyteller
- Many low-priced auction items
- Several big-ticket auction items

Notice how fanciful, even silly, ideas, such as "performance by Fran and Spencer" could lead to more viable options, such as "murder mystery dinner." Likewise, viable ideas, such as "talent contest," could lead to other options, such as "athletic contest(s)" and "cook off." Moreover, various ideas were improved by add-ons. The cook off idea was improved by having different categories of food, prepared ahead and brought in to serve as the event dinner.

So far we've focused on what to talk about—interests and multiple optional solutions. But you've heard the saying, "It's not what you said, it's how you said it." Maybe you've even quoted it to someone else. The next few chapters will show you how to express yourself in a more bridge-building manner, beginning with when not to speak at all.

Key Points from Chapter 8

- To optimize consensus, we look for a number of alternative ways to address both parties' interests before deciding which ideas to adopt
- Asking yourself and the other person questions can inspire creative ways to address interests
  - o Ask, "What would help?" to inspire appropriate ways to address feeling interests
  - o Ask a fanciful question to boost your thinking out of the box
    - Start with, "What would _____ do?" and fill in the blank with the name of someone (real or fictional, past or present) very different from you
      - Don't fill the blank with names such as Jesus that carry heavy emotional weight for you or the other person
    - Or start with, "What would we do if we lived in _____?" and fill the blank with a different time or place
    - Identify the kernel of goodness in your fanciful answer, then modify the answer to make it workable while retaining the kernel of goodness
  - o Ask, "How can I...?" to help another appreciate and contribute to your interests
  - o Ask, "How else can you...?" to help another consider alternate ways to address his own interests
  - o Ask, "How can we satisfy both (one interest) and (another interest)?" to start pulling a consensus together
  - o Ask, "How can we do more?" or "How can we do it better?" to move beyond an acceptable consensus to an optimized consensus

PART III: THE BASIC SKILL SET—HOW TO TALK ABOUT IT

CHAPTER 9
USING THE BRAKES TO GET THERE FASTER

The real art of conversation is not only to say the right thing in the right place, but, far more difficult still, to leave unsaid the wrong thing at the tempting moment.
- Dorothy Nevill

You've seen the driver who weaves in and out of traffic, tailgates, accelerates and brakes abruptly, and blasts through an intersection the instant the light turns green. Clearly, he's in a hurry. Experiments have compared such drivers with normal drivers on the same routes. Even on a long cross-country trip, the shave-off-every-second driver saves little time at best.

"At best" assumes he does not, in his haste, take a wrong turn or wreck his car, in which cases he actually loses considerable time and possibly incurs major repair expenses or even physical injuries. Moreover, impatient driving burns more fuel. In short, the antsy driver only *feels like* he gets there faster. His tactics are counterproductive.

This chapter deals with the advantages—in efficiency and effectiveness—of **investing in time at the front end** when resolving differences and building consensus. **Using our conversational brakes to slow down the process actually brings results faster.** Time investment pays off handsomely.

Many factors and situations can drive people to speak too soon, dump too much information at once, make premature decisions, and push others to do likewise:

- You're stretched thin juggling work, home, family and friends.
- The person you're talking to is stretched thin juggling work, home, etc., and you're well aware of it.
- You have set an amount of time for a meeting, and you have set an agenda. The committee members feel they must reach a decision on every item on the agenda within the allotted time.

- The next meeting isn't scheduled for a month, and the item must be dealt with before then. You don't want to call an extra meeting or to delegate the item.
- Your temperament prefers quick thinking. You're the type who deals well with emergencies. It's agonizing to wait for the reflective thinker to lumber through his thought processes, especially when "the perfect solution" is so obvious to you.
- Or perhaps you are the more reflective thinker. You sense the impatience of others and agree to something that seems okay in the moment, setting aside your past experiences of seeing things differently, and better, after a break.
- The subject matter is unpleasant to talk about, so you want to get it over with.
- The subject matter is dull and tedious, so you want to get it over with.
- The other person(s) is unpleasant, dull or tedious, so you want to get it over with.
- You're chairing a meeting. Someone makes a suggestion, then asks, "OK?" One or two others nod. The rest remain silent. You assume silence means consent.
- The conversation moves along at a comfortable pace till the other person says something that stumps you. You say something just to fill what feels like an awkward silence.
- You've worked hard to reconcile two different views, and the other person finally seems to be coming around. You want to get his agreement, quick, before he changes his mind.

The temptation to move too quickly in these and other situations is very strong. We feel like we're making progress when we do, and we feel like we're spinning our wheels—or even going backward—when we don't.

In addition to whatever personal circumstances impel an individual to move, think and act fast, modern culture is wiring our brains to feel an almost constant sense of urgency. Recent studies have indicated that viewing the logo of a well-known fast food chain causes people to make quicker—and poorer—decisions, about financial matters, for example. We don't even have to eat the fast food. The glimpse of the logo may be so brief we aren't consciously aware of it. Yet the neural paths in our brains that have come to associate speed with satiety kick in, impelling us to speed up our next decision(s).[30]

Have you ever wondered why, as technology enables us to do things faster, we don't experience (or take) more leisure time? Why, instead, do we push ourselves to accomplish more and more in less time? Why do some of us feel uncomfortable, like something's wrong, if we *aren't* multi-tasking? I believe it's because the very speed of computerization and other technological advances wires our brains to feel that slow is bad in much the same way that fast food wires us to feel speed is good.

However, just as driving so fast you miss your turn costs more time in the long run, speaking or deciding prematurely results in mistakes that cost time, money and good will. When dealing with others, take your time— time to prepare, to think, to listen well, to communicate well, to gear down when necessary, and to engage in effective process. As a bonus, exercising the discipline to slow down will begin to counteract and balance out that cultural wiring, so that you to feel more and more comfortable investing in time in the future.

Time to Prepare

Preparing for a conversation is like preparing for a trip. If you consult a map beforehand, fix some major streets and key landmarks in your mind, and print out a copy to refresh your memory, you can drive straight to your destination without pulling over to figure things out or backtracking after mistakes. A more modern version is taking the time to put your destination into your on-board navigation system.

In Chapter 5, we saw the benefits of asking the *Three Magic Questions* before an important dialogue to ground yourself in your interests and get a head start on identifying those of the other person. Time spent preparing to use the other tools in this book will also make your dialogues more efficient and effective.

You can begin planning ways to address the interests uncovered by the Three Magic Questions, that is, *Solution Smorgasbord items*, before you speak with the other person. Again, it is helpful to make notes.

---

30 Hara Estroff Marano, "Food Chain," *Psychology Today* 43 no. 5 (2010).

In addition to his notes on interests, Spencer might make the following Smorgasbord list before approaching Fran:

- Games plus speaker
- Games instead of speaker
    o Move speaker to a different event
- Other speaker-getting project(s) for Fran
- Games at a different event
- Guest speaker at service same weekend as fundraiser with games

Don't get stuck on an idea you find especially appealing, "the perfect solution." Leave your mind open to alternate or additional solutions suggested by the other person. And remember to pace yourself when presenting your own ideas. Explore his interests before making suggestions. When he seems to feel you understand him, you can begin offering ideas, but don't overwhelm him by spilling your entire list at once. He's more likely to buy into a solution that he helped to develop at a pace that allowed him to get his mind around the ideas in small, digestible bites.

You can also prepare to use virtually *any communication tool*. For example, you can plan some useful open and closed questions using the guidelines in Chapters 8 and 10. Again, don't spit them out like a toy robot. Consider them options that you can draw on as the conversation develops. You can even prepare some useful lines for requesting the time you may need to think, or suggesting that the other person take time to think, during the course of the dialogue, as we'll see below.

I usually make four lists when preparing:

- Interests
- Possible Smorgasbord items
- Possible Communication points
- Walk-Away Alternatives (or "Plan B," covered in Chapter 12)

Such preparations typically take me thirty to ninety minutes. Compared to the hours I used to spend aimlessly stewing over an upcoming meeting, and that meeting's often-disappointing results, I never doubt the value of preparation.

Time to Listen

The most effective communicators often listen more than they talk—easy to say, sometimes hard to do. But when you try listening well, and experience the results, you'll want to make the effort.

Sometimes we translate the importance of a matter into a false sense of urgency. Someone else begins verbalizing a train of thought about a matter that could affect you a great deal. The first sentence or two puts your mind in gear. Perhaps you think you already know where this train is heading and/or you feel you must be prepared to respond as soon as the other person finishes. So you tune out and begin planning your response, losing the benefit of the other person's complete thought. Your response doesn't fully address what she meant to convey. Now she tunes you out and plans a better way to restate her original idea. Can you see this conversation sliding downhill?

Contrary to what our instincts tell us, *we actually get more ideas, and better ideas, when we concentrate on what the* other *person is saying.* The unconscious mind works while you listen, and you'll often find you're ready to respond by the time she finishes.

Think of her words as gifts. She's giving you more and more information about her interests, more ideas about various options for addressing these interests. Her tone of voice and body language help you to see her ideas through a more accurate lens and provide clues to those all-important feeling interests. As a bonus, *listening to her is the best way to get her to listen to you.* When she feels you understand her, she's not tempted to tune you out while she plans another way to get through.

Don't toss her word gifts aside. Having skillfully applied the Three Magic Questions to your particular situation, soak up the answers like a sponge. If, after she's finished speaking, you need more time to think of how to respond, you can take that time. The next section shows how.

If your mind tends to wander, jotting the occasional note may help you focus on the other person's words. Don't write everything she says. That would disconcert her. But noting a few key words here and there keeps you listening and also shows her you're interested.

Time to Think as You Go

OK, you've listened so carefully you could write an essay on what someone else has said and how he feels about it. Now it's your turn, and you don't know what to say. But it's your turn. You have to say *something*, right? Wrong. Dialogue is not a tennis game. You won't lose points if you fail to volley back before the verbal ball flies out of bounds. However, you can lose points if you say something ill-considered just to fill the silence.

Silence itself is a communication tool. Use it. When you take time to think, the other person will often spend that time doing some thinking of his own. He may reconsider something he said, or consider your statements more carefully.

I once gave a training course for a department of a major corporation. I had asked an acquaintance in that department to serve as my partner in an unscripted improvisational role-play demonstration. He played his role aggressively, raising his voice louder and louder and making increasingly offensive statements.

I listened calmly, letting him "vent." Though I knew ways to ramp things down after he'd said his piece, those measures proved unnecessary. After reaching an apex, he ramped back down on his own—a great lesson for the class.

Does it occur to you that this friendly acquaintance ramped down to make me look good to the class? Consider a real-life example. On another occasion, I was sitting with my attorney as she negotiated by phone on my behalf. At one point, the other lawyer began bullying, saying things like, "This is taking too long. If you don't..., I might just have to..." Catching my attorney's eye, I put my finger to my lips. We sat in silence for what seemed like an agonizing length of time. At last, the other lawyer broke that silence by offering us a deal even better than we had requested.

Ideally, when you are trying to bring about a meeting of minds, each thing you say on the issue should further the process. *All too often, however, our instincts lead us in the wrong direction*, and the more important the matter, the more counterproductive our instincts may be. They can prod us to make others wrong, for example, escalating their resistance.

Take all the time you need to think before you speak.

The silence may seem longer to you than it does to the other person. He might not be as impatient as you feel. He might be glad you're actually thinking about what he said. Or he might fill the silence himself—another gift of information.

However, *if a sense of awkward silence is so distracting* to you that it prevents you from doing what silence is for—thinking, *fill the gap with a non-response.* Sip your water or coffee. Jot a note. You can interject a neutral word or phrase that shows you're thinking without showing what you're thinking, "Hmm," or one of my favorites, "That's interesting."

If you need even more time, you can *suggest a short break* and walk down the hall, even if you don't need the restroom. When your mind is stuck, moving your body can trigger fresh inspirations.

Another approach, when a short pause doesn't provide a ready answer, or when answering at all is against your better judgment, is to *shift the conversation to a different aspect of the matter at hand.* Your unconscious mind will work on the stickler while you focus on the new aspect. You can return to the original point later, if need be. However, sometimes the newly introduced aspect will prove so fruitful that returning to the original point becomes unnecessary.

Here's an example of a fundraiser dialogue in which shifting gears in this manner works well for Fran:

Dialogue 6: Fran shifts gears

	Dialogue:	**Fran's View:**
S:	I was thinking we might have games at the fundraiser this year instead of a speaker. What do you think?	Fran feels upset. She recognizes this feeling as a cue not to speak at this moment.
F:	Let me grab a cup of coffee and we'll sit down and talk about this.	She buys time to let her emotions settle down.
S:	Sure.	

F:	(Returns with coffee) So, you were saying?	Asking Spencer to restate his point buys additional time till she's ready to respond. And maybe she'll learn more from his restatement.
S:	Well, I've heard some of the younger folks favor games.	Maybe this wasn't his idea.
F:	By younger folks, you mean?	She begins to explore whose interests she really needs to address.
S:	(Laughs) Well, younger than you and me.	
F:	So not kids. Young working adults?	
S:	Yeah. But that gives me an idea. We could have different sets of games for different age groups—toddlers, grade schoolers, teens, young adults, middle-aged, seniors. That way everyone could find something they like.	Fran thinks, *Brother, you have no idea what an organizational nightmare that would be.*
F:	Have you been dissatisfied with the speakers in the past?	**Fran decides to shift to a different aspect instead of responding directly to Spencer's nightmare plan.**

S: No. I like them. But, I mean, I just think some of the younger folks, well they're so used to having something to look at—computer screens, slide shows. They weren't raised on lectures like we were.

Spencer has revealed more about the interests of those who suggested games. Maybe love of games isn't driving this, but rather dislike of lecture-style presentation.

F: One of the speakers I was considering is an astronaut who has some great slides and exhibits to show.

Fran suggests a different way of addressing these interests.

S: Wow! I'd like to see that. But, on the other hand, I still like the idea of all age groups having something.

This further refines the interests to be addressed.

F: Suppose we have games for the smallest kids only, at the same time as the speaker? And any young adults or teens who don't want to sit still for a speaker can run the toddlers' games and tend the infants.

Fran suggests a way to address all Spencer's known interests without going back to the nightmare plan.

S: That could work.

F: I'll check around and see if enough people are willing to give up hearing an astronaut in order to run games.

Indirectly suggests that perhaps only a few people don't want the speaker.

S: Hmm. Even the toddlers might hate to miss an astronaut. But they wouldn't sit still for a program that would interest the adults.

He's not entirely happy with her alternate plan, but she can modify it.

F:	Maybe the astronaut can first do a very short thing for the toddlers, then a longer multi-generational program for everyone else. I could get sitters for the tots during the long program.	She modifies her plan to satisfy all interests better.
S:	Yeah. That sounds good. Keep me posted on what you find out.	*Whew! Dodged that bullet.* She didn't have to accept Spencer's nightmare plan, nor offend him by rejecting it.

How to Ask for a Longer Break

What if the stumper must be addressed, and none of the above techniques have inspired a response you feel good about? Perhaps the stumper is of the essence of the matter. Perhaps the other person insists on a response. Perhaps you yourself wish to go on record, but don't yet know how. You need a longer break. You might say, "I do my best thinking when I let important things percolate awhile. Can we stop for now and schedule a time to talk again?"

Here's another way to make someone comfortable with a longer break. This works especially well when the person is pushing you for a response:

Him:	Well, what do you say?
You:	You've given this a lot of thought, haven't you?
Him:	Yes.
You:	I'd like to honor that by thinking about it too, rather than shooting from the hip. Can we resume this discussion tomorrow at 2:00?

Note that a person is unlikely to admit he has not given much thought to an issue he's pressing. However, if he answers your question, "No," simply change your next line to, "This is an important question. I'm glad you raised it. Let's both sleep on it, then talk again. Would tomorrow at 2:00 work for you?"

Note also the importance of agreeing on a specific day and time to resume your dialogue. It lets the other person know that you aren't just putting him off in hopes he will drop the matter.

When You Feel Impatient

Putting the shoe on the other foot, you may sometimes feel like pressing. Your instincts tell you, *I must get his agreement now, while he's leaning my way, before he changes his mind.* That might be true for a shopkeeper selling goods to a tourist he'll never see again; but when you have a relationship with someone, you benefit when he thinks through a question thoroughly and buys into the decision whole-heartedly.

For our purposes, having a relationship simply means that you wish to, or have to, deal with the other person in the future. The relationship can be temporary. For example, even if Sal and Trudy agree on terms for the sale of Sal's boat today, they probably can't close and transfer titles and property today. If, this evening, Trudy feels she was duped by Sal's fast-talking pressure, she can back out of the deal. If Sal tries to re-open the discussion, he'll now have to overcome her distaste and distrust for him.

In a long-term relationship, such as clergy-congregant or co-membership in the same congregation, it is all the more important that the way you deal with a person today builds a bridge for future dealings, on the current issue and/or other matters that may arise. Giving in to pressure when you really need time to think teaches someone that applying pressure works. On the other hand, pushing him to agree to something he'll later regret knocks the props out from under any bridge between you. But by showing him that you wish to address his interests, if possible, and that you intend to satisfy your own interests as well as you can, you lay a foundation for that bridge, a bridge of mutual respect and consideration.

Thus, *actively encouraging others to take think breaks can work to your benefit.* Every time you take a break, whether a few seconds to sip your beverage, or a week to research and reflect, you give him a break too. Even if he didn't think he needed more time, he may come up with ideas that will work better for both of you. And if he comes up with objections or new issues, better now than after you began to execute a plan you thought you had agreed on.

In groups, absence of discussion can be a sign that people need more think time. Asking, "Any objections?" doesn't help; silence does not mean consent. Unless the issue is patently simple and straightforward, tolerate silence for a while to give all present a chance to get their minds around the issue. If there is still insufficient participation, re-docket the matter for a future meeting.

Time to Gear Down

Strong negative emotions such as fear, anger, or resistance to being made wrong, can serve us well in the kinds of situations for which they evolved— atack by a saber-tooth cat, for example. However, when trying to bridge from conflict to consensus through reasoned dialogue, these emotions prevent our best thinking. In consensus building, the stronger the urge toward a knee-jerk reaction, the greater the need to take a break.

This doesn't mean you should ignore the emotion. During the break, ask yourself what caused the emotion. The fear might have been spawned by a valid instinctive sense that the other person spoke dishonestly. The anger could have arisen from a sense that the other person's "nice" comment was actually patronizing, in other words, disrespectful. *When you can identify the source of the emotion, and think calmly about how to deal with the dishonesty, disrespect, or the like, the break has done its job.*

On the other side of the coin, *when a conversation goes well, we can get carried away by euphoria and agree too quickly to a half-baked plan.* A break before consenting to anything important is always a good time investment.

Time to Communicate Effectively

Easing someone around to a sound conclusion in small digestible bites takes longer than simply telling her your conclusion at the outset. But if she doesn't accept your conclusion, if your pushing triggers resistance, how much additional time do you spend before she accepts that conclusion—if, in fact, she ever does? What is the value of saving time on the physical process of talking if she never comes to agreement with you at all? What did you save if she gives in grudgingly and carries that grudge forward into your relationship or into half-hearted execution of the project? What if your conclusion is totally or partially mistaken, and you could have done better if you'd had her carefully considered input?

Judging the efficiency of our communication only by the time it takes to deliver a message is misleading. We should judge efficiency by the total time it takes to achieve our ultimate objectives. We should also factor in the effectiveness of the end result.

Of course there are situations where we have no reason to expect resistance to our requests. In those cases, it makes sense to jump right to the point. "If you're going past the post office, would you take my mail?" However, where the matter is complex or likely to generate a range of initial reactions from different people, we arrive at a sound result faster if we slow down the process.

Some of the communication tools in this book involve a small investment of time at the front end that pays off many times over in actual results. In addition to those covered in preceding and subsequent chapters, *carefully consider the means by which you choose to communicate—in person, by phone, or in writing.*

I once knew a man who owned and directed a good-sized business. One of his children, whom I'll call Travis, helped him run the firm and was groomed to take over the presidency in due time. The man died, leaving shares in the business to all his children—those who weren't involved, as well as Travis. The legal technicalities of the bequest (probably unknown to the father) were such that, for example, any of the siblings could have taken it upon themselves to license company-owned technology or lease company property.

This legal fluke could have made it impossible for Travis to run the business effectively, which would have hurt them all. He wanted his siblings to change the nature of their rights, so that he could make the decisions, provided the others got their fair share of profits and proceeds. Yet, Travis worried that, if he simply wrote to, or phoned, his siblings (who all lived far away), they might think he was trying to pull something on them. After all, he was asking them to give up certain legal rights.

The situation was so technical, that he would need his attorney to help him explain it. His sister and brother, in turn, would hire their own attorneys. Travis would not know what spin their lawyers put on his lawyer's communications when they relayed them to their clients. His siblings or their attorneys might turn this into a fight or drag their feet.

Wisely, Travis asked all the siblings and their lawyers to fly in for a meeting at the company headquarters. His attorney was then able to explain the situation to everyone concerned and to answer questions and clear up any apparent misunderstandings on the spot. Everyone got to hear everything that everyone else said, instead of going through a drawn-out process of letters between attorneys, who in turn would relay information and advice to their respective clients.

Moreover, Travis and his attorney had the advantage of a face-to-face encounter complete with all the good will and credibility they conveyed through facial expressions, body language and tone of voice. They could observe the faces, bodies and tones of the others to better assess how their comments were received and deal with any disconnects.

It took only about an hour for all to agree on the changes Travis wanted. Afterward, his siblings said they were glad to see one another, but wondered why they had to fly all that way for something "so simple." The fact is that the matter was simple *because* they flew all that way to get together in person. Any expense Travis incurred in air fares for his siblings was more than balanced in the savings of time, trouble and attorney fees that would have accompanied a long and indirect letter-writing process.

People sometimes think, *I'll set things out in black and white so they will be perfectly clear.* But sometimes writing can be more easily misinterpreted than oral communication.

In general, writing is the worst way to begin discussion of a topic on which people's views are likely to diverge, where they will have doubts and disagreements. Writing is also risky with respect to *matters with significant emotional weight* (feeling interests). We all view events through different lenses. Speakers and listeners hear enough different messages even when they speak aloud. Why make matters worse by depriving ourselves of the tools of tone of voice, facial expression and body language?

Text messaging and email exacerbate the ambiguities inherent in the written word. When you write a letter, you tend to put more thought into your choice of words. You have to wait for it to come off the printer, and when it does, you usually reread it before signing and mailing it. That short pause and reread alone can show you how someone else might attach a different meaning to your words than you intended.

Because the physical process of keying and sending an email or text message is faster, it generates a false sense of efficiency. It also prods us to work quickly, not choosing our words as carefully, not reading the entire message before we click "send," much less letting that message rest for awhile and rereading it later. We judge our efficiency by the time it takes to send our emails, rather than by the time it takes to achieve our objectives.

In addition, people often justify their use of email and text messages as "efficiency" when the real motivator is reluctance to discuss a touchy issue face to face, or even by phone. They don't want to hurt someone's feelings or cause a huge blowup, but they end up doing just that.

An Example of Email Mischief

Consider how such email mischief might play out for Fran. Let's assume that, before Spencer has a chance to raise the issue, Fran hears on the grapevine that Yolanda wants to get rid of "boring" speakers and update the fundraiser with active games. Yolanda has always rubbed her the wrong way. Now Fran is downright angry. It hurts to feel like anyone over forty no longer counts. The fact that Yolanda sees it this way just goes to show how much the young snip still has to learn.

Fran feels she must defend herself, but fears losing control if she tries to speak to Yolanda. She also worries about embarrassing herself in front of Spencer if she approaches him. She tells herself she's "playing it safe" by emailing. Since Spencer is big on avoiding triangulation, she writes to both of them, "I've found some great speaker options for the fundraiser—an astronaut, a professional story teller, and a professor of religious studies. Comments?"

As Fran sees it, she has kept her communication positive and upbeat, leaving out her negative emotions. She has shown what interesting speakers she can line up and has put the ball in Yolanda's court to bring up her objections directly to Fran or not at all.

Spencer wants to know more about everyone's ideas and interests. His mind is open to any programming that will achieve his ultimate objectives, which include keeping both Fran and Yolanda involved and happy, if possible. He knows this is too important a matter, with too much potential for emotional content, to decide by email. He's right. But then he makes the mistake of sending a short, and in his view, innocuous reply to all, "Please hold off until we can speak in person."

Fran feels worse than ever. Why would Spencer request this delay if he liked her ideas? She envisions Spencer already in Yolanda's hip pocket and anticipates the upcoming conversation as negative and humiliating. She dreads this conversation, and her fear of losing control increases, as does her anger toward Yolanda.

Meanwhile, Yolanda wonders why she was copied on this email since she's not on the fundraiser committee, at least not yet. Someone must have told Fran that Yolanda was talking up games. Probably that big mouth Tommy. She fires off an email telling Tommy she'll never trust him again.

Then Yolanda decides to get some advice from someone she *can* trust, Nigel. She forwards Spencer's email, with Fran's original entrained below, to Nigel and asks him what he would think of games as opposed to any of the three proposed speakers. Nigel decides that twelve heads are better than one, so he forwards to a dozen of his pals and asks what they think.

Soon half the congregation is busily adding to the chain of emails. Fran's anger and embarrassment soar. The other half of the congregation sends replies to all asking to be deleted from the list because they feel spammed and harassed by all these messages. This offends the message senders, who thought their feedback was wanted and replied in good faith.

You see where this is going?

As a general rule, your *first communications about a topic with potential for emotional content and/or controversy should be face to face if at all possible.* Failing that, at least pick up the phone. Realize that, even if you have to wait awhile to get the appropriate people together, or play phone tag for awhile, you'll attain your objectives better and faster in the end. *Save email and other writings for sharing purely factual information and for confirming understandings and tying up loose ends once you've reached a basic agreement.*

Consensus skills help people discuss difficult matters that formerly daunted them. With practice, instead of hiding behind the written word, we gain the confidence to plan that meeting or make that call. Once we see how much sooner and better we achieve our objectives, we find ourselves using our voices, instead of our fingers, even for non-controversial matters.

Try This: Rewinding an Email

The next time you've typed a quick email, instead of clicking "send," save it and turn to another task for a while. Then print and read the saved email from the point of view of a particularly obtuse mind; look for every way your written statements could be construed in a different manner from the one you intended. (Do take the time to print. Reading hard copy of something you've been viewing on a screen helps you see its content from a different perspective.)

Now, still in the point of view of that obtuse mind, compose a response to your email. How would you react to that response?

Asking the right questions can be every bit as important to reaching consensus as knowing the right answers. Chapter 10 shows how.

Key Points from Chapter 9

- Slowing down the communication process often brings results faster
- Invest in time:
  - Time to prepare
    - Get clear on your interests
    - Get a head start on Solution Smorgasbord items
    - Plan some communication options (developed further in Chapters 10 and 11)
    - Know your Plan B (Chapter 12)
  - Time to think as you go
    - Use the tool of silence
    - When stumped on one thread of conversation, shift gears and discuss another aspect; your unconscious

mind will work on the stumper while you focus your conscious thoughts on something else
- Take short breaks
- Ask for longer breaks
  - Mention your interest in thinking things over
  - Explain that you want to do justice to the thought the other person has put into the matter
  - Set a specific date and time to resume
- Encourage others to take think breaks too
- Time to gear down from possibly counterproductive feelings
- Time to communicate effectively
  - Don't judge efficiency by the time it takes to say your piece, but rather by the total time it takes to reach a sound consensus
  - Begin important conversations in person, if possible, or by phone
  - Save writing such as emails, text messages and letters for pure facts and confirming a final consensus

CHAPTER 10
OPEN A DOOR, CLOSE AN AGREEMENT

If we would have new knowledge, we must get us a whole world of new questions.
- Suzanne K. Langer

You'll find that questions are among the most important tools in your kit. It's often said that the best communicators listen more than they talk. Likewise, when they do speak, those who excel at resolving differences and building consensus often ask more than they opine.

This chapter is packed with many useful questions and a number of ways to use them. As with any chapter in this book, you don't have to try to learn everything at once. In fact, you'll do better if you read the chapter through, working through the "Try This" segments as you go. Then choose one type of question and one way of using it to try in real life. For example, you might decide to try using open questions to draw people into a collaborative frame of mind. Try your selection out a few times in real life. Then review the chapter to select something to try next.

To help you get organized, we break questions down into two major categories—open and closed.

Open Questions Open Doors

The Three Magic Questions are examples of open, or open-ended, questions. So are the six Smorgasbord-building questions laid out in Chapter 8. *Open questions can't be answered "Yes" or "No."* Thus they usually employ one of the words *"who," "what," "when," "where," "how,"* or *"why."*

Try This: Practicing Open Questions

Sit with another person and think of a topic you'd like to discuss. Try to go five minutes asking only open questions, no closed (yes-or-no) questions.

Ask your companion to try to catch you. If you ask a question that can be answered "yes" or "no," she is to answer that way, without elaborating. You can make this more fun by paying a penny every time she says "yes" or "no."

Then switch roles.

In addition to uncovering interests and building a Solution Smorgasbord, open questions serve you in many other ways.

Open Questions Draw People In

When people are invited to express themselves, rather than simply answer yes or no, they sense that you are truly interested in what they have to say. They feel respected when you seek their detailed opinions. When they hear themselves answering fully, they have a greater sense of being heard. Feeling heard, in turn, makes them more willing to settle down, listen to you, and work with you. Open questions draw you and the other person together into a collaborative frame of mind.

Put yourself in Fran's shoes and compare these two approaches by Spencer:

1. I think we should try having games instead of a speaker this year. Is that OK with you?
2. What would you think of having games instead of a speaker this year?

Which approach makes you feel better about yourself? Which makes you want to work with Spencer?

The format of Number 1, a statement of Spencer's idea followed by a closed (yes or no) question, can be quicker and perfectly acceptable when the issue is not important and/or the two parties' views are not likely to differ. But Fran has been proudly programming the fundraiser with speakers for fifteen years. It's likely she will at least hesitate, and more likely resist.

Format Number 1 only exacerbates this resistance. It pushes her away from Spencer. She feels he is not all that interested in what she thinks or wants; she must either suck it up and have games or else try to argue with someone who has already made up his mind.

Number 2, the open question, draws Fran in toward Spencer. A question that can't be answered yes or no shows that he wants her actual opinion, and he wants it in detail. So her opinion must count with him. Consequently, Spencer's opinion counts more with her. His open question sets a collaborative mood, and collaboration implies his desire to agree on a plan they both like. Fran is more likely to work with Spencer because he has shown that he wants to work with her.

Open Questions Draw People Out

Instead of the quick and easy, yes-or-no reply, open questions encourage people to elaborate. They gain you more information. What's more, people convey this information in their own words, which more accurately express their original thoughts, rather than their reactions to your thoughts.

You can use open questions to correct or expand upon what you believe might be another person's interests. In Dialogue 1, when Fran told Spencer, "We can't gear it [the fundraiser] to the young folks," he asked the open question, "What's the downside of that?" to get her own perspective on the interests behind her position. He probably expected to hear something about middle-aged and older members representing a majority and/or giving the most money in support of the church. But Fran's choice of words, "It's us mature people who can afford to spend the most on the silent auction," notably the "us," provided him with an important insight: Fran counted herself among those who donate a lot and prefer speakers. Her words might even suggest that she, and others like her, fear being shunted aside or discounted.

In Dialogue 2, Spencer began to explore Fran's feeling interests by asking the open question, "How does it feel knowing it's time to start planning once again?" He learned that her feelings were mixed: "Well, there's a little sigh, because I know how much work it is. But there's a lot I enjoy about it." He could have predicted that.

But when he sought elaboration with another open question, "What do you enjoy the most?" he got a surprise. Fran enjoys "selling" prestigious speakers on appearing for a reduced fee, selling people on making donations to the auction, and even selling volunteers on remaining active and motivated. Later, he used this newly discovered interest to suggest an alternative volunteer job that Fran might find more rewarding—tapping her selling skills for a larger inter-denominational lecture series.

"What does it mean if...?" is another good form of question for drawing out feeling interests. A close relative is, *"What does it say about you/us if...?"* If Fran becomes irritated during the discussion of games and says, "I don't know why we're even talking about games and polling people. Nobody wants games except Yolanda," Spencer might ask, "What would it mean if we found that a number of people prefer games to speakers?" This could help Fran recognize and communicate the feeling that a preference for games devalues what she does best and has worked hard to do for fifteen years. By implication, this preference could also seem to devalue Fran herself. Now Spencer can address the feeling interest that's really bothering her.

Whether they realize it or not, congregants often resist, or advocate, a particular position because of what it seems to say about them as a group. If a meeting about whether or not to dismiss the music director becomes heated, the leader could ask, "What does it say about us if we fire our music director?" and "What does it say about us if we fund a full-time music director position?"

In addition to exploring interests, *you can use open questions to encourage people to elaborate on any subject*. Open questions can serve virtually any purpose that will advance the dialogue. For example, you can invite people to offer ideas for meeting interests, "What other auction items can young people give?" You can troubleshoot suggestions with minimum wrong making. "How could we fit games into the fundraiser schedule?" You can flesh out general ideas with the details that make them workable, "What kinds of games might attract which age groups?" "How much should we charge for children's games?" "How much for adults?"

In Dialogue 1, Spencer used an *implied question* to solicit creative ideas. "Let's think about modestly priced items people can donate to the auction," is equivalent to, "What modestly priced items can people donate?" When you occasionally shift away from literal question-type sentence format, other people are less likely to feel as if they are being interrogated or as if you are not contributing your fair share of information and ideas.

You can also change format, and avoid interrupting another's mental flow and energy, *by simply repeating a key word or two* on which you'd like elaboration, while letting your tone of voice provide the question mark. Suppose Mike accosts Laurel about the window she broke.

Mike:	It must be nice to rate such special treatment in this congregation.
Laurel:	Special?
Mike:	The rest of us have to pay for our damage, but you don't.
Laurel:	Damage?
Mike:	The window you broke. I had to pay for the sign I backed over, you know.

Another variation is putting the tonal question mark after your own word. For example, "Why?" can be replaced with "Because...?"

Of course, no amount of variation in sentence form will avoid the impression of interrogation if you only ask questions and never make statements. People need to feel that their ideas are welcomed, but *they also need to feel that you are contributing as well.*

Even if you only ask a few questions, the wrong manner can make people feel grilled. You know that manner. It's the way a trial attorney in a TV drama approaches a hostile witness. It's a tone of voice and set of jaw that tells the other person that, no matter what she answers, your next move will be a "Gotcha!"

The best way to match your manner to the drawing-out nature of the open question is to cultivate an attitude of sincere curiosity about the other person's thoughts and feelings. As we've seen in the chapters on the Three Magic Questions, the more you understand the other person's perspective, the better your chances of reaching a consensus that satisfies your interests as well as hers. Curiosity pays you well, but you can't fake it. It must be genuine. As you begin to utilize consensus skills and experience the value *to you* of understanding and addressing another's interests, your sincere curiosity will grow.

In the following prelude to Dialogue 5, Laurel uses various open questions to advance a discussion in several ways.

Dialogue 7: Laurel asks Mike open questions

Dialogue:	Laurel's View:
M: Must be nice to be special.	Mike's sarcastic tone clues Laurel that he has ill feelings about something.
L: Special?	Though unprepared, she begins to search for driving interests with an open question.
M: Yeah, I heard you got off without paying for that window you broke.	Laurel doesn't understand why Mike is miffed about this, but he doesn't sound ready to volunteer his feelings.
L: You sound angry. Are you angry with me?	She takes a guess, hoping he'll correct her if she's wrong.
M: Well, yeah, I guess I am, a little.	Mike feels that feelings aren't the right stuff, so he downplays them.
L: I'd like to understand why.	1st Magic (open) Question
M: I just think a church, of all places, should play fair with everybody.	Sounds like Mike perceives different treatment for different people.
L: What else happened? What makes forgiving the window unfair?	Follow up open questions.
M: I had to shell out big time when I backed over a sign.	Progress. Mike is beginning to reveal what's really bothering him.

L: You had to pay for your ac-   Laurel paraphrases.
     cident, and I didn't.

M: Right.

L: Oh. Now I can see how   Empathizes with his reac-
     you might feel I got special   tion, given the limited in-
     treatment.   formation he has.

M: It doesn't just seem like it.   He's getting riled up again,
     You did.   but Laurel doesn't panic. He
                                     needs to vent, and she needs
                                     to know still more.

L: So your paying for the sign   She combines empathy with
     must have felt bad, like—if   an open question about pre-
     Laurel's special, that makes   cisely how he feels.
     Mike...?

M: Chopped liver.

L: Nobody wants to feel like   More empathy.
     that.

M: It's like there's three cat-   Above series of open ques-
     egories of people around   tions plus empathy have
     here—the really poor folks   drawn him out. Even
     who get all the sympathy   though Mike has not put a
     and help, you fat cats who   label on his feeling, Laurel
     donate big bucks and have   now understands.
     time to hang around here
     and work, and us shmucks
     who get lost in the shuffle.

L: I wouldn't want to be lost   Now that she understands
     in the shuffle either. How   the feeling, she empathizes
     might I help?   again and asks what would
                                     help.

M: Either you pay for the window, or I get a refund for the sign.

Laurel knows this won't really resolve everything. Money doesn't heal hurt feelings. But she can work from his suggestion.

L: I'd like to be sure that whatever we do gets things completely OK between us. Would you humor me for a minute? Let's say I pay for the window. At the next church social, you see me walking toward you. What will you feel like doing—in your guts?

Laurel expresses her interest in a good relationship with Mike.

Since he has trouble naming his feelings, she asks an open question about a specific hypothetical situation.

M: I wouldn't mind talking to you.

He can't seem to say he'd welcome her company.

L: I'd like it better if we actually enjoyed talking to each other.

After lots of attention to Mike's feelings, Laurel can now express an opinion.

Sounds like my paying for the window wouldn't get us there.

M: Yeah.

L: What else could help?

She solicits more of his ideas.

M: I can't think of anything else you could do.

Laurel picks up on the word "you."

L:	Who *could* help?	Akin to "What would help?" this question steers him toward options that might better address his true interests.
M:	The leaders who make these decisions about who pays. The ministers who only schmooze with the fat cats.	More progress.
L:	Middle-class people form the majority of our congregation. It bothers me that they might feel lost in the shuffle. What would you think of discussing this with Rev. Black?	The open question, "What would you think of...?" introduces a suggestion in a way that lets him know his true opinion is wanted.
M:	I'll think about it.	

This dialogue demonstrates all uses of open questions discussed so far. *Laurel drew Mike in.* She used some of the magic questions to explore his interests, and "How might I help?" to generate ideas for addressing them. Laurel knew Mike's first answer wouldn't really work, but can you see how these questions and his answers advanced the conversation? By asking *him* how she might help, Laurel showed she was truly interested in mending the fence. This started them down the road toward a collaborative, cooperative mood.

She drew him out. Mike's answers to Laurel's questions gave her information that inspired further questions. These follow up questions eventually drew out the real feeling issue: Mike feels ignored and discounted by the church leaders.

Now both Laurel and Mike know more. Mike can see that his anger at Laurel was misdirected. His feeling interest toward her might be satisfied by the very act of her asking open questions. His answers help him realize that payback for the sign won't assuage his feelings. He shifts his viewpoint and is now in the right frame of mind to better address his true feeling interests.

Some readers might think, if I were in Laurel's shoes, and Mike insulted me, I'd simply walk away. The matter doesn't justify the effort. Again, none of our dialogues are intended to indicate *what* you should do in a given situation. Rather, they are about *how* you can manage those situations in which you don't find it so easy to walk away. And you'll find that open questions, used the way Laurel used them above, serve you in whatever matters you do find worth resolving.

Open Questions Minimize Wrong making

As we learned in Chapter 4, people resist threats to their sense of rightness, and the stronger they feel about a concept, the more they resist changing it. But if the change is their own idea, they accept it more readily. Open questions come across as less challenging, less threatening. We can use them to steer another person toward their own reflections on a different perspective. Laurel did just that in the above dialogue. The other person may still be skeptical, but open questions, as opposed to statements, can help him listen to you, think about what you say, and continue conversing, rather than shutting you out.

When using questions to introduce someone to a different perspective, it is especially important to avoid the air of the courtroom drama "gotcha" question by cultivating an attitude of genuine curiosity and compassionate interest in what the other person has to say. You just might hear something that will help you address interests—yours and theirs—even better.

Remember Salvador who listed his boat for $40,000? Suppose prospective buyer Trudy has no RV or other item to trade, but she does have research indicating that sales of used boats comparable to Sal's average $20,000. Trudy might invite Sal to a more realistic price.

Dialogue 8: Trudy uses open questions to invite Sal to another perspective

Dialogue:	Trudy's View:
S: I want $35,000.	Sal focuses on what he wants, rather than on what the boat is worth.
T: Help me understand how you arrived at that figure.	This implied question recognizes that Sal might have reasons for his asking price. Contrast wrong-making statement such as "It's not worth that much."
S: It's what I need to buy an RV.	Reveals an interest, but also confirms that Sal has not considered the value of the boat.
T: What does your research show about the value of the boat?	Suggests a different perspective while still showing Sal that she wants to hear his ideas.
S: Well, it's $5000 less than I paid for it.	
T: How about recent sales prices for comparable boats?	Contrast this question with a statement, "Well, I've looked up comparables."
S: Uh, I don't have any.	
T: I've seen several comparable boats that went for $20,000 recently.	At this point, Trudy injects a respectful statement of fact.

S: If you can find one that low,
       go for it, but I need that RV.

T: How does time factor in?   Contrast   a   statement,
       How long will it take to   "You'll never get that much.
       find a buyer who's willing to   And the boat is depreciating
       pay $35,000?   while you wait.

S: Hmm.

Trudy has brought home the realities of the boat's value while minimizing resistance. By the end of this sequence, Sal is at least thinking about value, rather than simply focusing on what he wants. In her last question, Trudy hopes to inspire Sal to consider that he might never find a buyer willing to pay $15,000 more than the boat is worth, and that the longer he waits, the more his chances diminish. If he does not come around to these ideas, she can follow up with more direct statements.

Put yourself in Sal's shoes, and compare your likely reactions with the contrasting statements in the "Trudy's View" column. Can you vicariously feel that unpleasant little crunch in your guts when you hear an argumentative (wrong-making) statement? Now reread the dialogue. Feel the difference? There may be no way to broach the issue of value without at least a little suggestion of wrong, but using questions, Trudy minimizes this effect. Sal keeps talking, rather than walking out, as he might do if she made challenging statements.

Open Questions for Introducing Your Point of View

Two open questions, in particular, can open another person to your point of view, especially if their demands cut against your interests, so that it would make no sense for you to comply.

What Would You Do?

Most people love to give advice. Asking them to put themselves in your shoes (assume your interests) and advise you leads them to your point of view while minimizing wrong making.

Let's say Fran refuses even to consider any changes in programming for the fundraiser. Compare two approaches by Spencer:

1. You've done a great job in the past, and I really appreciate it. I also have an obligation to see to it that the fundraiser appeals to as many of our members as possible.

2. If you were me, you had a highly valued volunteer who wanted to continue along the same track, and you also had to try to address all congregants' preferences, what would you do?

Option 1 is good. It goes about as far as a statement can to minimize wrong making and resistance. But Option 2 is even better. By asking Fran's advice, Spencer shows he respects her opinion. Thus he positively makes her right. Moreover, the open question invites her to think and come up with her own answer, rather than simply asking her to agree with his.

Better still, if you can shorten the question and still make yourself clear to the other person, do so, then ask follow up questions, as needed, breaking the problem down into smaller steps:

S: What would you do if you were me?

F: I'd stick with what's been working all these years.

S: What would you say to the younger people who've asked for games?

F: I wouldn't worry about them. It's probably just Yolanda, anyway.

S: If I ignore her, what do you think she'll do next?

F: Well... She might complain.

S: To whom?

F: Her cronies, I guess.

S: Anybody who'll listen?

F: I suppose so.

S: Any ideas how I could maintain my overall credibility with as many of our members as possible?

F: Hmm.

Tone, of course, is always important. The caveat with this form of question is that it can sound rhetorical, and thus, strike the other person as an argument for your own point of view. Genuine curiosity and sincere interest in the other person's advice lead to a credible tone.

Suppose Spencer is the one insisting on an elaborate program of different games for various age brackets, from toddlers to senior citizens—an organizational nightmare. Fran could ask him, "If you were me, how would you set up the various venues and organize the volunteers to run all the different games?"

Perhaps Brandon insists that Molly lend him her dollhouse and tries to guilt trip her about disappointing the children. She might ask, "If someone wanted to borrow your most precious possession, a delicate heirloom, and put it in a roomful of boisterous kids, what would you do?"

"How would you feel?" and "What would you say?" are useful variations on "What would you do?" Laurel could ask Mike, "What would you say if you had been doing a volunteer job, and paying a lot of sundry expenses out of your pocket without reporting them, then you accidentally broke something trying to prevent a more serious accident?" Molly might ask Brandon, "How would you feel if you had loaned several things to fellow members, and they were returned in worse condition? Then someone wanted to borrow your most prized possession?"

Putting the question before the description of your interests is a nice touch, especially if your interests inherently involve an implication of wrong on the other person's part. If Molly says, "Suppose someone had broken one of your tools and then wanted to borrow your most prized possession, what would you do?" Brandon first hears wrong making (he has broken her things in the past), so he's already in a resistant frame of mind when Molly asks his opinion. His resistance could dilute, or even eliminate, the benefits of the request for advice.

Now compare *"What would you do if* someone wanted to borrow your most prized possession, but had previously broken one of your tools?" This first lets Brandon know his advice is being sought. A little shot of right making puts him into a positive frame of mind before he hears about his past behavior.

How (or Why) Would That Make Sense for Me?

This form of question is *especially helpful when a person insists that you do something that cuts against your interests*. Here are a few examples:

- Molly: "Above all, I want to maintain my prized heirloom in top condition. How does it make sense for me to lend it to a roomful of boisterous children?"
- Spencer: "Why would it make sense for me to ignore a certain segment of our membership?"
- Fran: "How would it make sense for me to double or triple the number of volunteers I need?"

Some follow up questions may be in order to reinforce the other's focus on your interests:

- Molly: "Yes, the children would love the dollhouse. And how would that help me preserve my heirloom?"
- Spencer: "Perhaps a speaker might prove to be the best choice. And why would it make sense for us to just impose that on the younger adults without at least discussing their suggestions?"
- Fran: "True, games at many levels would make for a lively evening. What would the logistics mean for me?"

In each case, the speaker acknowledged a correct aspect of the other person's previous statement, making the other right. The speaker followed with an open question that further minimized wrong making, demonstrated respect, and invited the other person to think about the downsides of their suggestion.

Open Questions Get Others to Help Create the Content of Consensus

There are many advantages of others' input into the end result of a dialogue. *When people help craft a plan or agreement, they are more likely to buy into it and execute it.* In Dialogue 1, as Fran began to contribute ideas for engaging the young people in the fundraiser, her energy and enthusiasm grew. It doesn't take a psychologist to know that she will work harder on a plan that excites her. In Dialogue 5, Laurel used fanciful questions to inspire Mike's imagination, so he helped to craft a plan.

Sometimes we think we know just what would satisfy the other person's interests or objectives. It's tempting to offer our ideas as soon as they pop into our minds. However, other people often have, or think they have, even better ideas about satisfying their own interests. They need to be heard. And they may offer pleasant surprises for satisfying your interests, too.

We instinctively feel that, if we generate most of the content of the agreement, we will get the best deals for ourselves. But in reality, those who contribute the most content sometimes end up giving more than their fair share of the cost and/or effort of implementing the agreement.

The Smorgasbord questions in Chapter 8 are open questions specifically designed for inspiring ideas about consensus content, but you need not limit yourself to these. You can, for example, simply ask, "How can we _____?" filling the blank with one of your interests. Or, if what the other person wants cuts against your interests, ask, "What other ways could we _____?" and fill the blank with a broader statement of the interest behind his demand.

Open Questions Buy You Time to Think

Many of us generate our best ideas given ample time to reflect, and all of us occasionally get stuck. We don't know what to say. Our guts may tell us, *Say something to fill that awkward silence. Quick! It's my turn.* However, if you are not sure what to say, don't make a significant statement.[31]

Instead, you can ask an open question. Then remember to listen, not tune the other person out while she's answering. You come up with better ideas if you concentrate on her words. Feeling stuck sometimes means we don't yet have enough information, and as we've seen, open questions elicit more.

Don't worry that listening deprives you of the time you need to think. While you listen carefully to the other person, your mind works subconsciously on the basic issue. You'll often find breakthroughs occur while you are in the act of listening. But if they don't, if you need more time, simply say, "That's interesting. Let me think about that for a minute."

What if the shoe is on the other foot? The other person asks you an open question, and you aren't sure how to answer? Just take the time you need. If the silence gets too long or awkward, "That's a good question. I'd like to think about it."

---

31 Time investment is discussed thoroughly in Chapter 9.

Caveat: *Sometimes people change open questions to closed questions by suggesting an answer.* You ask a friend, "What should we have for lunch, sandwiches?" If your friend answers, "No," you still don't know what he wants for lunch. And if he says, "Yes," you lose the benefit of his unbiased thoughts; he might have suggested something you'd like better than sandwiches.

Likewise, don't dilute an open question by turning it into a cousin of the closed question—multiple choice. Spencer: "Why don't you want games at the fundraiser, because you don't like playing them, or because they're harder to organize?" Having answers suggested to her, Fran might choose one of them even though her interests would be more accurately represented if she came up with her own reason, "Because good speakers attract visitors." Since Spencer's purpose in asking the question is to learn about Fran's interests, he will gain more if he leaves the question truly open, "Why don't you want games at the fundraiser?" then *waits* for the answer.

Try This: Converting Statements to Open Questions

For each of the following statements, substitute an open question:
1. You never bring me flowers any more.
2. (To teenage child) You can't have a refrigerator for your room. You wouldn't like it anyway; it would take up too much space.
3. No one helps me clean up after the post-service coffee hour.
4. You're not listening to anything I say.

You'll also find it helpful to reread some of the previous dialogues and notice how our characters used open questions.

Closed Questions Close Agreements

The closed, *yes-or-no*, question closes agreements both large and small. It can, of course, save time and effort when discussing small matters that are neither complex nor highly contested. "Will you fold if I staple?"

However, *in building consensus, the primary use of the closed question is to confirm mutual understanding*. After creating a Solution Smorgasbord, we narrow down our thinking and refine our ideas to create an agreement or consensus. It's like planning to share a plate of food and agreeing on which foods to put on that plate. Before sitting down to eat, both people check over the selections to be sure these foods meet all their requirements for taste and nutrition (positive interests) and that there's nothing on the plate they can't tolerate (negative interests).

When you think you've reached agreement, use a closed question to verify that you and the other(s) are on the same page. First state your understanding of the agreement, then follow with a closed question such as "Have I got that right?" or "Correct?" Spencer might say to Fran, "OK, so you're going to speak to Yolanda about working together on the fundraiser for a transition year, while I help you set up a Caring Committee, right?"

"Right?" makes this a closed question. Spencer needs a yes or no to be sure that he and Fran have the same understanding of their final plan. If she answers, "No," then he needs to learn how her understanding differs from his so that they can keep trying till they agree on a joint statement of the plan.

Like looking at actual foods on a plate, viewing the plan in writing can help you ensure all needs are covered. The writing also serves as an aide memoir for future use as you implement the plan.

Likewise, *you can use closed questions to verify agreements about matters that precede the final plan*. They can confirm your understanding of others' statements, "If I understand correctly, you're saying having both games and a speaker would get too messy logistically. Have I got that right?"

They can also confirm temporary agreements. "OK, so you're going to seek more information from Yolanda, I'm going to take Interfaith Ministries' pulse about a lecture series, then you and I meet again in two weeks to discuss our final plan, correct?"

Other Uses of Closed Questions

Sometimes *people in the throes of strong emotion can't answer an open question*. The emotional activity in their brains blocks that kind of thinking. Suppose Fran is so crushed by the suggestion to change the fundraiser programming that she just sits and hangs her head. Perhaps she can't tell

Spencer "What would help?" at that moment. But if he asks, "Would it help if I bring you a glass of water?" she can probably nod or shake her head. She probably can't respond to the (implicit) open question, "Help me understand how you're feeling," but she might be able to answer an easier yes-or-no, question, "Are you feeling hurt?"

Notice that *Spencer's closed questions revolve around Fran's feelings and needs.* Now is not the time to direct her attention to his interests. She can't shift gears that abruptly. Rather, his compassionate questions about her concerns can start a more gradual transition.

Sometimes it's better to imply the "Right?" rather than state it aloud. If Mike accosts Laurel in a rage, she might say, "Mike, it sounds like you feel very angry indeed." Voicing "Are you?" in this situation, asking about the obvious, could seem ludicrous. Mike might even feel insulted or patronized by such a question.

Yet an angry person will usually respond to the implied, "Right?" Often, he will vent about why he's angry and just how angry he is. Though hard to listen to, this is what they both need before he can settle down and have a meaningful discussion. Meanwhile, his venting gives Laurel information on his interests, especially his feeling interests.

Occasionally someone whose anger is noted will deny it. That's OK too. Mike might scream, "I'm not angry!" in which case Laurel knows he's really, really angry. And she learns a second of his interests—he doesn't feel comfortable owning his anger. Or suppose Mike assumes an air of unnatural serenity and says, in a low tone of voice, "I'm not angry, I'm just disappointed in you." Now Laurel knows three interests: (1) he's angry, (2) he doesn't want to own it, and (3) he wants to feel one up with respect to her.

Alternatively, though not yet ready to think creatively, Mike might respond to a closed question in the form of *a simple, reasonable request,* "Will you set down the baseball bat while we discuss this?"

Once the other person begins to settle down, the closed question "May I," *asking permission for what you want to say or do next,* shows respect, continuing to ramp down unproductive emotions, while leading into dialogue. After Fran begins to respond to Spencer's closed questions, he might ask, "May I tell you how much I admire your work in getting us top flight speakers?"

Watch and listen for the other person's remarks to begin to reflect fresh thinking. She might ask a question, "What is it that the young people don't like about the speakers?" Or she might express a new insight, "I suppose we could incorporate more than one activity." Now test the water with an open question that offers little or no threat, "What do the mature folks like about speakers?" If you get a thoughtful answer, green light! You can resume normal conversation.

We've seen how helpful questions can be. But sooner or later, we have to make statements as well. As the next chapter shows, you don't need to strain your brain trying to think of brilliant arguments to persuade another person. You can build better consensus faster in much easier ways.

Key Points from Chapter 10

- Open questions can't be answered "yes" or "no." They open doors in many ways
    - Open questions draw people in to a collaborative frame of mind by helping them feel respected and heard
    - Open questions draw people out by encouraging them to elaborate on their ideas in their own words
    - Open questions minimize wrong making
    - Open questions can introduce others to your point of view
        - By asking advice: "What would you do if you were in my shoes and..."
        - By asking how what they are demanding would make sense for you
    - Open questions get others to help create consensus content
    - Open questions buy you time to think
        - While the other person answers, listen and concentrate on what he is saying
    - Don't turn your open question into a closed question by suggesting an answer
    - Don't dilute it by making it multiple choice

- Closed (yes-or-no) questions confirm understandings, large and small, temporary and final
  - Closed questions can also help settle someone who is too emotionally engaged to answer an open question. Helpful types of closed questions in this situation include
    - Questions about whether a given action on your part would help them
    - A simple, reasonable request
    - A request for permission for what you'd like to do next

CHAPTER 11
MAGIC MIRRORS

You can taste a word.

- Pearl Bailey

Just as a mirror reflects a visual image, we can reflect others' statements. This chapter deals with various forms of reflection—paraphrasing, repeating, rephrasing and reframing; and with some of their close cousins—agreement, validation, and what I call the "But Out" tool. You'll find these tools as useful as the mirrors in your car.

Like all our tools, the Magic Mirrors enhance the basic approach of meshing the interests of all parties to build consensus. Thus, in using them, we maintain our awareness of those interests and remain alert to further interests—our own as well as the those of the other person—which may come to light as we reflect their statements.

If I am totally self-centered, trying to use the Magic Mirrors as gimmicks to manipulate another into caving in to my demands, sooner or later, this attitude will reveal itself, thwarting my efforts and burning a bridge. Conversely, if I seek only to placate the other person, and fail to mesh my own interests with his, I will grow disheartened, perhaps even bitter.

However, *if, as I use these tools, I calmly focus compassion and curiosity not just on me, not just on him, but on us, the results can seem as magical as the mirror in a fairy tale.* The Magic Mirrors not only draw others to our side, but their very use synergistically helps us develop those core values that make them shine.

Paraphrasing

To paraphrase, *re-state the other person's remark in different words. Then confirm by asking a closed question about whether you got it right.* Laurel says to Mike, "So you feel the approaches to our two accidents were inconsistent. Correct?" In some cases, the confirming question can be incorporated into the paraphrase by your tone of voice, "So you want to borrow the dollhouse for two weeks?" However, voicing the question shows your respect for the other person more clearly, which helps to engage him.

A nice touch is introducing the paraphrase by a statement of your intention such as:

- Let me be sure I'm following you.
- I'd like to check my understanding before I answer that.
- If I understand you correctly...
- Let's see if I'm tracking that right.

For those who don't wish to leave the impression that they agree with the other person's statement, the introduction clarifies—you neither agree nor disagree at this point; you're only checking what you think you heard. In addition, introducing a paraphrase helps the other person to follow your train of thought.

The most obvious use of paraphrasing is to *verify your understanding of another's statement before you decide how to respond*. In one of my short programs, "Miscommunications You Never Knew You Had and What To Do about Them," I begin with a quote from Suzanne K. Langer's, *Philosophy in a New Key*, "Language is, without a doubt, the most momentous and at the same time the most mysterious product of the human mind." Next, I explain that, more often than not, a speaker and listener have at least slightly different understandings of the speaker's statement, that these misunderstandings can turn into conflicts, but that learning to detect them teaches us that not all the "conflicts" in our lives need to be conflicts.

I follow this introduction with a question, "What was the gist of my opening quote?" Someone always says, "Language is mysterious." Others will say things like, "We have more misunderstandings than we think," and "We can reduce the conflicts in our lives." The answers prove my very point by showing that some understood the words "my opening quote" to mean the quotation from Langer, while other's took it to mean all my opening remarks. Among the latter, people took away different notions of the gist of the opening even though they heard those few sentences only moments before.

I once saw a talk show where the host described a situation in which a woman buys a new outfit for an important event and models it for a friend.

The friend says, "That outfit is all wrong for you." The talk show guests argued heatedly about whether the friend had been unkind or had done the lady a favor. I could see that the "favor" proponents took the friend's statement to mean that the outfit was inappropriate for the occasion, while most of the "unkind" proponents understood that it was unattractive.

Such *misunderstandings can stem from different understandings of words* per se, as in the examples "opening quote" and "all wrong for you." *They can also arise from the fact that people don't always take in every word we say.* Qualifiers like "sometimes," or "it's possible that," or in the talk show example, "for you," might not register. Our long-term and short-term experiences color what we hear. If I've been roasting a turkey, I might hear a person say, "Baste," but if I've been watching a war movie, I might hear, "Based." Communication diversity, as described in Chapter 2, also spawns many misunderstandings.

Because the very nature of the problem lies in different understandings of a given series of words, the paraphrasing tool requires that we use *different* words to restate the other person's point. Say the lady in the talk show scenario thinks her friend finds her outfit unattractive, but the friend meant that it wouldn't suit the occasion. The lady wants to be sure she understood correctly before expressing hurt feelings. If she says, "Are you saying this outfit is all wrong for me?" she won't discover the disconnect. She repeated the same words that meant different things to her and her friend. However, "Are you saying the color makes me look washed out?" might do the trick.

Try This: Paraphrasing

Paraphrase each of the following statements:
- If anything happened to that dollhouse, nothing could really make it up to me.
- We know we make good income with speakers. Games represent an unknown.
- I broke the window trying to prevent a worse accident.
- Kayla has worked hard for a modest salary. How we treat our music director says something about who we are.

When to Paraphrase

Sometimes another says something that we know we don't understand, so we naturally seek clarification. "Use the order of service template from last week," might inspire you to ask, "You mean the one for Wednesday or the one for Sunday?" The dilemma, of course, is that unnecessary conflicts arise precisely because we think we do understand exactly what the other person meant. Misunderstanding means difference in what we firmly believe the words meant. *Sometimes we believe our understanding so implicitly that we don't think to check it.*

Paraphrase "Unreasonable" or "Offensive" Statements

So what would inspire us to paraphrase in cases of true misunderstanding, *when we believe we know* what the other person meant? One sign of misunderstanding is our own reaction to the person's statement. The statement seems unreasonable or incredible. You feel angry or hurt. Before arguing, before lashing out in anger or skulking away to lick your emotional wounds, paraphrase and confirm. How do you come up with different words? The easiest way is to state your own understanding.

For three days, Uri has been analyzing spreadsheets till his eyes are falling out, and he goes into Vera's office to vent. After awhile, Vera says, "Give it a rest," and Uri feels hurt. He might paraphrase in terms of his initial understanding of her words, "It sounds like you want a break from listening to me. Am I right?"

A more refined touch is to *ask yourself, How would (s)he have to understand those words in order to consider them reasonable (or credible, or polite)?* Then paraphrase in terms of the other person's possible understanding. This often requires a pause to allow your knee jerk reaction to settle down and your mind to work its way around the other person's statement. After such a pause, Uri might think to ask, "Did you mean for me to give the spreadsheets a rest?"

Paraphrase Important Matters

Another cue to paraphrase is the importance of a statement. For example, if you have asked one of the three magic questions, and the other person has answered, paraphrase. Paraphrasing and confirming also solidifies the concept in your mind, and it reinforces the other's recognition that you are interested in him and in trying to understand his interests.

Always paraphrase apparent agreements as explained in the preceding chapter. If Brandon and Molly believe they've arrived at a plan for the children's program, before proceeding, they should restate that agreement to be sure they're on the same page.

Other Uses of Paraphrasing

Aside from its obvious use in correcting misunderstandings before they grow into conflicts, paraphrasing has other virtues and uses.

Like asking open questions, *paraphrasing buys you time to think*. In an important interaction, your statements should be purposive. Because our knee-jerk reactions often work against consensus, blurting out your first thought can derail your efforts. If you aren't sure what you think, how you feel, or what to say, a paraphrase can give your unconscious mind enough time to figure it out, and as a bonus, you might learn something more from the other person's reply.

In addition, *correctly paraphrasing is the best way for you to get heard*. When someone repeats the same point for the fourth time, that usually means she feels you didn't get the point the first three times. Starting right in to argue your counterpoint reinforces her feeling. If you only understood her, she feels, you'd see it her way. So what does she do? While you present your flawless counterargument, she tunes you out and devises a better way to phrase her original point. Or worse, she doesn't even wait for you to finish that flawless argument. She interrupts and shouts you down.

Accurately paraphrasing proves you got another person's point, eliminating her urge to devise a better way to convince you. Now she's ready to listen. The candy flower on the icing of this cake is that, when you prove you understand others, you come across as intelligent, and therefore, even more worth listening to.

Again, repeating another's exact words doesn't work well for this purpose. It can sound like mindless parroting. It can even seem patronizing or dismissive. Re-stating others' points *in different words* proves you really understood them. And if you didn't understand them, your request for confirmation elicits correction, sparing you the embarrassment and inefficiency of launching into a discussion of the wrong point.

Beware of paraphrasing's evil twin—telling others what they think or how they feel before they express it themselves. This has just the opposite effect of a skillful paraphrase. I used to work with a man who would introduce an opinion with, "*I* know *you* think…, but…" Once I'd heard his intro, it didn't matter what he said next. I'd already donned my mental boxing gloves.

The value of grounding this Magic Mirror in attention to both parties' interests bears repeating. If, once you've been heard, you proceed from a totally self-absorbed point of view, you undo the effect of the paraphrase. The other person once again feels you aren't hearing them, and tends to argue, rather than collaborate.

Repeating

The above section on paraphrasing points out several contexts in which repeating someone's exact words doesn't work well. However, repeating has its uses in certain situations.

- *When trying to establish trust* with a new acquaintance or a highly suspicious person, you might begin by repeating his key points, then move on to paraphrasing when he seems more comfortable.

- *When someone is highly excited*, too excited to converse normally, particularly if the person is angry, repeating key words or phrases can begin to calm things down.

- *When* you want the other person to open up, to elaborate on her interests or contribute to a Solution Smorgasbord, for example, and she does, *you don't want to break the momentum or distract* her while she's on a roll. Yet you might like to let her know you're following her. You can repeat a key word from time to time.

> Fran: Once we get the younger adults involved in do-
> nating social events, we can expand to teen in-
> volvement. It takes a long time for everyone to go
> through a buffet line. If teens help in the kitchen
> and wait tables, we could have table service.

Spencer: (Nodding) Kitchen.

Fran: Or the older kids could run games for the younger ones while the adults attend the speaker.

Spencer: Games.

Fran: Or adults who aren't interested in the speaker could do that. We could charge chump change for the kids to participate in the games, and have small prizes—toys or treats.

Spencer: Prizes.

Fran: People wouldn't have to hire sitters for the evening, so they'll have more to spend at the auction.

Spencer: More to spend. I like it.

Rephrasing

"Rephrasing" can be synonymous with paraphrasing, but as used here, it refers to *restating something in more clear, concise or memorable terms*. People thinking aloud tend to ramble, repeat themselves, and jump from one idea to another in a disjointed manner. A clear, concise rephrase can sum things up in a way that everyone will understand and remember.

At the end of the conversation snippet just above, either Fran or Spencer might say, "So twenty-somethings donate socials to the auction, teens help with dinner, and people who don't like speakers run little kids' games with prizes."

Reframing

When someone phrases something in an unhelpful manner, say their wording is tactless, accusatory or inflammatory, casting a different light on one of their key concepts can promote a more positive tone without overtly making the speaker wrong. Reframing is particularly helpful to the person facilitating or mediating a discussion between others.

Suppose Molly and Brandon sit down with their minister, Joan, to discuss the children's program for which Brandon wants to borrow Molly's dollhouse. A portion of the conversation might go like this:

Dialogue 9: Rev. Joan reframes inflammatory statements

	Dialogue:	Joan's View:
M:	Brandon never returns anything he borrows.	Accusatory statement using absolutes "never," "anything."
J:	So you've had trouble getting some things back in the past. Right?	Reframes more accurately and less offensively.
M:	Yeah. And he breaks things and doesn't give a hoot.	
B:	She's just a pill.	
J:	Sounds like you two have different ideas about what's an acceptable amount of wear and tear. Can each of you give me an example?	Reframes last two statements to put focus on what happened, rather than on people's perceived faults, followed by an open question to learn more about what actually happened.

When you reframe on your own behalf, rather than to facilitate a discussion between others, the person whose statement you reframe might feel corrected, and thus made wrong. To avoid sounding uppity, foster sincere curiosity about whether your reframe correctly reflects what the other person thinks and feels. Sincerity helps keep the schoolmaster tone out of your voice. Still, be alert to signs that others feel made wrong—they deny, rationalize or project—and be prepared to regroup.

Agreeing and Validating

Many of the practices presented throughout this book help us avoid making people wrong. The good news about the power of wrong making is that right making is just as strong. It helps to build the bridges that carry us across the chasms of difficult conversations. The following group of skills actively makes people right, drawing them to our side. *We agree with ideas. We validate feelings.*

Agreeing

Agreeing with someone who's fighting you can feel like giving in. You might think, *Now he'll run right over me.* However, just as wrong making triggers resistance, agreement and validation inspire affinity.

This doesn't mean you should pretend to agree when you don't. However, when you do agree with an idea, and say so, the other person is generally more likely to listen to, and seriously consider, your ideas. We've learned that correctly paraphrasing others' ideas suggests that we are intelligent and worth listening to. Agreeing with at least some of their ideas raises that dynamic to an even higher level.

When someone presents his case, fully expecting a counterargument, and you agree with one of his points, you give him nothing to push against. You arouse his interest and curiosity. He listens. Even if he argues heatedly, your agreeing with valid points begins to ramp down a tense situation.

Caveat: Some people wonder, with good reason, whether agreeing with one point can psychologically set them up to agree with additional points that cut against their best interests. Sales people and fundraisers are taught to seek a small concession early on, which makes it more difficult for the subject to refuse a later, and larger, request. A similar dynamic was at work in the experiment where homeowners who had displayed a small sticker later agreed to accept a big ugly sign.

When you consciously choose to agree in order to calm someone down and help them listen, take these mindfulness steps to prevent your being sucked into additional agreements:

1. Be aware of the sticker-sign dynamic.
2. When you agree with a point for a purpose, to restore calm, for example, remain mindful of that purpose.

3. Always maintain awareness of your own interests, alert for solutions that might work for the other person as well.

4. Take a think break before final agreement on an important matter, and review your interest list during that break.

In my experience, the benefits of judicious agreement outweigh any risks, especially when I consciously employ the four mindfulness steps listed just above.

Here are a few examples of judicious agreement:

Example 1:

Molly: It wasn't fair to tell the kids they were getting the dollhouse without asking me. You set me up.

Brandon: You're right. I should have checked with you first. Where do I go from here?

Example 2:

Fran: I wouldn't lose sight of what us mature people want. We're the ones who spend the most at the auction, and we like speakers.

Spencer: True. We don't want to increase one group's participation only to decrease another. How might we interest both?

Validating

Validating can mean acknowledging that a feeling is natural under the circumstances, that you'd feel the same way in the other's shoes, that you have felt the same way in similar situations, or simply that the feeling must be unpleasant.

Sometimes, with our hearts in the right place, we tell another that she shouldn't feel hurt, sad, angry, or whatever. This usually makes her feel even worse. Avoid telling someone that she should not feel as she does. Better to validate the feeling. Later you can offer thoughts that might help her feel better, but leave it to her to decide what to do with them.

> Her: I'm meeting my future in-laws for the first time next weekend. They invited us to their country club. I'm so nervous. I'm just sure I'll screw up something or other.
>
> You: I remember when I met Mary's parents. It felt like I was going into a job interview. Nerve-wracking, isn't it?
>
> Her: Yeah.
>
> You: You looked really poised and put together when you chaired the meeting last week. I bet your in-laws will love you.

Validating feelings can be even more powerful than agreeing with ideas. Suppose Joan tries to mediate between Brandon and Molly. She aims to get each to understand how the other feels before moving on to settle the dollhouse issue. So far, her strategy is good. But if, when Molly expresses an ill feeling, Joan immediately points out how Brandon feels, she seems to take sides. Molly's defenses go up. The same thing happens if Joan tries to get Brandon to empathize with Molly's feelings without first validating his. Put yourself in Molly's shoes and consider this exchange:

> Molly: Brandon has no respect for me or my property. He borrows things, and if he returns them at all, they're late and damaged.
>
> Joan: I'm sure Brandon feels hurt when he hears that.

As Molly, you feel discounted. Your feelings don't matter. All Joan seems to care about is making you feel sorry for Brandon, the one who disrespected you. You've been made wrong, and a sense of righteous indignation springs up.

Now compare this:

Molly:	Brandon has no respect for me or my property. He borrows things, and if he returns them at all, they're late and damaged.
Joan:	I can understand how you might feel disrespected. Sometimes, when we believe our things aren't cared for, we extend those feelings to ourselves.
Molly:	Yeah.
Joan:	And if Brandon believes he does respect you, he might be surprised when he learns that the damaged pitchfork left you feeling disrespected.

As Molly, you might still feel a little huffy, but you see Joan as fair, and you're willing to think about what she said.

Validation Variation—The Power Apology

Those who find it hard to admit mistakes or to apologize often suffer from one of two inaccurate assumptions. These assumptions would be easier to correct if they formed part of our conscious reasoning. All too often, however, they fly way below our conscious radar screens. These assumptions are:

1. If I apologize, I admit I'm bad or stupid.

2. You're either right or wrong, good or bad, strong or weak; if I admit I did or said one thing wrong, I lose it all.

In short, those who fear apologies usually harbor self-doubts. Contrary to what our knee jerk reactions tell us, a sincere apology or admission of error, delivered at the right moment and in the right manner, can be a powerful tool for those who are self-assured enough to use it.

Tone is paramount. *The tone you want arises from respect and esteem for yourself as well as for the other person.* It's neither a breast-beating *mea culpa* nor an uppity "SOR-ry." You can't fake this tone.

If you feel like one mistake makes you a loser, if you feel the apology itself makes you a loser, this will come out in your tone. You will, as many fear, project weakness. Offered to an aggressive type who is inclined to prey on the weak, such an apology can backfire on you, escalating his attempts to take advantage of you.

On the other hand, if you turn the apology into a way to put the other person down, you can antagonize even a mild-mannered sweetie. "I'm sorry *you* took it that way," or even a simple "I'm sorry," uttered with nose pointed skyward, is better left unsaid.

To be effective, ***the apology must be credible***. Don't apologize unless you believe you made a mistake that inconvenienced or hurt another. Don't apologize unless you truly regret that inconvenience or pain. But if your error caused harm that you regret, *know* that this makes you neither worse nor better than she is, and express that regret sincerely. The right tone will often follow.

A good apology is powerful. Traditionally, attorneys used to advise a doctor whose actions had harmed a patient not to apologize. From a strictly legal point of view, this made sense. In the event of a malpractice suit, the apology could be taken as an admission of wrong doing that would work against the doctor at trial. However, later studies showed that, when the doctor apologized, the patient was far less likely even to file suit, so there was no trial.

Put yourself in Molly's shoes, and contrast these two possible approaches by Brandon:

1. Look, I know you were upset when I broke your pitchfork, but I promise I'll take care of the dollhouse. Please don't make me disappoint the kids.
2. I did break your pitchfork, and I got defensive and flip when you pointed it out. I'm sorry for both of those things. What would it take for you to feel comfortable letting us use the dollhouse for our program?

In the first approach, Brandon told Molly how he thought she felt, but did not actually apologize, or even validate her presumed feelings. Molly senses Brandon is about to argue why she should not feel as she does. Brandon follows this ambiguous observation with an attempt to guilt trip Molly.

In the second approach, Brandon acknowledges specific past behaviors and clearly expresses his apology. He follows up with an open question that shows he wants Molly to feel comfortable and for her to decide what she needs.

From Molly's perspective, which approach is more engaging? Which draws you into conversation with Brandon, and which makes you want to walk away?

As always, continue to advocate for your own legitimate interests. Remember that material things can't satisfy feeling interests. If your mistake cost the other person money, you might need to pay her because the hurt was monetary. But if your mistake insulted her without causing any material loss, money won't cure the hurt anyway. Why penalize yourself when payment won't achieve your objective of building a bridge to a positive, collaborative relationship?

What if you've had an unpleasant argument with someone, but he started it? What *if you feel you really did nothing wrong*? Yet, for one reason or another, it's in your interest to patch things up. Perhaps the two of you serve on the board and have to continue working together for the rest of the year. Yet you know him well enough to realize he's unlikely to make the first move. Without actually apologizing, you might try expressing regret for the situation. "I've felt unhappy with the turn of our last conversation and was *hoping we could rewind and clear the air.*"

Validation Variation—The Detailed Legitimate Compliment

Phony compliments, or "stroking," won't fool anyone with a bit of people smarts. It can even work against you, making you seem manipulative and untrustworthy.

All too often, however, we truly admire someone, or we're grateful for his efforts, but we neglect to say so. Sometimes his attributes or accomplishments seem so self-evident it never occurs to us that he might want or need to hear them expressed. He does. We all do.

A sincere compliment is one of the best ways to address feeling interests. However, you don't need to save up your compliments until you are trying to build consensus out of divergent views. In fact, compliments may work better as background—building a relationship of mutual regard—than as fixes for controversies.

Pay your compliment as close as possible to the time when someone manifests the characteristic or behavior you admire, and she will find it more credible. If she did a great job chairing a meeting, tell her so as soon as the meeting is over. If you admire his restraint in defusing a verbal attack instead of firing back, tell him at the first graceful opportunity.

Well-framed compliments are particularly useful to clergy and other church leaders. In *Please Understand Me II*,[32] author David Kiersey writes:

> ...the surprising thing is that followers do what the leader wants primarily to please the leader... Is not the paycheck and the satisfaction of doing a good job enough? Apparently not... We all want appreciation, *and we want it from the person in charge*.[33] [Emphasis added]

Many clergy, to their credit, take great pains not to lord it over the laity. Yet, no matter how egalitarian they try to be, no matter how much authority may actually be vested in a board, vestry, or the like, people feel that their minister is "the person in charge." Like it or not, the minister is the figurehead of the church. If you doubt this, just notice whom people blame if things don't go their way. When people feel dissatisfied with the course of affairs in their country, they blame the head of state. When they're unhappy with the course of the church, they blame the clergy. The "one in charge" is also the lightning rod.

Clergy and other leaders can lay the groundwork for more realistic assessment of difficult times by letting members know they are appreciated and precisely why they are appreciated.

On the other side of the coin, people often fail to pay legitimate compliments to their clergy. It's not that they don't appreciate them. They just assume those compliments go without saying. No news is good news. They may even feel that the minister is so far above them that it would be impertinent, for example, to compliment her on her sermon.

But clergy want appreciation too. Like everyone else, they want it from "the boss." And the Protestant congregation that calls a minister, and can likewise dismiss her, is her boss in a very real sense. Even if a denomination,

---

32 (Prometheus Nemesis Book Co., 1998).

33 Ibid, p. 288.

such as Roman Catholic, appoints clergy to congregations and decides when to move them, the priest still values words of appreciation from parishioners.

One of the most unfortunate situations I see is the minister who wants to resign in the face of complaints from a small but vocal minority, not realizing that the silent majority value and appreciate her.

Though compliments from "the person in charge" are particularly inspiring, all compliments are valued. They build bridges with anyone—superior, subordinate or peer. Even if a person is a contented worker bee with no aspirations to a leadership role, the sincere compliments we pay establish mutual respect that will stand us in good stead if and when we need to resolve a difference of opinion.

People value detailed compliments more than general ones. Imagine you worked hard cooking dinner for a guest. As he pushes his chair back at the end of the meal, he says, "Thanks. That was delicious." He might have enjoyed the meal, or he might just be saying what he thinks is polite. However, if he says, "I loved that glaze on the carrots. Was it a maple syrup base, or molasses?" You *know* he enjoyed it.

If, after a service, someone shakes the minister's hand and says, "Thanks. I enjoyed the sermon," that's good. But if she says, "I think that technique of meditating on ambient sounds would work well for me. I'm going to try it tomorrow," that's even better.

Suppose Fran and her committee pull off a great fundraiser. If Spencer says, "You all did a wonderful job. Many thanks," everyone feels good. But if he tells Fran how the well-planned event came off without a hitch, tells Chris how much he enjoyed the dessert, tells George what a relief it was to see all the chairs and tables wiped down and put away within thirty minutes of the end, and tells Pat that he heard good things about the speed of the auction check out, they all feel *great*. It takes time for a leader to seek out individuals and customize compliments for them, but it's time well-invested.

Detailed compliments work better, and *compliments directed to individuals' fortes, the things they're most proud of, work best of all. Please Understand Me II* offers guidance for identifying a person's strong points according to temperament.

Kiersey also recommends following up the compliment with detailed questions about the person's achievement. I believe detailed questions prove appreciation in much the same way as paraphrasing proves understanding. Spencer might say to Fran, "You planned this event well. Everything went off without a hitch. How did you manage to get all those teenagers to work the kitchen and wait tables without making a big mess?" He might ask Chris, "What was in that icing? I could eat a bowlful of it." To George, he could say, "It was so nice to have the tables and chairs cleaned and put up so quickly. How many helpers did it take?" To Pat, "I heard lots of compliments about how much faster the auction checkout went this year. What's your secret?"

Words of *thanks also validate*. Again, the sooner the better, and the more detailed the more credible.

Try This: Detailed Compliments

Think of the last thing your minister did well. If you are the minister, think of the last thing a volunteer did well.

Compose a compliment for the person who did well.

Now go back and make your compliment even more detailed.

Validation Variation—Linguistic Devices

Any phraseology or grammatical structure that lessens wrong making is relatively right making or validating. Therefore, (just in case anyone hasn't heard) complaints expressed as *"I statements"* are, relatively speaking, more validating than "you statements." Instead of telling Brandon, "You never return anything on time, and when you do, it's broken," Molly might try, "I've had things broken in the past."

Writing instructors, especially those who teach fiction, tell us to favor active voice, in which the subject of the sentence performs an action, "He ran the red light," over passive voice, in which the subject is acted upon, "The red light was run by him." This makes our writing more stimulating to the reader. Fiction writers want their readers to sense the action and feel the emotions of the characters in a story. Conversely, when the goal is to foster a calm atmosphere, *passive voice* tends to work better. Instead of, "You broke my pitchfork," Molly might say, "My pitchfork was broken."

Writers are also generally encouraged to avoid overuse of the verb "to be" in favor of "action verbs," again to make their work seem lively and stimulating. "The skier struggled to free herself from the snowdrift" is more exciting than "The skier's efforts to free herself from the snowdrift were a struggle." Conversely, when your goal is a calm, civil conversation, *the verb "to be"* often serves you better. Instead of "Yolanda hurt me," Fran might say, "Yolanda's words were hurtful to me."

Caveat 1: I have observed, however, that some people view a particular linguistic device as a magic bullet. They seem to think, *As long as I stick to "I statements," no one will take offense, and everything will be fine.* Molly tells Brandon, "I need to be sure my dollhouse stays in its current condition, so I owe it to myself to consider that things I've loaned previously were broken." Brandon snaps, "So you're accusing me of being irresponsible?" Molly now feels dumbfounded, cheated, as if Brandon broke the rules. Guard yourself from this attitude.

No linguistic device, nor any other consensus tool, is a panacea. Many people recognize a complaint as a complaint no matter how you phrase it. In fact, learning communication skills can enhance such recognition. If both Brandon and Molly heard about "I statements" in a recent sermon, Brandon is more likely to realize that Molly tried to complain, albeit in what she hoped would be a less inflammatory manner.

This doesn't mean that either the sermon or Molly's I statement proved useless. Brandon not only recognizes that Molly has a complaint, he also recognizes that she is trying her best not to make him feel bad. Her good intentions still go a long way toward tempering his response.

Moreover, whether or not Brandon heard the sermon, and even though he was offended by the "I statement," he continued the discussion. If, instead, Molly had said, "I can't loan you the dollhouse. You have a history of returning things late or damaged, if you return them at all," can't you just imagine Brandon storming away?

Caveat 2: Validating linguistic devices work by reducing the directness and emotional load of a complaint. But *reducing directness sometimes reduces understanding as well*. Due to communication diversity, some people simply don't get certain indirect messages.

Suppose Ms. Tardy habitually arrives late at committee meetings and leaves early. This distracts the other members. They also lose time repeating things for her. The committee chair tries all sorts of tactful—thus less direct—ways to let Tardy know that they would like her to arrive and depart on time in order to hear everything. Over and over, Tardy replies, "Oh, don't worry about me. I'm OK with whatever portion I do hear." She doesn't get the point.

In all likelihood, the only wording Tardy could understand would go something like this, "We aren't just worried about you. We're concerned about ourselves. It's distracting when you arrive late and leave early. More importantly, it's frustrating to deal with your comments and questions when you haven't heard all the background. We're willing to consider altering the start and stop times so you can make the entire meeting. Otherwise, we'd like you to drop out."

Unfortunately, the chair has to decide whether to make such a statement, and risk offending and angering Tardy, or to continue tolerating her habits.

The "But Out" Technique

This variation on agreeing not only breaks through resistance, but can even disarm an outright verbal attack and effectively introduce a different perspective to the attacker. The But Out tool includes three steps.

Step 1: Find something the other person has said that you can honestly agree with, and say so. For example, say Mike verbally attacks Laurel, "You rich bitches think you deserve special treatment, and our 'leaders' are so spineless, they suck up and give it to you." Laurel's Step 1 could be, "It's true I've been blessed money-wise." By agreeing, Laurel begins to disarm the attack, giving Mike nothing to push against.

If you can't agree with anything precisely as the other person stated it, *try reframing*. Laurel did this by reframing "rich bitches" as "blessed money-wise."

If you can't find a point of agreement, you can almost always validate a feeling if you predicate your validation on the other person's perspective. "If

I believed the church had discriminated against me, I'd be angry too." Notice that Laurel did not have to agree that the church discriminated. She only said that, if she believed what Mike believes, she'd feel like he feels.

Sometimes you have to repeat this first step until the other person seems ready to listen to a different perspective. If you agree with one point, and he repeats it, try paraphrasing. If you agree with one point, and he angrily raises another, try to agree with something about the new point or validate the feelings associated with it. Keep agreeing and validating until things settle down:

M: You rich bitches think you deserve special treatment, and our 'leaders' are so spineless, they suck up and give it to you.

L: It's true I've been blessed money-wise.

M: And you just love all that special treatment.

L: You sound angry, and—

M: (Interrupting) Damn right, I'm angry.

L: If I believed the church discriminated against me, I'd be angry, too.

M: You bet I am. I can't donate as much as you, but I do what I can and that should count for *something*.

L: Of course it should. Everyone contributes in their own way, and they all deserve appreciation and support.

M: Well, I'm glad you see that.

Step 2: Don't say "but." The agreement step has calmed the atmosphere. The other person is listening to you. Now you're ready to introduce your perspective. Because your perspective contrasts with his, the natural segue is "but" or a synonym like "however" or "nevertheless." In fact, it is extremely difficult not to say "but" in such situations. It rolls off the tongue before you can catch it. And what happens when you say "but"? Laurel says, "If I believed the church discriminated against me, I'd be angry, too, but…" The attack she just disarmed begins to rise from the ashes. Mike hears "but" and thinks, *Here it comes.* His defenses spring into action, and the discussion moves backward.

Getting Past No by William Ury[34] points out that, in formal logic, "and" is equivalent to "but." So Ury suggests using "and" as your segue. For this reason, he calls this three step process the "yes… and" technique. *"And" makes for an especially smooth transition*, entraining your next point. "And" suggests that you intend to build on his ideas, rather than argue with them.

However, if you find it too difficult to say "and" when "but" is battering the inside of your mouth trying to escape (and believe me, it will be), simply move on to your perspective without a segue. The most important thing is not to undo what your agreement or validation has accomplished by saying "but." Thus, I've re-titled this the "But Out" tool.

Step 3: State your point or perspective. Laurel's complete statement might be, "If I believed the church discriminated against me, I'd be angry, too, and there were facts about my accident nobody but those present had any way of knowing."

In some cases, where the other person has been very heated, you can begin with a reasonable request for a hearing, instead of a counterpoint. "If I believed the church discriminated against me, I'd be angry, too. May I tell you some facts that nobody but those present at my accident had any way of knowing?" By requesting Mike's permission to introduce a different perspective, Laurel demonstrates respect and concern for his feelings.

We've seen one example of the But Out tool in the above exchange between Joan and Molly. Joan validated Molly's feelings, then used "and" to segue into the idea that Brandon might also have legitimate reasons to feel hurt.

Here are some other examples:

- I agree the past speakers have drawn many donors to the fundraiser, and I'd like to maintain that demographic while also attracting younger adults.
- It's true the pitchfork had four tines when I borrowed it and three when I returned it, and I noticed before I started using it that one of the tines was bent.

---

34 (Bantam, 1993).

- Yes, our minister did suggest Kayla for music director, and the board met in closed session without the minister to discuss whether it was appropriate to hire a member of the congregation.
- If I were in your shoes, selling a boat, I'd try to get as much for it as possible. And as a buyer, I owe it to myself to be sure that the boat is worth what I pay.

The But Out technique takes practice because it's so very natural to interject "but" before a counterpoint. You need to *practice in low stakes situations* in order to draw on this powerful skill in those tense encounters where the other person goes ballistic. Practice first on an ordinary disagreement. If Butting Out can ramp down a verbal attack, imagine what it can do for, "Aw, Mom, I don't want to."

You can even practice in situations with no stakes, no controversy at all, such as in describing your own mental decisions. Suppose you're sitting in a restaurant deciding what to order for dinner. Instead of "I'd like enchiladas, but I had spaghetti for lunch, so I'll just take a salad," you can say, "I'd like enchiladas, and I had spaghetti for lunch. I'll just take a salad."

You're not doing this because "but" is a bad word. "But" is a perfectly good word and often enhances the clarity of our statements. Because the matter of why you chose a salad is unimportant, you can use it to practice Butting Out, even though a "but" segue would actually make your remark easier for your dinner companion to follow. You're not trying to eliminate "but" from your vocabulary. You're just practicing.

Set aside a short time of casual chit chat, say from the time you place an order until the food arrives. Try to But Out during that time period. Then relax and enjoy your dinner—and the conversation. Later, when you experience the near-magical results of Butting Out under tense resistance or verbal attacks, you'll know the practice was well worth the effort.

Sharing the Magic Mirrors

Sometimes, once we have experienced the magic of mirroring, we worry whether someone whose motives are less than admirable can use these tools to bend us to their will. As mentioned at the outset, such tools work best when the user focuses, compassionately and curiously, on your interests along with his own.

However, even if someone approaches you in a state of complete self-absorption, don't worry if he uses the Magic Mirrors. Would you rather he dismissed your statement out of hand, or paraphrased it before offering his own view? In order to paraphrase what you said, he must think about it. And if he gets it wrong, the paraphrase plus confirmation invites you to correct the misimpression.

If you should lose your cool, would you rather he shouted back, or Butted Out? Butting Out requires him to think of something you said that he agrees with. If he hurts you, would you like an apology? Would you like him to try to bully or harangue you, or would you prefer that he try to address your interests, albeit only to get you to address his, and not because he cares about you?

The practices themselves, even if first undertaken from a self-absorbed point of view, can draw the user toward compassion and curiosity. It is difficult for him to paraphrase you without gleaning at least some understanding of your point of view, difficult to disarm your attack by Butting Out without keeping himself calm as well.

These right-making practices are ways to address others' feeling interests, and isn't that what we all want?

Are you wondering what to do if the other person never uses consensus skills at all. What if he doesn't even seem interested in consensus? Chapter 12 provides some answers.

Key Points from Chapter 11

- To **paraphrase**, re-state the other person's remark *in different words*. Then confirm by asking a closed question about whether you got it right
    - o Paraphrase when:
        - ▪ You want to make sure you understand
        - ▪ The other person's statement seems incredible or unreasonable
        - ▪ To confirm a final understanding or other important point

- You need time to think
- You want the other person to listen to you
  - Don't tell others what they think or feel. Rather, let them state it, then confirm what you think you heard
- Repeat key words when
  - You want to establish trust
  - The other person is highly excited
  - You don't want to break the other's train of thought
- Rephrase confusing or rambling statements
- Reframe statements worded in an inflammatory or unhelpful manner
- Agree with ideas
  - To build bridges of affinity
  - To defuse resistance
- Validate feelings
- Apologize from a basis of respect and esteem for yourself as well as for the other person
- Make your compliments legitimate and detailed
  - Emphasize attributes the other person is proud of
- Use linguistic devices as aids, not panaceas
  - I statements
  - Passive voice
  - The verb "to be"
- But Out
  - Find something you agree with and say so
  - Don't say "but"
    - Segue with "and" if you can
  - State your point
- Share the Magic Mirrors
  - You'll want others to use them when conversing with you

CHAPTER 12
BUT WHAT IF...?

Trouble, like the hill ahead, straightens out when you advance upon it.

- Marcelene Cox

There comes a time when my clients and trainees have had so much fun and enjoyed such success practicing role play exercises with both parties using their consensus system that it almost seems too easy. Inevitably, someone will ask a question beginning with, "But what if..." The sentence usually ends with something more or less equivalent to, "...I'm dealing with Attila the Hun."

However, Attila is not the only "what if." People want to know:

- What if the best we can do, using all the skills, still doesn't satisfy my interests?
- What if the other person is unreasonable?
- What if the other person lies, reneges, stonewalls or bullies me?
- What if we just don't have time to keep using the skills until we reach a consensus?
- What if there's no way around making someone wrong?

The "but" in "but what if" suggests an assumption that, when things get really difficult, we abandon the consensus skills that normally work so well and use something else. It's as if the person asking the question envisions two separate toolboxes, one for use with reasonable folks, and the other for the Attilas of this world. I sometimes suspect that the client asking the question has not actually tried using the skills she's learned with Attila.

In fact, *the tools in the preceding chapters form the foundation* for dealing with almost any situation, even the most challenging. *We can add to them, but we don't abandon them in favor of an entirely different set.*

If you want to finish a piece of rough wood to a high gloss, you begin with chisel, plane and sandpaper. *Then*, you use more refined treatments to bring out the luster.

This chapter explains some of the refined tools of consensus building and how they interface with our basics. As you read about these refined tools, you'll see that they are intimately interwoven with those in previous chapters, and in particular, with identifying and focusing on ultimate objectives or interests.

What Would Make That Reasonable?

This is an open question to ask yourself, briefly introduced in Chapter 11. When someone's words or behavior seem unreasonable, before you write him off as Attila the Impossible, ask yourself how he would have to view the situation in order to see his own actions, positions, opinions, etc. as reasonable. If he behaves in a manner that he himself considers unreasonable, he makes himself wrong. Being made wrong is so stressful that people rarely do it to themselves. So he most likely considers his words or actions reasonable.

This person might have rationalized himself into this belief, his mind working so quickly that he was unaware of the rationalization process. Culture, temperament or the like might make his behavior seem normal to him. Or he may interpret words differently than you do. But however he arrived at the belief that he is reasonable, he holds that belief now.

You don't have to agree with him, but if you want to change his mind, you do have to know what's on his mind at present. If you discover that what you're really dealing with is a difference in interpretation, rather than an intractably unreasonable person, that's good. Differences in interpretation, once uncovered, are usually easier to handle.

Suppose Mike and Laurel take their dispute to Megan, chair of the Building and Grounds Committee. Mike tells her that he's angry because he paid for the sign he backed over, but Laurel didn't pay for her broken window. Megan says, "Well, Laurel, that's right. We have to be fair." Laurel explodes, "What about me? What about being fair to me?"

It would be natural for Megan to think Laurel is impossible. She projects: *Laurel breaks a window, doesn't pay for it, and she's mad at* me*? Apparently, Laurel's definition of "unfair" applies any time she doesn't get her way. How unreasonable! How can anybody deal with a person like that?*

But then Megan stops and asks herself, *How would Laurel have to see this situation in order to believe it's unfair for her to pay for the window?* It occurs to her that Laurel might be considering facts that she is not aware of.

So Megan asks Laurel for those facts, "Help me understand why it's unfair for you to pay for the window. What else do I need to know?"

Laurel replies, "Mike just wasn't looking out when he backed over the sign. But I broke the window trying to stop a little girl who was running with a sharp pair of scissors. That's different."

Megan may or may not agree that those circumstances should excuse Laurel from paying, but at least now she knows what she's dealing with, and she can use her consensus skills accordingly.

One way to help answer the question, "What would make that reasonable?" is to *zero in on a key word, such as "fair,"* and consider how it might mean different things to different people or under different circumstances. You can also ask the other person what the word means to them in the present situation. "What would fairness look like to you?" or "How do we decide what's fair?" or simply "Fair?"

Suppose Spencer says he'd like different kinds of games for different age groups. Fran throws up her hands. "How in the world am I supposed to know what kinds of games all those different people would like?" Spencer is dumbfounded. Fran seems to think he's being unreasonable, when she's the one off in left field. *If we know what kinds of curricula to present to different age levels in religious education, we can certainly tell which games appeal to preschoolers, grade-schoolers and teens,* he thinks. Apparently Fran is stubbornly resisting games and grasping at any excuse not to have them.

But he steps back and asks himself what would make her reaction reasonable. What kind of situation would leave her at sea over which games to provide for different groups? A situation where personal taste figures in, perhaps, or a situation where age doesn't reveal much about preference. What kind of situation would produce that kind of dilemma? One example would be different groups of adults. *Wait a minute! We were talking about the young adults wanting games and the middle-aged and seniors wanting a speaker. Maybe she thought I meant different games for different age levels of adults.*

Now he can ask Fran, "What different age levels are you thinking of?" or "Did you think I meant different age levels of adults?"

Try This: Making Things Reasonable

Reflect on an exasperating incident when you mentally or physically threw up your hands at how unreasonable someone seemed. Write down any ways the exasperating person might have viewed her situation, her words, or her behavior so that they seemed reasonable to her.

Turn Off Your Resistance

In each of the last two examples, the "unreasonable" statement of one person made the other feel made wrong. Committee chair Megan felt Laurel considered her unfair. Spencer felt Fran considered him unreasonable. To enable themselves to answer "What would make that reasonable?" each of them had to let go of their instinctive resistance—denial, rationalization, or projection. They had to take the focus off themselves and concentrate on the other person's point of view.

Though viewing things through another's lenses doesn't mean agreeing with them, on a visceral level, it feels akin. When the other person has made you wrong, anything that feels like agreement is uncomfortable.

Whatever you can do to *relieve your own reaction to being made wrong* will, therefore, boost your ability to make that mental shift. As in the above examples, a pause helps. Practice and experience help. When you begin to see how often different interpretations masquerade as, or turn into, conflicts, you will come to *feel* (not just think) that asking "What would make that reasonable?" is not about right and wrong—neither yours nor the other person's. And the key to turning off your resistance is to turn off the *feeling* of being wrong.

Any regular practice that helps you keep your balance—meditation, exercise,[35] laughter—will stand you in good stead when you feel made wrong.

---

35 Regular exercise helps your general ability to turn off the feelings of being made wrong. Note, however, that during, and in the immediate aftermath of, vigorous exercise, anger is temporarily increased. So allow plenty of recovery time after a workout before approaching a person with whom you have a disagreement.

Another trick is to *keep a grounding trigger* handy, something small you can handle or look at to remind you of good feelings. A reminder of someone who loves you unconditionally can serve. You can touch your wedding ring, for example, if you feel made wrong. Recalling love works like an antidote to feeling made wrong because giving or receiving love makes you right. When mediating or facilitating meetings, I like to keep a photo of one my unconditionally supportive nephews under the table. If I feel myself tilting off balance due to the high emotions of my clients, a glance at that photo brings me back to center.

Try This: Grounding

Think of a time when you felt warmly loving and/or loved, a time when you felt very good about yourself. This should be a time *unrelated* to the exasperating person and incident in the preceding Try-This Segment.

Sit comfortably, close your eyes and relax. For a few minutes, make yourself right by concentrating on that warm, loving time. Try to recapture those good feelings.

Now open your eyes and try to improve on your notes from the preceding Try-This Segment.

Were you able to add more insights about how the exasperating person might have considered herself reasonable?

Think about your experience during the exasperating incident. Did that incident make you feel made wrong in any way?

Plan B

Your Plan

When, for any reason, a mutually satisfactory consensus does not come easily, you need to know how you will address your own interests if the other person can't or won't. What is the best you can do for yourself without him? This is your "Plan B." I also refer to such plans, or their components, as your

"Walk-Away Alternatives" because they're what you will do if, for any reason, you decide to walk away from your dealings with the other person.[36]

We may instinctively feel that designing a Plan B before trying to reach consensus is negative thinking, that it will impede our best efforts to reach consensus with the other person. In reality, *a Plan B actually increases your chances of reaching consensus while minimizing conflict.*

Develop your Plan B as soon as possible, and you lessen the chance that you actually have to use it. Remember my arm pushing experiments, how head talk about have-to's and needs literally weakens a person? Without a Plan B, you may enter a dialogue feeling needier than necessary. When you feel you *must* reach consensus with another, that your success or wellbeing depends on him, you inject an undercurrent of anxiety into your dialogue. That anxiety creeps into your tone of voice, choice of words and body language. Your discomfort can be contagious. The other person may not know why he feels uncomfortable, but he associates the feeling with you. He may see you as pushy or even a bit desperate.

How do you react to someone who seems too needy? If you're like most people, you shy away, sensing that this person's demands on you will become too much. How do you react to someone pushy? You push back or walk away. Do you want people to react to you in those ways?

Just as a leopard goes for the weakest animal in the herd, an aggressive or exploitative person grows bolder when he senses the weakness born of neediness. Moreover, neediness and desperation impair your ability to think well, to use your consensus tools at their best, and to make your best decisions.

Conversely, when you enter a dialogue knowing that you have options, you relax. You can approach the other person with a friendly confidence. You can open your mind to his interests, rather than simply scratching and clawing for your own.

But sometimes focusing on others' needs can become such an end in itself that we might neglect to advocate for our own interests. This is particularly common in church settings, where "getting along" with others is seen as

---

36 Harvard Negotiation Project materials, such as *Getting to Yes*, call such a plan a "BATNA," which stands for "best alternative to a negotiated agreement." In my experience, people find this term difficult to understand and remember. Therefore I coined my own terms "Walk-Away Alternatives" and "Plan B."

especially important. One may give in to another when a more balanced solution would have served both persons better. A Plan B maintains your wide-angle view to meeting *both* the other person's objectives *and* your objectives.

While *it is best to develop your Plan B before beginning a consensus-seeking conversation*, you can find yourself in the midst of one before you realize the need for a Plan B. Of course you can use any of your consensus tools impromptu in these situations. However, if you feel needy, anxious, or just unsure what to say, take time to think through your Plan B before resuming the discussion.

Like a Solution Smorgasbord, **Walk-Away Alternatives are inspired by your list of interests.** Suspend judgment and list every option that occurs to you, even those that seem unattractive or unfeasible at present. You might be able to improve them by asking a fanciful question as explained in Chapter 8.

In listing your Walk-Away Alternatives, be careful to include only actions you can take on your own without any cooperation from the other person. If there is a cooperative solution you favor, but the other won't agree to it, a step down from that solution is not a Walk-Away Alternative because it still requires her agreement. **Walk-Away Alternatives are self-help measures.**

For example, let's say Brandon has asked Molly to show and explain her dollhouse at one of the children's meetings then leave it with them for use as a go-by while they build their own. Molly refuses. Brandon might think, *Well, maybe she'll at least do the show and tell and let us take pictures to go by.* And maybe she will. In fact, she almost surely will. Allowing photos would be an easy and reasonable thing for her to do, and would run little or no risk to the dollhouse. But this almost-certain solution is not a true Walk-Away Alternative because Molly must agree to it and act on it.

Brandon's Walk-Away Alternatives include things like taking the children on a field trip to a museum featuring dollhouses, showing the children a video about how to build dollhouses, or buying a book about dollhouses. These are true Walk-Away Alternatives because Brandon doesn't need any cooperation from Molly to do any of these things.

Developing a Plan B

Let's look at a more detailed example. Assume that Spencer recently approached Fran to suggest that she change the fundraiser programming this year, from speaker to games. Fran had heard that Yolanda was talking up the idea of this change, and had garnered a little support among a few new members. Fran suspects that neither Spencer nor these new people have seen Yolanda's true colors.

Fran knew Yolanda's parents, who retired young and moved away before Spencer's time. Last year, after being out of state for college and a first job, Yolanda moved back to her hometown and rejoined the congregation. Her lively personality made a good first impression on many people, including Fran, who had not seen Yolanda since she was a teenager. After a few months, however, Fran noticed Yolanda's popularity waning. People were still polite to her, but not as engaged as they had been.

Fran did not understand this, and tried to make up for it by reaching out more to Yolanda. However, Fran eventually began to see why others had backed off. She found that Yolanda has a know-it-all attitude and difficulty believing that others could reasonably disagree with her, much less that they might have good reasons for their disagreement—a kinder way of saying that she is stubborn and narrow-minded. Her word is unreliable, as she tends to jump to conclusions and exaggerate. Yolanda is also flighty. She'll bubble over with enthusiasm for something for a while. A few months later, she's moved on to something new and different.

A few months ago, Yolanda tried to talk Fran into choosing a contro-versial alternative medicine guru as speaker for the annual fundraiser. Fran's refusal put the deathblow to her already-cooling friendship with Yolanda.

In Fran's brief conversation with Spencer, he not only seemed excited about switching to games, but had worsened the prospect, envisioning a very complicated program with different games for each of eight or nine different age levels of children and adults—in short, an organizational nightmare.

Fran even got the impression that Spencer considers Yolanda potential leadership material, and might like to start steering her that way by getting her involved in this year's fundraiser.

Fran feels insulted that Spencer doesn't show her a little more consider-ation and deference, given her maturity and experience running successful fundraisers for fifteen years.

Knowing she needed time to prepare to use her consensus tools, Fran told Spencer she'd like to think things over and meet with him in one week. Now she begins by writing her answers to the Three Magic Questions, continuing to ask "Why?" to each answer till she can't go any further. Then she underlines those things she considers her broadest interests.

Fran's Interests

1. Have speaker at fundraiser (or a darned good reason not to)—*Why?*

   - Successful in past—*Why?*

     o Middle-aged and older people like it—*Why do I care about that?*

       ▪ They can afford to <u>attend, donate</u> more to the auction <u>and spend more at the auction</u>
       ▪ They represent a <u>majority of the congregation</u>
       ▪ They can't or <u>don't want to be on their feet</u> for a long time
       ▪ Speakers attract <u>visitors</u> from outside the congregation—*Why?*
         - <u>Maximizes income</u>
         - <u>Introduces potential new members to our church</u>
       ▪ I'm one of them and they are my friends

   - <u>I like speakers</u>

   - I want to <u>use my gift for getting good speakers at reduced prices</u>—*Why?*

     o <u>Feel proud of my work</u>

   - It's <u>easier</u> and more <u>fun</u> for me to do something I already know how to do well

2. Avoid Spencer's nightmare plan—*Why?*

   - <u>Keep</u> things relatively <u>simple</u>
   - <u>Keep</u> things relatively <u>easy</u>
   - Don't require too many volunteers—*Why?*

     o <u>More people participating in auction</u> and hearing <u>speaker</u>

   - I have no experience with such a thing and will make more <u>mistakes</u>

3. Minimize involvement with Yolanda—*Why?*
- Her narrow mind and flightiness increase complications and hassle and possibility of things going wrong—*Which means I want*
  o Relative <u>simplicity</u>
  o High probability of <u>success</u>
- I find her unpleasant—*Which means I want*
  o <u>Pleasant working conditions</u>
4. <u>Appreciation</u>—from Spencer & congregation generally
5. <u>Respect</u>—from Spencer & congregation generally
6. Deference (let me run it or let me get out)—*Why?*
- My temperament
  o What I'm good at—proven <u>gift for leadership</u>
  o The way I like to work
7. Remain on good terms with Spencer and as many other members as possible—*Why?*
- I have <u>invested a lot in these relationships</u>
- I <u>value these relationships</u>
- I'd rather <u>not have to start over at a new church</u>

Fran makes a separate list (not shown) of Spencer's probable interests and is encouraged to see that some of her broadest interests, such as maximum income, potential new members, and more people participating, are probably shared by Spencer

She has learned that she has a greater chance of reaching consensus with him if she develops her Plan B now, and has it mind when they meet. Referring to her interest list, especially the underlined interests, Fran now lists all her Walk-Away Alternatives—things she can do to satisfy her interests without any cooperation from Spencer. In a sort of Self-Help Smorgasbord, Fran notes every idea, even those unworkable in their current form, without censoring herself.

Fran's Walk-Away Alternatives
- Give in—do the fundraiser as Spencer and Yolanda want
- Give up leadership of the fundraiser
- Don't work on the fundraiser at all
- Use my gifts for leadership and getting speakers for another organization

- o Another congregation
- o Inter-denominational group
- o Non-religious non-profit
- o Business
  - ▪ Look for opportunities within my present company
  - ▪ Change jobs
- o Start my own organization
- o Start a consulting business engaging speakers for other organizations
  - ▪ Expand to event planning
- Look for other ways to nurture my relationships with Spencer and other members
  - o Plan least contentious, but honest, way to explain my decision if I resign from the fundraiser
  - o Look for other ways to be involved and contribute
    - ▪ Without spending too much time in view of my new work for other organization
      - • ? Help with occasional special field trips for children?
      - • ? Give rides to church for elderly people who can't drive?
- Leave the congregation

Reviewing this list, Fran decides that giving in is not a good option for her. She would have such a bad taste in her mouth that she wouldn't enjoy the work. Therefore, she probably wouldn't do as good a job, and certainly wouldn't take much pride in it.

Fran decides on **her best Plan B**: Give up leadership of the fundraiser and use her gifts for another organization; don't even work on the fundraiser; that would require a Herculean attitude adjustment for Fran as well as her former committee members. If she has to execute her Plan B, she will look for ways to nurture relationships, and defer deciding whether to leave the congregation until she sees how her interactions and relationships shake out. However, before her meeting with Spencer, she will strengthen her Plan B by researching other outlets for her talents. Then she will have an even clearer picture of her Plan B.

Imagine how much more calm and grounded Fran will feel when she begins her interest-oriented dialogue with Spencer, using her best efforts to reach consensus with him about the programming for the annual fundraiser event, but knowing she has this backup plan for comparison with any potential agreement with Spencer. Instead of a vague general feeling that "it will be awful" if she can't do the fundraiser her way, she knows exactly what will happen, and it's not all that bad.

Of course, Fran should not become so enamored of her Plan B that she launches into it prematurely, or decides not to attempt agreement with Spencer at all. As long as she keeps all of her own objectives in mind, objectives that include a strong interest in maintaining present relationships, she will realize that no unilateral action on her part will satisfy her as well as a consensus that adequately addresses her interests. Interests are the hub around which all the other skills revolve.

Try This: Plan B

Place yourself in the shoes of Brandon. You can review his situation on p. __. Use the Three Magic Questions to develop his list of interests. Then working from that list, develop his Plan B. Any two people will do this at least slightly differently, so don't be concerned if your answer differs from the sample in Appendix B.

How and When To Use a Plan B

So how do we know when to actually execute Plan B? When do we walk away from dialogue with the other person? *We walk away when it becomes quite clear that Plan B will satisfy our interests better than any consensus we could possibly reach with the other person.*

Sometimes we know this from the outset. Suppose a wealthy and eccentric collector offers Salvador $50,000 for his boat. (Recall that Sal needs about $35,000 to buy the kind of RV he wants.) Before he can seal the deal with the collector, Trudy contacts him to say that she can't pay any cash, but can trade her RV for the boat. Trudy's RV is worth about $25,000; it needs $5000 in repairs. With respect to Trudy's offer, Sal's Plan B is the collector's firm offer of $50,000. It so clearly satisfies his interests better than Trudy's offer, that it would actually be a disservice to Trudy to waste her time trying to negotiate.

In most situations, however, especially when dealing with those with whom you have ongoing relationships, we should make our best efforts to reach consensus, using all the other tools, before turning to Plan B. In congregational interactions, the decision to walk away should not be taken lightly. Before a person walks, he should ask himself:

- Have I really considered *all* my interests, including the kind of relationship I want with this person?
- Have I really tried my best to apply all my consensus-building skills, including taking adequate think breaks for both parties?

Use Your Plan B as a Test of Whether or Not to Agree with the Other Person

Suppose you have tried your best, using all your consensus skills. Perhaps the other person has tried, too. You just can't come up with a solution that fully satisfies all your interests. Should you accept the best the other person has been able to offer you? Your Plan B answers this question. If her best offer satisfies your interests better than Plan B, accept her offer. It's the best you can do. But if Plan B meets your objectives better than her best, simply express your appreciation for her efforts, explain that your interests are better served if you take another direction, then do so.

Viewed another way, Plan B ensures that you don't enter into a bad agreement. If you have identified *all* your interests, and if her offer meets them better than the *very best* Plan B you can devise, it's only logical to conclude that you won't make a big mistake by accepting her offer.

Allude to Your Plan B to Defuse Difficult Dynamics

When dealing with difficult dynamics—aggressive behavior, stonewalling, reneging and the like—alluding to your Plan B sometimes helps. *Frame the reference to your Plan B as a way of satisfying your interests, rather than as a threat.* Let's look at some examples:

- Fran has tried her best to reach consensus with Spencer, but he refuses to consider anything other than his eight level nightmare plan. Fran can ask, "What would you do if you were me and needed an outlet for your special gift for getting excellent speakers at reduced prices?"

- If the open question doesn't work, or as an alternative to the question, Fran can specify her Plan B, "I owe it to myself to make good use of what I see as my special gifts—finding good speakers, negotiating good prices, and organizing the type of event we've had in the past. I would prefer to do that for this congregation, and failing that, I guess I would have to look for another outlet for those gifts." Note her use of "and" instead of "but."

- Suppose Laurel has been reflecting Mike's angry statements—paraphrasing, asking questions, butting out—for quite awhile, but Mike continues to scream at her and insult her. She can't discuss interests because he keeps interrupting. Laurel has decided that her Plan B is to simply stop trying to deal with him. It's in her interest to defuse anger of any other member of the congregation, but if he's going to be angry no matter what, exposing herself to expressions of that anger only makes matters worse. A think break might help him as well. Laurel says, "I'd like to make things right between us, and I owe it to both of us to do that at a time when we can engage in a mutually respectful dialogue. Now is not that time." Then she demonstrates her Walk-Away Alternative by literally walking away. Laurel also uses "and" instead of "but."

- Every time Molly thinks she's reached an agreement with Brandon, he backtracks and asks for a little more. They agree she will bring the dollhouse to show and tell. Then he asks if she can leave it till next week for the children to refer to until they come up with a plan for their own dollhouse. Molly says she doesn't want to leave it at church, but she will bring it back two weeks in a row. They shake hands on the deal. But then Brandon calls her and says he doesn't think the kids can remember the details well enough after only two sessions. Why can't they just borrow the dollhouse? He promises faithfully to take good care of it and watch the kids like a hawk when they are around it. Molly says, "I don't see how it's in my best interests to keep renegotiating agreements that don't stick. And it's beginning to look like, if I even bring the dollhouse to the first show and tell, we'll end up rehashing our agreement at the end of the session."

Notice how the above examples deal with various "what-ifs." Spencer *stonewalled*. Mike was *unreasonable* and *bullied* Laurel. Brandon kept *reneging*. In each case, in one way or another, our skill user alluded to their Plan B in as non-threatening a way as possible. Since threats have much the same effect as wrong making, minimizing the threat helps to minimize the push back.

Some savvy readers might have paused in reading the third bullet above. Laurel stated that now is not the time when they can engage in a "mutually respectful" dialogue. Doesn't this implicitly make Mike wrong? Doesn't it suggest that he is disrespectful? Won't he be likely to go home and deny, rationalize and project? Yes. However, even the Silver Rule has its exceptions. Here, Laurel has decided that her interests in being treated respectfully, setting boundaries, and looking to her own spiritual and emotional wellbeing outweigh her interest in making things right with Mike. Her Plan B is the lesser evil.

Note, however, that she tried other means before even implicitly making Mike wrong. And when she decided it was time to overtly set the boundary, she chose her words carefully. Not, "I won't listen until you can speak respectfully," but rather, "I'd like to make things right between us, and I owe it to both of us to do that at a time when we can engage in a mutually respectful dialogue. Now is not that time."

The questions "What would you do if you were in my shoes and [insert your interest]?" and "How would it make sense for me to [insert the other's demand] can indirectly suggest that you have a Plan B and that it meets your objectives better than anything you've heard from the other person so far.

If alluding to your Plan B doesn't bring the other person to a more reasonable stance, then it's time to consider whether or not to walk away and execute your Plan B. Compare the best you can do for yourself with the best the other person is willing and able to do for you, then decide accordingly.

You Can Enhance Your Plan B Before You Speak with the Other Person

When faced with a situation that is highly conflicted or otherwise difficult, it pays to take positive steps to enhance your Plan B before entering into dialogue. If music director Kayla has been called to a board meeting to discuss whether the congregation can continue to employ her, she can research, and interview for, other positions before the meeting. She might get an offer or two, or she might conclude that it would be very difficult for her to find other employment at the present time. Maybe she learns that she would have to relocate or take a salary cut in order to get another job. In any case, her educated Plan B will help her assess more reliably if, for example, the board proposes to cut her back to three-quarter time.

Others' Plan B's

Sometimes the reason to walk away from dealings with a person revolves around her interests, rather than yours. Perhaps she has a Plan B that satisfies her interests so well you can't hope to better it. Suppose Trudy tells Sal she has been approached by an eccentric collector of RVs who offered her $50,000. No point in Sal trying to negotiate a trade for a boat worth much less. Why waste his time or hers?

Just as you get a jump on understanding the other person's interests by trying to imagine them in advance of a conversation, you can increase efficiency by thinking ahead to his Plan B. In both cases, remember that he always knows more about his situation than you do, so be careful not to lock into your projections.

You can encourage others to think about their own Plan B, if they have not already done so, and/or to consider how well it will meet their objectives. In Dialogue 8, Trudy did this when she asked Sal the open questions, "How does time factor in? How long do you think it will take to find a buyer who's willing to pay $35,000?"

A question about the other person's Plan B takes the form, "What will you do if we can't agree on anything?" Sometimes the other person will take a mental step back and think. At other times, he will answer with an unrealistic abstraction, rather than a plan, in which case, you can follow up with more specific open questions, as Trudy did with Sal. Here's another example:

Dialogue 10: Rev. Spencer helps Fran think about her Plan B

Dialogue:	Spencer's View:
F: If some people don't appreciate the value of my speakers, that's their problem. I won't dumb things down with games.	
S: What other options do we have for attracting both groups?	Open, interest-oriented question.
F: I don't know and I don't care. I don't have time for this foolishness.	Stonewalling.
S: It sounds like you don't want to discuss this. Is that correct?	Paraphrase and confirm.
F: It's taking a lot of time I could spend on the fundraiser.	
S: **What will you do if we can't find a solution we're both happy with?**	Question about her Plan B.
F: What I'll be happy with is everybody letting me get on with planning this event the way I know how to do it. If that doesn't make you happy, well, you're the boss, so I guess I'm out of the fundraiser picture.	Fran probably hasn't thought through her Plan B, but threatens to walk away, not only from the discussion, but also from the fundraiser.
S: You're saying you won't work on the fundraiser?	Paraphrase/confirm.
F: (Nods)	
S: **What *will* you do?**	Second Plan B question.

F: That's not your problem.

S: True, not my problem. It is But Out technique.
     one of my interests.

F: (Shrugs)

S: (Remains silent)   He uses silence to help Fran
                               settle down and think.

F: I'll be all right.

S: I'd like to find a way for you   Interest talk followed by a
     to be more than all right. I'd   more specific question about
     like you to be happy with   her Plan B. This question
     your role in the congrega-   leads her to think about the
     tion. If you only give up the   long-term results of making
     fundraiser and do nothing   good on her threat to walk
     else, how happy will you be?   away.

F: Not happy, but better than   Fran reveals some interests.
     if I work a fundraiser I don't
     agree with. At least I'd go
     out with some self-respect
     and dignity intact.

S: I think we can do better for you.   Spencer addresses those in-
     I still think that, if we invest a terests and ties them to his
     little time, we might find a   interest in continuing the
     fundraising plan that you'd feel   dialogue.
     good about—perhaps one that
     still includes one of your fine
     speakers. But if not, I'd like to
     see you involved in some other
     meaningful role that you like.
     Would you be willing to spend
     a little more time thinking out
     loud with me?

F: Well, OK. A *little* more time.

Joint Plan Bs

An individual's Plan B addresses what will happen if he can't come to consensus with the other person. When people do reach consensus, agree on Plan A, it is often advisable to deal with what will happen if, for any reason, Plan A doesn't pan out. This can serve as a reality check for both parties. Have they thoroughly considered their ability to play their parts in Plan A?

For example, suppose Molly agrees to loan Brandon the dollhouse for two weeks, and he promises to be sure no harm comes to it. Molly can say, "No amount of money would make up for the sentimental value if something happened to the dollhouse. But we should agree on what redress I will get just in case the dollhouse is damaged."

The upshot of this suggestion could be Brandon backing out of the deal. In that case, the suggestion did its job—bringing home the seriousness of Brandon's obligation and ferreting out whether or not he will really take responsibility.

If Brandon does agree to pay a certain amount in the event of damage, or to pay for professional repairs by Molly's choice of model maker, or any other joint Plan B, they minimize the chance of future arguments about what to do in the event of damage.

People May Resist Discussing Joint Plan B's

Many people shy away from discussing such matters. They can be just as reluctant to ask for a contingency plan as to commit to one. There are many reasons for this reticence.

Some fear they will offend the other person. This fear is not unfounded. Indeed, some people do puff up with indignation when asked to deal with the possibility that their part in Plan A falls through. They may even take offense when asked to commit to their part. Sometimes, those who react this way are the very ones whose intention and/or ability to fulfill their role in Plan A is shaky.

Whether or not his prospects of doing his part are shaky, a person may be so sensitive that he takes any mention of a Plan B as a negative judgment about him. He feels made wrong or as if he is being treated like a child.

Others feel that it should not be necessary to deal with such matters in a church setting. *We're people of good faith. We have a Golden Rule of Love. We should be able to trust one another.* Providing for a Plan B seems to make a negative statement about who they are—a suggestion that they are untrusting or untrustworthy, lazy, half-hearted, or mercenary—especially if money is involved.

Still others fear that providing a joint Plan B sets a lesser goal that people will live down to, almost as if they are jinxing Plan A.

In those situations where you have an interest in a joint Plan B, you can deal with such fears and resistance by applying your consensus skills to the Plan B issue. *We can step to one side and apply the entire consensus system to this ancillary topic.*

Dialogue 11: Molly persuades Brandon to consider contingency plans

Dialogue:	Molly's View:
M: What if someone carrying the dollhouse trips and drops it?	Instead of beginning with a position, Molly expresses a concern (interest) and asks an open question.
B: Oh, come on! How likely is that?	
M: We all have accidents. I sure have my share, and when I do, I often think, *Who could have predicted that?*	Molly puts herself and everyone else on the same level—people who could have accidents. This helps Brandon not to feel made wrong.
B: You're saying you don't trust me to do the right thing if I have an accident?	He still bristles, but he remains in dialogue.
M: I'm not saying that. I'm not even sure what "the right thing" would be. What do you think?	Solicits Brandon's input to build the content of an agreement using another open question.

B: I'd pay for it.

M: Pay for what? A commer-   More questions help
     cially available dollhouse?   Brandon come to his own
     Repairs by a model-maker?   conclusion about the com-
     Or what?   plexities of the issue without
                                       arguing with him.

B: I don't like the direction   Again, he may be uncomfort-
     this conversation is taking.   able, but he remains engaged.

M: It's uncomfortable talking   Validates his feelings.
     about such things, isn't it?

B: So let's stop.

M: Humor me for a minute. On   Another open question to
     a scale of one to ten, with   begin leading Brandon to a
     ten being perfectly comfort-   different conclusion in small
     able, and one being excruci-   steps.
     ating, how uncomfortable is
     talking about this now?

B: One.

M: I guess I'd give it about a   Another open question
     five.   leading toward a conclusion
                                       that will relate to Brandon's
     Now let's say the dollhouse   interest in minimizing
     is smashed, and I'm crying   discomfort.
     about how much it meant
     that my grandfather made
     it, and that nothing could
     really replace it. Where's
     that conversation on the
     scale?

B: One.

Brandon boxed himself in by giving the first scenario the lowest possible score, but he would probably find the second scenario even more uncomfortable.

M:

Molly maintains a calm, pleasant affect and uses a long pause to give Brandon time to think.

B: (Sighs). Okay, minus five.

Brandon breaks the silence.

M: Me too. If we can't handle this conversation now, I hate to think about having it after an accident occurs.

Molly agrees, then appeals to Brandon's interest in avoiding uncomfortable conversations.

B: Well, maybe I shouldn't borrow the dollhouse. I can't replace something that's irreplaceable.

If he summarily drops the matter, he may still resent Molly.

M: That's up to you. But if I can agree with you now about what I will accept in the event of damage, I'll abide by that agreement—no tears, no fears.

So she shows him a possible way to satisfy both their interests.

B: So, if the dollhouse were smashed—and I don't think it will be—but if it were, what would you accept?

He begins to collaborate with her.

M:	If the damage were repairable, repairs by an experienced craftsperson. If not repairable, money wouldn't help. Maybe some type of tribute to my grandfather?	Molly suggests some agreement content, and seeks further input from Brandon.
B:	What about a pretty bench for the church courtyard with a plaque dedicating it to your grandfather?	This is his idea—a good one that Molly might not have thought of, and one he is more likely to buy in to and abide by without ill-feelings later on.
M:	Done.	

Depending on the personalities and the subject matter, a less extensive suggestion of the mutual interest in a contingency plan will sometimes serve, "On the outside chance that something unforeseen happens, say you are carrying the dollhouse, a bee stings you, and you drop it. We might as well decide now what redress I'll get for damage. That will ease any future conversations and avoid misunderstandings."

Prioritizing Interests

When you compare a prospective consensus with your Plan B, or several possible agreements with one another, don't be misled by the sheer number of interests addressed by each option. You should also take into account the *relative importance* of those interests and *how well* each one is met by the various alternative plans. Prioritizing interests leads to sound decisions in those less than perfect situations where neither your Plan B, nor any Plan A from your Solution Smorgasbord, provides an ideal solution.

Here's an example of how prioritizing interests can affect a choice between continuing to work for agreement versus going to Plan B. Laurel may have multiple interests in dealing with Mike's anger:

- Her own peace of mind
- Things will be more pleasant when she and Mike meet

- How Mike will speak of her to others
- Her interest in the general health of the congregation

However, if despite her best efforts, Mike continues to yell at her, call her names, or the like, one single interest will outweigh all the others—her interest in respect. Setting appropriate boundaries, respecting herself by demanding respect from others, is paramount. She will go to her Plan B, whether that be to avoid Mike, to ask their minister to intercede, or whatever.

Prioritizing interests can also help us decide which of two Plan B's to execute or which of two potential agreements to select. Recall the committee meetings in Chapter 11 where Ms. Tardy didn't seem to get the point of the more tactful (and therefore less direct) statements of the problems she caused. The committee had to make a difficult decision. They could continue to tolerate her tardiness, or they could express the problem in a more direct (and therefore more wrong-making) manner, along with an ultimatum. These two options could be viewed as two Plan B's.

The committee could make its best decision by listing the relevant interests. Their list might look something like this:

- Eliminate frustration
- Minimize misunderstanding
- Avoid backtracking and repetition to bring Tardy up to speed
- Respect for ourselves and our time
- Help Tardy learn how her behavior affects others
- Avoid the discomfort of an unpleasant dialogue with Tardy
- Harmony with someone we will see and deal with at other church functions, even if she withdraws from the committee
    - o She speaks well, or at least not badly, of us to others
    - o She remains enthusiastically involved in the congregation

How they prioritize this list, and how heavily they weight each interest, is for them, not us, to say. The point is that they will come up with their best decision if they do prioritize and weight them.

It helps to prioritize before you begin your dialogue. However, just as new interests can come to light as you converse, so can new priorities. So be prepared to adjust as new insights present themselves.

Identifying Stealth Interests

It's hard to develop a Plan B, a Solution Smorgasbord or a priority among interests if some of those interests don't show up on your radar. These stealth interests can be the most important ones, the ones really driving people's behavior and decisions.

Suppose a person states a certain objective, you suggest one or more ways to meet that objective, but he doesn't come to agreement. Perhaps he says something like, "Well, I don't know. I still don't feel right about this." This means either that he needs more time to think or that he has additional interests he has not mentioned. He himself may or may not realize what those stealth interests are.

Or maybe he says, "Yes, but..." and raises a new interest, then another and another each time you address the last one he came up with. As mentioned above, it is natural for people to identify additional interests as they use consensus skills. In fact, that is one of the advantages of practicing them. However, a continuous string of add-ons means that the person is unwilling or unable to tell you what's really behind his failure to come to consensus.

Feeling interests are particularly prone to flying below our radar screens. When someone fails to mention a feeling altogether, but can't come to agreement even when all his material interests have been addressed, at least we can be pretty sure there's a feeling interest driving his refusal. But what if he misstates or understates his feeling? He says he's disappointed when he's really hurt, or she says she's a little miffed when she's really boiling with anger. Misstatements and understatements can intensify the stealth character of an interest because we are no longer looking for an unknown feeling interest. We think we've already identified the feeling interest.

Four Ways to Uncloak Stealth Interests

Identify Your Problem with the Process

One way to deal with stealth interests is to simply describe what you think is going on. Indicate how the dynamic is creating a problem for you:

- You know, I feel like the solutions I've been suggesting don't address what's really driving your hesitation.

- I'm beginning to feel like, no matter what I suggest, there's no end in sight.

Notice that this is a form of interest talk. You allude to your interests in clarification and better process and invite the other person to address those interests.

It's tempting to follow such a comment with a question. However, this is a good time to use silence. Wait a good long time for the other person to respond.

If he does not, you can ask a follow-up question such as:

- Is there something you're not comfortable telling me?
- What would it take for you to come to a final agreement?
- What do you think is really going on here?
- What would you think if you were in my place reflecting on the pattern of our discussion so far?

Suggest a Break

If statements and questions of the type explained just above fail to inspire a breakthrough revelation by the other person, you can follow up with something like, "It can be hard for people to identify the interests that are behind their hesitation. I know it sometimes takes awhile for me. Why don't we take a break so you can mull that over, while I get back to work on my other projects, and we'll speak again on Wednesday, OK?"

Notice that this type of statement includes a subtle suggestion that time is becoming an interest for you, that there are limits to how much time you will spend letting him string you along.

Indicate a Time Interest, Carefully

Time can be an interest in itself. However, we must take great care not to see it as an overriding interest when it is not (see Chapter 9). Permanently discontinuing a consensus-building process "because it's taking too much time" is tantamount to going to your Plan B. So before you do so, ask yourself the following questions:

1. What will happen if I don't reach agreement with this person, in other words, what's my Plan B?

2. How much time will be involved in meeting my own objectives if we don't reach agreement? In other words, how long will it take to execute my Plan B?

3. How well will my Plan B meet my objectives?

If you decide to state a time interest without permanently shutting down the discussions, bear in mind that this can read as pressure, or even a threat, to the other person. She may push back even harder if she feels threatened. Or she may give in, although she has reservations, only to regret the decision, resent you, and fail to execute the agreement. Here are some ways to avoid or minimize such results:

- As with all your interests, ask yourself the magic question "Why?" about your time interest. Then state the time issue to the other person in terms of this more ultimate objective. "The time I've been taking in these meetings is causing problems at home."
- Use open questions. "How can we reach agreement while also allowing me to do justice to myself and family?"

Make a Guess

You'll recall this technique from the section on dealing with feeling interests in Chapter 5. In the context of stealth interests, it has two variations.

You can guess out loud. This is similar to our paraphrasing tool. For example:

- "It sounds like you're feeling uneasy, but are having a hard time saying why. Is there an unpleasant feeling you can't identify?" If he says, "Yes," help him identify the feeling by asking for an analogy, "Can you help me understand by comparing this feeling to some other situation where you've felt the same way?"
- "I sense there's something you're not comfortable discussing. Are you concerned about hurting my feelings if you tell me?" If "Yes," follow up with, "What I'm imagining in my own mind could be a lot worse than what you're really thinking."
- You can make a more specific guess, "Are you having trouble telling me that you agree with Yolanda that my programs are boring?"

A person who couldn't or wouldn't clearly state his interest to begin with, will often correct you if you guess wrong. Be careful, however, not to go to the closed question/guess prematurely. Use it as a fallback when neither identifying the apparent problem, nor asking open questions, works.

You can guess at the stealth interest and test something that would address it. When dealing with someone who has extreme difficulty identifying or acknowledging feeling interests, you can try making an educated guess in your own mind, then testing something that would address the feeling interest you envision, rather than asking him about it. Carefully observe facial expression and body language when running your test comment up the flagpole.

For example, consider this dialogue involving Mike, Laurel and their minister Joan in the broken window scenario:

Dialogue 12: Rev. Joan tests stealth interests

Dialogue:	Joan's View:
J: I would like to try to help you to resolve your disagreement in a way we can all feel good about. Let's start with each of you giving me your view of the issue.	Although Joan could call on each of them in turn to comment, she can learn something from who speaks up first and how long it takes them to do so.
(Long pause)	
L: Mike's mad at me because I was excused from paying for a window I broke.	Laurel breaks the silence, so Joan suspects Mike is the more reluctant to speak candidly, at least to his minister.
J: Mike, what's your take on this?	At this point, Joan directs a specific question to Mike to show she intends to be even-handed and consider both perspectives.

M:	I just think the same rules should apply to everyone. I had to pay for the sign I backed over, so she should have paid for the window.	Joan observes facial and body tension, hears a crackle in Mike's voice. There's probably a feeling interest at work here.
J:	How did you feel when you heard that Laurel was excused?	Joan tries an open question.
M:	I felt like she should have paid for the window.	He restates what he *thinks*, rather than answering the question about what he *feels*.
J:	What does that mean to you, if you had to pay and she didn't?	Joan tries a different open question.
M:	(Clenches his jaw) That it's unfair.	Again, he states what he thinks. Joan senses that Mike has extreme difficulty speaking about his feelings, though they are obviously very strong.
J:	Laurel, what do you think about the discrepancy?	Joan turns her attention to Laurel to give Mike a break, to keep him from feeling picked on, and to show even-handedness to Laurel.
L:	I didn't know Mike backed over a sign and had to pay for it. I guess I could pay for the window if it's really all that important to him.	Laurel offers to address Mike's money interest, but may not see that this will not address his stealth (feeling) interest. Meanwhile, she might abandon legitimate interests of her own. For her to do so will not serve anyone in the long run. So Joan doesn't follow up on her offer.

J: Why do you think you were excused?

L: Maybe because of how it happened. I knocked a chair into the window trying to catch a child who was running with a pair of scissors.

Joan sees Mike's eyebrows raise as if he's a bit surprised by this information.

L: It also might have to do with my volunteer activities. I pay for a lot of sundries out of my own pocket without mentioning them or turning them in for reimbursement. Many of the lay leaders are aware of that.

Mike tenses up again. Maybe he resents the idea that Laurel has a higher status because she can afford to do more for the church than he can.

J: Just speaking hypothetically, Mike, would you feel all better if she paid for the window?

Since open questions haven't worked, Joan tries a closed question about Mike's feelings.

M: (Angrily) Damn *straight*!

His statement literally says one thing, but his choice of words and tone imply another. He probably will not feel all better, but may not understand that.

J: As an aside, but an important one, I'm hearing about kids running with scissors on our premises, signs that are apparently hard to see and easy to back over. Do you two think we should take some proactive steps to address safety issues?

Joan wants to test Mike's interest in feeling valued, but her test won't work if it comes too close on the heels of direct questions about Mike's interests. So she changes the subject.

L: Yes.

M: Maybe a professional safety expert should review our whole set up.

Mike relaxes when he is asked for, and gives, his opinion. This suggests his stealth interest in feeling valued or esteemed.

L: Yes, not only the physical plant, but also what actually happens around here on Sunday mornings. How did a little girl get her hands on a sharp pair of scissors anyway?

M: And Wednesday nights— with choir practice, committee meetings, and all. If people bring their kids then, they probably have even less supervision.

J: Mike, do you have connections for finding a suitable consultant? Would you be willing to make some calls and suggest someone?

Joan now tries a more overt test—showing esteem for Mike by asking him to take on an important responsibility that not just anyone could do well.

M: (Nodding) Yeah, I can do that.

Positive test result.

J: I appreciate that, and I'll look forward to hearing from you.

Joan directly expresses appreciation.

Well, then, about the window...

L: Like I said, I'm willing to pay if you all think it's the right thing.

M: Well, I didn't know about the little girl. I guess I'd have done the same thing you did.

J: So what should we do?

M: I don't want to make a big deal out of this window. But maybe you should have a word with the officers about making sure their decisions are even-handed.

J: I'll be happy to do that. Meanwhile, if either of you have any follow-up points after you reflect on this, I want you to call me.

Wisely, Joan encourages follow up. People need time to digest and process things. She won't know if the stealth issues have really been satisfied without a touch back.

You've now seen a complete basic consensus system. You may wish to try it out before moving on to Part IV of this book. Part IV deals with even bigger "what ifs." What if someone's problem behavior doesn't change even after you've tried all of the above? What if you're seeking consensus among a larger group?

If you defer reading Part IV, do skip ahead and read Part V, which will help you see how our basic system comes together.

Key Points from Chapter 12

- In more difficult situations, don't abandon or replace the skills of the basic system, but rather build on them

- When someone seems unreasonable, ask yourself what perspective might make their statements or behavior seem reasonable to them
  - Try to address *their* probable perspective
- Turn off your resistance to being made wrong
  - Pause and give your brain a chance to overtake your visceral reaction
  - Refer to a grounding trigger, such as a photo of a loved one
- Develop your Plan B
  - Before an important or difficult conversation
  - Lay out a smorgasbord of Walk-Away Alternatives, self-help measures for addressing your interests
  - Take any actions reasonable under the circumstances to enhance your Walk-Away Alternatives
  - The best combination from your self-help smorgasbord of Walk-Away Alternatives is your Plan B
  - After thorough dialogue with the other person, compare the best Plan A he is willing to agree to with your Plan B
    - If Plan A satisfies your interests better, enter consensus
    - If your Plan B satisfies your interests better, walk away
  - Alluding to your Plan B can sometimes help defuse difficult dynamics by helping the other person to see your perspective on your own interests
- Help the other person think about his Plan B
  - Ask, "What will you do if we can't agree?"
- Consider incorporating a joint Plan B into an agreement with the other person
  - What will the two of you agree to do if Plan A falls through?
  - You can apply your consensus skills to the side issue of including a joint Plan B in your agreement
- Prioritize your interests
- Uncloak others' stealth interests (those they don't or can't express)
  - Identify your problem with the process

- ○ Suggest a break
- ○ Indicate a time interest, carefully
- ○ Make a guess at their stealth interest
  - ▪ Express your guess out loud and ask them if you are correct
  - ▪ Make the guess in your head, suggest something that would address the stealth interest you've guessed, and observe the person's reaction

PART IV: INTRODUCTION
TO ADVANCED APPLICATIONS

CHAPTER 13
DEALING WITH INTERESTS IN PROBLEM BEHAVIOR

Fear is the path to the dark side. Fear leads to anger. Anger leads to hate. Hate leads to suffering.

- Yoda/George Lucas

What about individuals who regularly lie, level personal attacks, or engage in submarine sabotage, so that problematic dynamics become a pattern of behavior? Several good books have been written about coping with such dynamics.[37] In this chapter, I will emphasize some of my favorite methods and how they tie in with our interest-oriented approach.

No matter what the behavioral pattern, no matter whether a person acquired it by imitating his parents, through the trial and error of his own personal life experiences, because it is a symptom of substance abuse or other mental illness, or in any other manner, that person thinks, or subconsciously senses, that the behavior works for him. This may be true, at least in those cases where he chooses his victims skillfully. Or it may be that the behavior worked for him in childhood, and the adult can't turn off what seems normal; abandoning this behavior would feel like taking a stroll in his underwear.

This person may actually think the behavior works best because he's never been shown a better way. In other cases, not much thinking enters the picture. But whether conscious or unconscious, *the behavior* becomes so ingrained that it *takes on the character of an interest in its own right*.

When problem dynamics such as bullying and triangulating work, they do so by spawning unproductive feelings like fear of the bully and anxiety around the triangulator that can impair the victim's judgment. In dealing

---

37 See, for example, Muriel Solomon, *Working with Difficult People* (Prentice Hall, 1990); William Ury, *Getting Past No* (Bantam, 1993); and Sam Kaner et al, *Facilitator's Guide to Participatory Decision-Making* (Jossey-Bass, 2007).

with such behaviors, your interests typically include an immediate objective, such as not letting Trina the Triangulator manipulate you into taking on a third party for her, or not letting Butch the Bully stifle your opinion on a given occasion. You may also have an interest in a long-range improvement in the way these people interact with you.

Some readers might wonder, *Why would I want to build bridges with such a person? Why not just ignore them, avoid them, walk away?* It's not like they work in the next cubicle at the office or have been assigned to the same project team.

But walking away from someone at church isn't always easy either. What if you don't recognize how others are manipulating you till the damage is done? What if they manipulate others' reactions to you? What if walking away from them means walking away from an entire congregation where many other people have become like family to you?

Leaders, in particular, may find it difficult to just walk away. How can clergy totally ignore certain congregants? Leaders might also entertain broader objectives, such as discouraging Trina or Butch from causing repeated problems in congregational life. They may wish to show Trina and Butch better ways of relating to others for the sake of all concerned.

Of course it might be wise to walk away from a one-off incident. You may also do well to temporarily walk away from a repetition of the behavior if you wish to regain emotional equilibrium and think. Part of that thinking should include consideration of your Walk-Away Alternatives and Plan B, as explained in Chapter 12. However, if you find your Plan B unattractive, this chapter will help.

The techniques in this book are *tools, not rules*, and they all have their exceptions. *Even the tool of appealing to others' interests has exceptions. Where someone has an interest in continuing a behavior that causes us problems,* we do not want to satisfy that interest from either a short-range or long-range perspective. On the contrary, since the person perceives that this behavior works, *we try to make it not work for them when they deal with us.* This principle is at the heart of the advice given in all those good books I mentioned, though it may or may not be expressed in these terms.

But as you'll see, frustrating the problem behavior doesn't have to mean frustrating the person. Rather, look for the ways the problem behavior works, or seems to work, for them. What do they ultimately want to achieve? These things represent even broader underlying interests. Guiding them to better ways to address those underlying interests is the best way to help them change their problematic habits.

Understanding Behaviors and the Underlying Interests

Even though we don't want to reinforce an interest in problem behavior, we still benefit from understanding this interest. What exactly is the behavior? Why might the person sense that the behavior works? How does it work? What does it do for them? Or on the other hand, what problem do they sense would occur if they *don't* do the behavior? In other words, why would they resist change? What broader interest does the behavior serve? Can we steer them to address that broader interest in a healthier manner?

Putting a name to a behavior that troubles you can calm you and help you get your mind around which techniques will best deal with it. Muriel Solomon's *Working with Difficult People* is laid out as a reference guide in which you can browse a list of problems and look up a few pages of advice for dealing with each one. This list is one of the most complete I've come across.

Behavioral Clues

Sometimes *the kinds of things a person habitually accuses others of doing* provide clues to identifying the accuser's own behavior. We tend to assume others think, feel and behave as we do. So one who tends toward candor herself is less likely to leap to the conclusion that someone else is lying. Conversely, the one who often thinks others are lying *might* play fast and loose with the truth herself. The person who habitually says things like, "He's bluffing," or "You'll never go through with that," might tend to use threats to get his own way.

Of course we should not assume anyone who accuses another of lying is habitually dishonest herself. Perhaps growing up with an alcoholic parent taught her not to trust. But we can *notice patterns*. If she often accuses others of lying, and she also makes you uncomfortable for reasons you can't identify, it might pay to examine her statements more carefully.

Not everyone who accuses others of bluffing is a threat master. But what if he cries, "Bluff!" often, and he also raises the hair on the back of your neck? Replay his words in your mind. Do they contain an indirect threat?

Another way to discover *how* a behavior works for someone is by tuning in to your own knee jerk reaction to the behavior. ***Your reaction is often just what he wants.*** When confronted by a bully's insults or threats, do you fight or flee? You may know that, if you flee, the bully gets his way. But if you fight (argue), and he continues to threaten you on other occasions, the fighting itself is what floats his boat.

Triangulators often target those who are outgoing and eager to help. You hear of her problems or alleged mistreatment by third parties and leap into the breach to help her out, save the day, and restore "justice" to her world.

When someone blames and criticizes you (and calls it "honesty"), do you wilt with self-doubt or get defensive? Do you then sense your critic's satisfaction?

Likewise, observing how third parties react can enlighten us as to underlying objectives. Perhaps Leo pokes along, doing a slipshod job of setting up tables and chairs for an event. Frustrated with watching him, Richard steps in and finishes the task. Leo got out of doing something he clearly had no enthusiasm for doing. His habit of doing a poor or slow job works for him by getting others to do the work for him.

The situations in which the behavior occurs can also provide clues to underlying interests. Does the person bully someone only when third parties are present? He might feel that's the way to impress the others. If the behavior is directed primarily toward authority figures, he might get an emotional kick from the power struggle. If she triangulates only in one-on-one parking lot conversations, what might she fear would happen if she expressed her interests directly and in the appropriate setting?

How Fear Leads to Anger (and Triangulation, Lies and Tricks)

At the heart of many problem behaviors lies a negative interest, fear or anxiety. *A person might triangulate when she fears what will happen if she speaks directly* to the person she disagrees with. The other person will get his feelings hurt. I will be the one who hurt him. So, I will be wrong. He will retaliate and/or others will think ill of me.

People are especially tempted to triangulate when they already fear the person who causes them a problem. Such fear can rise from past experiences with the person, or from current behavior that seems aggressive through the triangulator's lenses. He speaks louder or stands closer than acceptable under her cultural norms, for example, or perhaps he shows clear aggression by almost anyone's standards. Anyone may fear confronting someone of higher status in the organization, which is one reason clergy are especially vulnerable to being criticized behind their backs.

People who carp and complain behind others' backs often feel as if there's nothing else they can do. They may feel powerless. This feeling can arise from the status or popularity of the person in question. Or the complainer may have been acculturated to fear directly confronting anyone, as in "Nice girls just don't..."

Similarly, *fear of losing can drive hostility*. Some people view *every* transaction as inherently up/down in nature. Their lives become a constant effort to be the one on top, for someone has to be on top and the other on the bottom; equal does not compute for them. *Working with Difficult People* describes several varieties of "hostile/angry people," in each case summarizing the hostile/angry person's thought process.[38]

- The Bully, Solomon writes, is thinking, "...I told them the right way to handle it. Yes, it *was* the right way... I must prove I am right."[39]
- The "Tackler," who attacks others personally instead of sticking to the issue, thinks, "She just wants to show me up, but I'll beat her to it."[40]
- The Intimidator sees a threat in the person whose ideas impress the boss; this other person must be prevented from "winning."[41]
- And Enviers, of course, are all about comparisons. For them, life itself is a competition.

---

38 Solomon's terminology is slightly different from that used herein. She refers to one type of hostile/angry supervisor as a "bully," while I might include several of them under a broad category of "bully." In any case, we can see the common denominator—fear of being one-down in some way.

39 Solomon, *Working with Difficult People*, 6.

40 Ibid., 14.

41 Ibid., 18.

Can you see the common thread of fear running through all these catego-ries? As between two opinions, one must be right and the other wrong; two aspects of a greater truth do not compute. One person must control, the other be controlled; working hand-in-hand as equals is a fiction. One must win, the other must lose; that's the way life is. This person's lens filters out both/and possibilities, allowing him to see only either/or alternatives. One who views the world through this lens may fear being the one who is wrong, the one who is controlled, the loser.

And as Yoda predicted, this fear leads to anger or hostility. This person knows no better way to relieve his fear than to control the other person, make him wrong, make him lose, whether his method be personal attacks, blame, or threats.

Dishonesty and tricks can also be fear-driven. Lying can emerge as a child's defense against an over-demanding (and therefore scary) parent. Those who grow up fearing they can never measure up, may also pick others' brains then take credit for their ideas, or disparage their "competitors" under cir-cumstances that don't allow those competitors to defend themselves.

Try This: Becoming Aware of Underlying Fears

Think of a time when you felt tempted to, or did in fact, become hostile. What was your underlying fear?

Now think of some specific instances when someone became hostile with you. What fears might have driven their hostility?

Other Driving Interests

While fear may lead to triangulation and usually does lead to anger, the con-verse is not always true. Not all triangulation, for example, is fear-driven. I once worked with a man I'll call Don who was a master of triangulation. I don't know if Don was afraid of bringing up touchy subjects, but I do know that he often got other people to do it for him. Thus, Don was rarely seen as "the trouble-maker" by anyone in the group. Staying on everyone's good side might have been motive enough for Don to triangulate even if he did not feel fearful of controversy.

A person might dread speaking to a particular individual in much the same way I dread preparing my tax return. I don't fear the tax return, I just don't like doing it. One might dread a conversation because the other individual is frustratingly long-winded, for example.

So, be aware of fear as a common driver of habitual problem behavior, but hold your mind open to other possibilities.

Frustrate the Behavior, not the Person

Once we get a handle on how a behavior works for someone, and if possible, a broader interest the behavior serves, we try to frustrate the problem behavior so it doesn't work, preferably without exacerbating the underlying fear. If we can *steer someone to an acceptable way to address their underlying interest*, we then reward that alternate behavior. Here are some examples:

Triangulation

Suppose Fran tries to triangulate Spencer into making Yolanda stop pushing for games. Once Spencer recognizes this, he can achieve an immediate objective of not interceding (unless all three of them participate in the process) by simply refusing to do so. But his refusal could punctuate Fran's underlying fear of speaking directly with Yolanda. Fran may be left feeling rejected, made wrong, and/or hostile toward Spencer. And as many readers know even better than I do, a hostile congregant can cause a cleric a lot of trouble, even if the hostility is not justified.

If Spencer wants to avoid alienating Fran and to help her learn to speak for herself, a more refined approach is more likely to achieve his long-range objectives. This interest-oriented approach minimizes wrong making as well as fear.

Dialogue 13: Rev. Spencer discourages triangulation

Dialogue:	Spencer's View:
F: I know Yolanda's exaggerating the games thing. It's just her personal preference, but she's making it sound like there's this big push for games among all the young people.	
S: So you're suggesting that we don't know how much enthusiasm there is for games, correct?	Spencer mirrors her statement in the form of a less-accusatory reframe.
F: Right. Yolanda probably mentions games to her friends. Maybe they nod or say, "Yeah," just to be polite, but they don't really care all that much.	
S: How could the situation be clarified?	Open question directed at an interest.
F: I think Yolanda just needs to be told to knock it off.	Fran indirectly suggests she wants Spencer to do this.
S: Are you planning to tell her to knock it off?	He doesn't reward this behavior. He asks a question to clarify her position, without suggesting that his involvement is on the table. Asking her *whether* she is planning to speak to Yolanda, rather than telling her she must, minimizes the fear she might feel when he doesn't offer to speak for her.

F:	She wouldn't take it from me.	Her bid for his intervention becomes more overt.
S:	Let's just hypothesize for a moment. Suppose someone told Yolanda that you were appealing to your friends to squelch her suggestion of games. I'm not saying you are, but suppose someone told Yolanda you were. Then someone else told you to knock it off. How would you react?	Open question. He hopes to steer her to the conclusion that his intervention will not address her fear of increased hostility or reprisal by Yolanda.
F:	That would depend on who told me. I wouldn't take it from Yolanda, but if someone in authority told me...	Spencer knows this is unlikely. Fran has not realistically predicted her reaction to an analogous situation. She would not like his telling her to knock it off. But that's what she wants him to do to Yolanda.
S:	Fair enough. Let's say *I* told you to knock it off. How would you react?	Open question, instead of making her wrong by directly contradicting her.
F:	Well...I'd be hurt. I mean, if I hadn't really done it, which I haven't, I'd be hurt.	She begins to see another perspective, but she's not all the way there yet. Her projection of how she would react is still unrealistic.
S:	Suppose, as a reality check on yourself, you had spoken to a few other people to gauge their interest in games versus a speaker.	An implicit, more specific, follow up question.

239

F: That's an OK thing to do. It's not squelching Yolanda.

S: True. So are you saying you'd still be hurt or angry in that case, if I told you to knock it off?

F: Sure. Wouldn't anybody?

S: I would. It's only human. And in my experience, people get just as huffy whether they did what they're accused of or not.

After validating her feelings, Spencer decides to venture a statement, rather than continuing a constant stream of questions. He doesn't want Fran to feel he's grilling her, and she has calmed down enough that the statement might get through to her. To minimize any wrong-making effect, he predicates his opinion on his experience, rather than presenting it as ironclad fact.

F: So Yolanda gets huffy. So what?

S: Sometimes huffy people become hostile. If I told you to knock off trying to squelch Yolanda, and you wanted to strike back at someone, who would it be?

Another question leading Fran closer to the conclusion that, even if Spencer is the one to speak to Yolanda, she still might become hostile toward Fran.

F: I suppose your point is that Yolanda might blame me. But wouldn't that be better than letting her sabotage the fundraiser?

Good. Now she's beginning to ask questions, a step in the right direction.

S: Perhaps. But what if we could find a way to avoid both of those unhappy results—optimize the fundraiser experience without spawning hostility?

Still another question suggesting the possibility of a win-win solution.

F: So we just ignore Yolanda and work hard on the current fundraiser plan?

S: I think some discussion with Yolanda might be in order. The preliminary work, and the event itself, will go better if Yolanda's remarks are addressed. I'm trying to find the most effective way to go about it.

Spencer indirectly suggests that he is not planning to intercede. Triangulation will not work. However, he is willing to help Fran in what he believes is a healthier way.

F: So you're not willing to talk to her?

Fran makes a last-ditch effort to triangulate Spencer.

S: What I'm asking is, if Yolanda had a beef with you, would you rather she came to you or persuaded me to speak for her? Which would be a more effective way for her to win your good will?

Rather than directly reject Fran and her request, Spencer re-directs the focus to how well his intervention would really serve Fran's interests.

F: I don't know.

More progress. She has stopped arguing for intervention and begun to question her original position.

S: What would you think if I gave you some communication pointers—see if we can get you comfortable with approaching Yolanda? We could even role play the discussion until you feel you have a handle on it. Then you can decide if you'd like to approach her one-on-one, or if you'd like me there as well.

Now Spencer offers help in establishing behavior he *does* want to encourage. This is a form of reward that promises to deal with her fears better than his direct intervention.

He wants her to succeed in dealing with Yolanda so that she will adopt the new behaviors to substitute for triangulation in the future. So he offers an empowering form of help.

F: (Sighs) I don't know. I need a break. I need to think about this.

She's right. This is not the time for Spencer to push for a decision.

S: Good idea. I'll take a break too. Just know that I'm here when you're ready to talk.

There are many possible results of Fran's think break, some good, others not so good. Spencer welcomes a touch back so he can deal with any unproductive feelings or decisions Fran might come up with. If he doesn't hear from Fran, he will contact her.

Fran might come out of this discussion disappointed, even a little miffed. But get into her shoes and compare her probable state of mind if Spencer had simply said, "This is between you and Yolanda. You need to speak to her yourself, or we all three speak together." That statement is absolutely true. It's assertive, rather than aggressive. Yet, she will likely feel implicitly dressed down (made wrong) and cut short (Spencer isn't interested in her or her problems). Whether she realizes it or not, part of Fran's discomfort with such a statement is the weakening effect of "You need to..." (recall my arm pushing experiment from Chapter 4). Finally, the statement reinforces her driving fear of speaking to the strong-willed Yolanda, and reinforces it at just the moment when she feels weakened and less able to succeed.

At that point, she might want nothing more to do with Spencer. He would achieve a short-range objective of avoiding the unhealthy triangle but not the long-range goal of helping Fran learn more productive behavior. Without a workable alternative, Fran will probably keep triangulating with people less able to resist than Spencer is.

Now, still in Fran's shoes, reread the dialogue. Can you feel yourself more inclined to think things through and open yourself to Spencer's guidance? If you were Spencer, and you had an interest in Fran's good will and cooperation in the future, which of the two reactions would you like her to have?

Address the object of the fear, rather than the condition of being fearful, unless the other person mentions it first. Note that Spencer offered to help Fran with *what* she was apparently afraid of, speaking to Yolanda. He did not directly ask her if she was afraid or anxious (or worse, tell her that she was). People can feel insulted or made wrong by a suggestion that they are fearful or anxious. Many will feel labeled whether you apply the label directly, "Are you afraid of...?" or indirectly "Do you have anxiety about...?"

Of course, if Fran had been the one to approach Spencer and told him that she was afraid to speak to Yolanda, that would have been a different matter. She had already owned her own fear.

However, in Spencer's situation in the last dialogue, had he found it necessary to be more specific, it would be preferable for him to ask Fran something like, "What is your concern about speaking to Yolanda?" or "What stops you from speaking to Yolanda?"

Another benefit of addressing the object of the emotion is that it can work for Spencer whether Fran's reluctance to speak to Yolanda did, as he imagined, stem from fear, or from some other cause, let's say dread of Yolanda's long-windedness. When Spencer offers communication tips, Fran can specifically ask him about how to keep the conversation from going on too long or wandering down too many side trails. When Spencer thought about what Fran might fear, the result of his reflections still helped him find the object to address. Addressing that object, dialogue with Yolanda, still helped him redirect Fran's attempt at triangulation. All this without the need to risk insulting Fran or making her wrong by raising the issue of fear or anxiety on her part.

Hostility

In the last dialogue, Spencer kept returning the focus to helping Fran deal with her own problem (interest), usually a good way to deal with triangulation. With other problem behaviors, like hostility (threats, insults, personal attacks and blame), as well as with various dishonest or tricky tactics, minimizing the wrong making becomes more challenging.

People instinctively feel that insults, threats and lies *are* wrong and that, as the moral authority of the church, the minister should call them out as such for the benefit of the congregation as a whole. However, the perpetrator who is called out, stinging with wrong making, can become a submarine saboteur.

As mentioned in Chapter 4, the more mature a person is, the more likely that he can overcome the biological urge to deny, rationalize and project when made wrong. The habitually hostile person is less mature than average, not more so. He is more likely to angrily resist accepting his own wrong.

If you want to, or must, deal with the person in the future, it's best to avoid overtly calling out his threats, insults or attacks if you have a reasonable alternative. Make him wrong only as a last resort. Hard as it may seem, helping him save face serves your interest in stopping the problem behavior.

Suppose, for example, Mike threatens Laurel, "If you don't pay for that window, I'll bring the matter to the next open board meeting. *You'll* be the one shown up in front of all the officers." Laurel calls him on his threat, "Go ahead. We'll see who's embarrassed." Now Mike must either make good on his threat or show himself up (realize his driving fear of being one-down to Laurel). And if he does go before the board, and if they decide to excuse Laurel from paying because she was trying to head off a worse accident, he will only be more resentful of Laurel. His hostility toward her, to her face and/or behind her back, is likely to escalate. Plus Mike may begin submarine sabotage against any officers who supported her.

Let's look at another way for Laurel to handle Mike's threat.

Dialogue 14: Laurel deals with hostility

Dialogue:	Laurel's View:
M: If you don't pay for that window, I'll bring the matter to the next open board meeting. *You'll* be the one shown up in front of all the officers.	A threat. The emphasis on "you" in *"You'll* be the one shown up..." suggests Mike feels shown up.
L: You're right. Neither of us likes being shown up. How might we both avoid that risk by settling the matter between ourselves?	In an elegant variation on the But Out technique, Laurel disarms him by finding something to agree with. Then she reframes his threat as a mutual interest.
M: By you paying for the window—or else!	He continues his threatening stance, but has backed off the specific threat to go to the board. He falls back on a vague "or else." This represents progress in the form of decreased certainty.
L: I'm confused about how this whole thing evolved between the two of us. How did it start and how did it become so intense?	Laurel ignores the threat and resists arguing against his position that she should pay. Instead, she begins to explore his view of the situation. What might he know, or think he knows, that would make his hostility seem reasonable to him?

M: It evolved from you think-   Another hostile
    ing you deserve special   behavior—accusation.
    treatment.

L: Help me understand what   She declines to argue but
    looks special to you about   asks for clarification.
    the way I'm treated.

M: Well, duh! Others pay for   "Duh!" A hostile put-down.
    their damage and you don't.

L: For example?   She refuses to take the bait
                                 to argue or get defensive.
                                 Redirects the conversation
                                 from personalities to issues.

M: I backed over a sign in the
    parking lot. I paid for that,
    and I bet it cost a lot more
    than your window.

L: So you're saying, all things Rephrases in less emotional
    being equal, everyone should terms.
    pay for their accidents.

M: All things aren't equal.   More hostility in "You fat
    That's the problem. You fat   cats," but he also reveals
    cats who can afford to do-   what's really bothering him.
    nate a lot to the church get
    special treatment.

L: (Genuine smile) I guess I   She reframes his name-call-
    should take it as a compli-   ing as a compliment, then
    ment that you think I have   tries again to paraphrase the
    that kind of clout. Are you   interest that underlies his
    saying that everyone should   demands that she pay.
    pay or not pay for damage
    that occurred under similar
    circumstances?

M: Yeah.

L: Tell me about your accident. How did you come to back over the sign.

    Open question.

M: Well, that sign's low to the ground. I just didn't see it.

L: May I tell you about my accident?

    She seeks his consent before telling how her circumstances differed.

M: I guess so. If you need to.

    He's still huffy, but not nearly so hostile and aggressive.

L: I saw a three-year-old child running with a sharp pair of scissors. I lurched to catch her and knocked a chair into the window.

M: So?

L: Maybe, for right or for wrong, nobody asked me to pay for the window because I was trying to prevent a worse accident, trying to do a good deed, you might say.

M: Hmph.

    Not the most accepting reply, but a far cry from his original attitude.

L: You sound unconvinced. Who contacted you about paying for your accident?

Since one of Laurel's interests is a lasting peace with Mike, she continues to address his apparent feeling interests.

M: Wendy.

L: What if we ask Wendy about the criteria for reimbursement for accidents?

She suggests an alternative to taking the dispute to the board, an alternative less likely to result in either of them being "shown up."

M: So she tells us. So what?

L: Several possibilities. If we think the criteria are unfair, we can say so. If it turns out that they do seem fair, we don't embarrass ourselves because we only asked for clarification. If the standards are fair, but Wendy slipped up in our cases, our enquiry reminds her to stick by the criteria, but without showing her up. Like you said, nobody likes that. If she agrees the standards aren't fair, she can help us present the issue to whoever sets the standards.

M: You can ask her if you want to.

L:	I want both of us to feel that the conversation with Wendy, as well as the outcome, is fair. I wouldn't be comfortable speaking for you. It only makes sense for me to go to her if you're there, too, to speak for yourself.	Addresses his interest in fairness. Also heads off any possible future complaints from Mike, for example about things Laurel and Wendy discussed outside his presence. If he was trying to set her up, she does not reward that behavior.
M:	I'll think about it.	He may or may not agree to speak to Wendy together, but he's likely to stop his hostile behavior toward Laurel.

Compare this dialogue to typical knee-jerk responses to hostility—fight (argument) or flight (avoidance or giving in). Arguing would mean making Mike wrong, and being in a hostile frame of mind already, he would have resisted vehemently, bringing more hostility down on Laurel's head. Flight would reinforce his impression that hostility works, and therefore, encourage him to try it more in the future. Perhaps the dialogue didn't leave Mike with a big case of the warm fuzzies, but it accomplished Laurel's objectives much better than fight or flight, and probably as well as possible under the circumstances.

Laurel used many of her general skills, such as open questions, Butting Out, reframing, and focusing on interests. *One noteworthy variation, often helpful in dealing with threats and attacks, is reframing a hostile remark.* She reframed his threat to show her up in front of the board as a mutual interest, "You're right. Neither of us like being shown up. How might we both avoid that risk by settling the matter between ourselves?" Notice how this avoids rewarding the objectionable behavior, since what Mike wanted was fight or flight. The fact that the interest on which she refocused was a mutual one added even more power to the technique.

What Mike wanted from the insult about fat cats receiving special treatment was for her to go on the defensive or feel bad about herself. Laurel reframed the insult as a compliment, frustrating the tactic, but without making Mike wrong.

In the case of another threat, the vague "or else," Laurel simply ignored it and kept calmly talking about the real problem, again frustrating the reward Mike expected.

Without honoring any of Mike's disrespectful comments with direct responses, and thus maintaining respect for herself, Laurel was also consistently respectful toward Mike. Thus, she avoided stirring up the fear of being one-down that underpins his hostile behavior. And when he began to drop his hostility, she rewarded him by assuring him that she wanted him to feel the final outcome was fair and offering to talk to Wendy together to that end.

Try This: Reframing Hostile Remarks

Try to reframe each of the following remarks as a mutual interest or as a compliment:

- Fran to Spencer: If I'm not appreciated anymore, I'll just take my talents and my money over to Fourth Street Church.
- Yolanda to Fran: You'd put on a concert by tone deaf singers if you thought it would bring in a few more dollars.
- Brandon to Molly: Those kids are going to be pretty unhappy with you if they don't get that dollhouse.

Dishonest or Unethical Tactics

We've seen that reframing is a particularly useful tool for dealing with hostility. Dishonest and unethical tactics, such as lying and breaking promises, can be difficult to reframe and also difficult to handle without making the other person wrong. In addition, when you suspect dishonesty, but are not absolutely sure, you might be the one embarrassed if you call it out directly.

Questions, asked in a tone of sincere curiosity, are more useful in cases of suspected dishonesty or tricks. If the other person is acting honestly and in good faith, such questions are harmless; no one loses face. But if your question uncovers an inconsistency or incorrect statement, the other person can save face by treating it as an honest mistake. His behavior will not be rewarded, so he will be discouraged from trying to trick you again. Yet, he is less likely to lash out against you with resistance to being overtly made wrong.

Let's look at how Spencer might speak to Yolanda when she approaches him about having games instead of a speaker at the fundraiser.

Dialogue 15: Rev. Spencer tests Yolanda's honesty

Dialogue:	**Spencer's View:**
Y: I have some concerns about the upcoming fundraiser that I'd like to discuss with you.	
S: Oh?	
Y: The younger adults, I mean people in their twenties and thirties, find those speakers a real snore. I'm worried they won't attend unless we have something more lively instead, like games.	Is Yolanda really speaking for a large number of people, or for herself? Is the "worry" that the young people won't attend true concern for the interests of the congregation, or a veiled threat?
S: Indulge me in what may seem like a silly question with an obvious answer, but I'd like to get your perspective in your own words. The disadvantages to us as a congregation if the young adults don't attend would be?	Spencer asks a clarifying question.

Y: Well, we wouldn't make as much money, obviously, and the young people might feel the leadership doesn't care about what they like.

S: So you believe the disadvantages would be reduced proceeds and possibly loss of good will among the younger folks, correct?

Paraphrasing.

Y: Right. After all, churches have to attract young members to replace the older ones who die or retire and move away. They are our future.

Spencer's suspicions deepen a little. Again he senses an insidious threat.

S: How do you feel about the speakers, personally?

Another clarifying question focused on her interests.

Y: Well, I don't want to hurt Fran's feelings, but speakers bore me. If it weren't for wanting to do my part for the church, I'd think, *Why pay to hear something I have to force myself to listen to and attend an auction where I can't afford most of the items?*

She *says* she wants to do her part for the church. Why does she elaborate about how she wouldn't want to attend if there is a speaker? Is she suggesting her Plan B?

S: How many other young people have complained about the speakers?

Having clarified Yolanda's interest, Spencer moves closer to uncovering any inaccuracy in how many people she speaks for, again with an open question.

Y: I'd say, twenty maybe.

S: What if we get together with all of them? I'd like to hear their concerns and ideas.

Spencer tries to make the triangle healthy by bringing the third parties into the process. This also takes another step toward discovering the true number.

Y: Well, I wouldn't want to embarrass anyone, like I'm going to you with something they told me privately.

If she's being evasive, that's another possible sign of dishonesty. Spencer needs to test further.

S: Are you thinking they want you to speak for them while they remain anonymous?

Y: Oh, I don't mean they're triangulating me. It's just, well, people are careful what they say to authority figures like you, let alone having someone else repeat things without their knowledge.

Evasiveness has not disappeared, nor been confirmed. He still needs to know more.

S: Fair enough. Let's do it this way. You go through them, person-by-person, in your mind, and without naming them, just give me a general idea, like, "A & B, a young couple with children; C, a single woman," etc.

Spencer speaks to her as if she is dealing with him honestly, even though he has his doubts. He offers a way to deal with the objection (interest) she raised.

Y: Well, gosh, I, well, there was a young couple with kids. Another couple without kids. And a single man.

More hesitation. Six people, not twenty. She exaggerated, whether intentionally or not.

S: So you're saying five people, plus you makes six. Right?

He confirms a number different from her first answer without overtly pointing out that they are inconsistent.

Y: Yeah, but I got the impression the childless couple heard some others mention the same problem. And I may have forgotten some.

S: And what were some of the things people said, specifically?

Now he wants to know how strongly these people felt about the speaker. Did they have this idea on their own or merely respond to a suggestion by Yolanda?

Y: Just, you know, they like the idea of games.

Sounds like they didn't feel strongly that the speakers were boring, and perhaps they were merely responding, casually and politely, to Yolanda's suggestion of games.

Everything up to now has been inconclusive. She might be in good faith, but despite every chance Spencer has given her, she has not cleared up the doubts raised by her inconsistencies, evasiveness, and possible indirect threats.

S: You've raised a good point about finding out what really attracts people to the fundraiser. Suppose we poll all the adult members concerning their programming preferences. What do you think about that idea?

Here is the acid test. Spencer first makes her right by agreeing with what he can, then makes a reasonable request. The result should give him a clear picture of what he's dealing with.

Y: You mean whether they prefer games or a speaker?

Yolanda seeks clarification.

S: Actually, I was thinking of something more refined. We work with Fran to develop a list of options, say three speaker topics and three activity options. Then we ask people to rate each one on a scale:
5. Wow! I love it
4. Good idea
3. OK by me
2. Don't like it
1. Wouldn't attend

It's called "gradient voting."[42]

Spencer has fleshed out his reasonable request. Yolanda can see that this plan will uncover just who prefers what, how strongly they feel, and how much their feelings about various options differ (it's possible some really like speakers and also really like games).

Ending I:

Y: That's a good idea. Anything I can do to help?

Either she was acting in good faith all along, or if she was dishonest, Spencer's failure to reward the dishonesty has persuaded her to give it up.

---

42 Gradient voting is described in Chapter 15 and in Kaner, *Facilitator's Guide.*

Ending II:

Y:	I don't know. This all sounds pretty complicated.	Now he knows she's playing him.
S:	I think I can make it simple enough, but it's not the only option for taking the congregation's pulse. We could have a town hall meeting.	Spencer offers another option for achieving his interest in serving as many members' preferences as possible. He helps Yolanda save face by speaking as if she shares his interest in good faith, even though he is now pretty sure she has not shared it up to this point.
Y:	That's even bigger, more trouble. Maybe we should just forget it.	She doesn't want the true majority view to come out.
S:	Let's both think it over. Meanwhile, thanks for calling it to my attention that some people like games.	Spencer closes with other face-saving measures—a sincere thanks for bringing up what might turn out to be a true interest of a fair number of members (games), and making her right by soliciting her further thoughts.

It is important to note that I have used terms like "good faith" and "dishonesty." However, not all untruths are deliberately perpetrated. If a person whose arm was electrically stimulated can believe he "decided" to raise it, Yolanda might well believe she was honest in her statements to Spencer. There are many times when we are not 100% accurate, and remain unaware of how quickly and silently our brains made our wishes look like facts. As Oscar Wilde wrote, "The pure and simple truth is rarely pure and never simple." One of the beauties of the approach Spencer employed is that it works without regard to Yolanda's level of honesty and good faith.

Save Their Face

The above sample dialogues and commentary illustrate the value of helping people who have engaged in problem behavior, such as hostile or dishonest dealings, to save face even while thwarting the behavior. This bears repeating. Helping people save face is tantamount to avoiding making them wrong, and therefore, defusing their resistance to your ideas.

Those who habitually engage in problem behaviors, those one might say are, in fact, the most wrong, are also the most resistant to admitting it. Behaviors such as hostile dealings and dishonesty are dysfunctional, so what are the chances that those who habitually engage in them enjoy the high functioning that allows them to easily self-assess?

So do yourself a favor. Saving their face saves you time and trouble. Saving face also minimizes the risk of downstream hostility or sabotage by the person whose problem behavior was frustrated.

Sometimes It Does Take a Village

All of the foregoing practices reduce the chances that the person exhibiting problem behavior will continue to try such behavior on the one using the skills. They also reduce the chance that the person who exhibited the problem behavior becomes hostile toward the one using the skills.

Yet old habits die hard. When problematic behavior patterns no longer work on one person, the perpetrator often simply turns to someone else. Despite Spencer's successful deflection of Yolanda's attempt to manipulate him, she may move on to more vulnerable members of the congregation, persuading them to advocate for a change of fundraiser programming.

Moreover, some people become hostile any time someone declines to do as they wish. In Dialogue 13, Spencer's approach to Fran's triangulation was not only tactful, but potentially empowering to Fran. Yet some people will take offense even at such a tactful approach. They take the refusal very personally, and consequently, may turn against the other person. They feel put down and, lacking the maturity or skill to overcome their knee jerk reactions to feeling put down, they retaliate by projecting put downs back at the "offender."

The higher the status or authority of the one who declined to do as they wished, the stronger their personal reaction. If, on the one hand, Laurel refuses to pay for the broken window, Mike may level a few more snide remarks—to her face and/or behind her back—but eventually lose interest in retaliation and move on. On the other hand, if music director Kayla declines to assign a solo part to a mediocre member of the children's choir, the child's parent may spearhead a campaign to fire Kayla. The real motivating factor behind this campaign may fly below the radar screen as a stealth interest. The parent rationalizes it with arguments about the congregation's limited finances and the worthwhile ministries that could be expanded if they eliminated the expense of a full-time music director.

Not all such stealth interests are justified by well-reasoned arguments such as the parent makes with respect to Kayla. Without the skills to directly approach someone who has offended them, people may complain to third parties about a plethora of unrelated human faults and foibles, actual or perceived, on a number of occasions. Listeners develop subtle negative feelings about the person being criticized.

This *birdshot criticism is all the more difficult to counter* precisely because it is based on a large number of small gripes, rather than one large complaint that is easy to identify and address. Sometimes, those who are influenced don't even remember the comments that gave rise to their vague negative feelings. The atmosphere is like a trap, all set and ready to spring shut on the "offender" the next time she puts a foot wrong.

Clergy are particularly vulnerable to such behavior. Other staff members and high level lay leaders can also be targeted. As mentioned in Chapter 11, compliments from clergy are highly valued and motivating because clergy have such high status in the group. Conversely, slights and offenses by clergy hurt more, feel more wrong making, than those committed by one's peers.

The leader who is criticized may find herself in a no-win situation. If the critic senses defensiveness, which can read as weakness to him, he feels emboldened to escalate the criticism. On the other hand, if he feels counterattacked, he not only escalates, but garners allies as well. Neither defensiveness nor counterattack work well, especially for a minister.

If she simply ignores the complaints, other congregants, who hear only the critic's side of things, may agree with him. Moreover, the victim's silence can be misconstrued. The minister may be seen as cavalier or uncaring. *She must*, people think, *be determined to stubbornly keep on doing what she's doing without taking others' concerns into account.*

Of course, the victim can try to speak to the critic, using consensus skills, but many factors can work against the success of such an effort. She might not become aware of the criticism until much damage has been done among the other members of the congregation. The critic may not open up to her about what's really driving the criticism, either because he doesn't own it even to himself, because he doesn't want reconciliation but rather to punish the minister, or for other reasons. He might discuss a host of other little peeves, leaving the stealth interest under cover. Or he may refuse to speak to the minister at all.

Some members, finding the critic's negative conversations distasteful and unhealthy, isolate themselves from the conversations or even from the church, thereby granting more influence to a small but vocal minority. Still others remain blissfully unaware of the problem until a lot of damage has been done.

Additional factors can compound such situations for clergy. The initial criticism begins in private conversations to which the minister is not privy. Matters can spin out of control before she even becomes aware of the situation.

In some cases, the disgruntled member's personal take on the minister's refusal to do his bidding may be exacerbated by transference of sexual or romantic feelings or past experiences of rejection. The minister's deflection of his attempts to manipulate her can feel like she's rejecting him personally. Such situations make it especially difficult for the minister to resolve the matter through direct communication with the critic, for almost anything she says can either exacerbate his feelings of rejection, or on the other hand, give him false hope.

The congregant fights back against the "rejection," but the results of his attack can't assuage his feelings of rejection. Twenty people jumping on his bandwagon do not make the minister accept him. On the contrary, the minister, quite understandably, may become even more standoffish. His attacks escalate as he tries harder and harder to make himself feel better using tactics that are doomed by their very nature to thwart his true underlying interest—acceptance by the minister.

What is a person in such a situation to do? *The cold, hard truth is that there are limits to what she alone can do.* If she can't win whether she defends herself, counterattacks, or ignores the criticism, the obvious solution is for a critical mass of supportive congregants to step up and defuse the problem behavior.

One of my fondest hopes is *to empower congregations to nip unhealthy attacks on leaders, or anyone else, in the bud before they spin out of control.* To this end, the minister can't be the only one skilled in consensus communication. The larger the number of members who are proficient at recognizing and handling problematic behavior, the harder it is for an unfair critic to garner a following. Better yet, the more congregants who acquire the skill and confidence to speak directly to the person with whom they have issues, the less likely they are to adopt problem behavior to begin with.

Examples of Villages in Action

I once took a short course titled "Conflict, Violence, War and Hope." Each session was taught by a professor from a different discipline—biology, history, sociology, etc. At least three of those professors came to one point from different directions: *The tide of human social development turned when the beta males figured out that, if they worked together, they need not suffer the dictatorship of one alpha male,* no matter how big and strong he was.

In one middle school in The Bronx, teachers have learned that *both a bully and his victim believe the children who remain silent approve of the bullying.* So the bully, feeling approved of, or even admired, keeps on bullying. The victim, believing that all the other children approve, doesn't sense the social support to resist. Direct intervention between teachers and bullies doesn't help much. What does work is teaching children who observe bullying to voice their disapproval to the bully.

The Value of the Village

We could all learn lessons from these children and from those prehistoric beta males. If one person, even the minister, expresses disapproval of unfair complaints about Kayla, the complainer, feeling made wrong, may intensify the behavior or change targets. But if enough people decline to reward his behavior, so that he can't find enough sympathetic ears, he has two choices. He may change his behavior, or he may leave the congregation. As we will see in the next chapter, his leaving is sometimes for the best.

However, consensus practices can reduce the risk of losing those of the bullies who are capable of learning to function better in the group. If those who intervene in the attack know how to minimize wrong making, as by rephrasing, reframing, and drawing out the real interests driving the problem behavior, it may be possible to help the attacker find better ways of satisfying his interests and feeling good about himself.

We're not talking here about unhealthy triangulation. I am not suggesting that victims manipulate others into fighting their battles for them. This is about recognizing when one person places another in a disadvantaged situation from which she has little realistic hope of extricating herself, no matter how assertive or how skillful she is. It is about offering the social support that makes it realistic for her to stand up for herself. It is about a critical mass of astute leaders choosing to intervene in the situation because of their own interests—interests in kindness and fairness, for example, or in the safety of the congregational environment. Depending on the circumstances, the interveners can engage the critic along with the victim, rather than for her, drawing all interested parties into a healthy triangle.

But *some people so dislike the idea of potential conflict within the congregation that they shy away from learning how to deal with it until it is upon them*, and by that time, they have two strikes against them.

Fortunately, the same practices that will enable them to deal with conflict also help them toward other goals in which they are keenly interested such as:

- Optimizing their plans for proactive endeavors such as ministries and events
- Improving efficiency
- Communicating more effectively with one another
- Demystifying temperamental and cultural differences
- Building or strengthening the bridges of community between them

They may be attracted to learning the practices for any of the above reasons, and as a by-product, they become equipped to deal with problematic behaviors and conflicts. *They learn that addressing such behaviors need not involve traumatic arguments, and thus, they gain the courage and confidence to address behavioral issues and to address them early on.*

I have mentioned that the various consensus skills in this book are tools, not rules. Even the Silver Rule of avoiding wrong making has its rare exceptions. The next chapter explains when setting boundaries trumps the Silver Rule and shows how to handle those rare situations.

Key Points from Chapter 13

- Those who regularly engage in problematic behaviors such as lies, tricks or hostile attacks think or feel that these behaviors serve their interests
    - o The behavior feels normal and comfortable to them, taking on the character of an interest in its own right
    - o This is one interest you don't want to appeal to
    - o Rather, to stop the person from engaging in this behavior with you, find a way to make the behavior not work for them
- To understand the behavior and what it does for the person
    - o Consider, but don't lock into, the things he routinely accuses others of doing
    - o Consider your knee jerk reaction to the behavior; it may be just what he wants
    - o Notice how others react to his behavior
    - o Fear drives many problematic behaviors
        - Fear of speaking directly for oneself can drive triangulation
        - Fear of losing can drive hostility
        - Fear of powerlessness or not measuring up can drive lies and tricks

- Frustrate the behavior, but not the person
    - Don't react in the way the person wants
    - Do try to steer him toward a better way of addressing the interest behind his fear
    - Deal with *what* the person is afraid of, but don't label him fearful or anxious
- Give him a way to save face
- Sometimes it takes a group effort to deal with one person's unfair attacks on another
    - Groups that learn consensus skills for upbeat purposes, such as enhancing communication quality and optimizing projects, can later use them to deal with conflicts, including unfair attacks

I don't know the key to success, but the key to failure is to try to please everyone.
- Bill Cosby

What about behaviors that, even after all the refinements in the preceding chapters, tempt the kindliest and most charitable among us to think, *This person really is impossible.* Maybe he learns not to bully you, but continues to bully others who, for one reason or another, can't handle him. Maybe she's a submarine saboteur who moves from one destructive project to another. In any case, the person seems unwilling or unable to stop a behavior pattern that harms other individuals and the group as a whole.

A thorough treatment of such situations is beyond the scope of this book. In this chapter, I will focus on aspects that flow most readily from what we've already learned.

Return to the Basics

Rethink and prioritize your current *interests.* If you have previously listed your interests with respect to this person, it's time to redevelop them from scratch because, in all likelihood, they will have changed.

Suppose Robbie was the star soloist of the children's choir until he hit his early teens and his voice began to change. Music director Kayla explained to Robbie that soon she would have to begin assigning soprano solos to a younger child. Robbie's father, Jake, spoke one-on-one to each of several congregation members who were unaware of the situation concerning Robbie but who were exceptionally interested in community outreach and social action. Jake pointed out how much more the congregation could accomplish in those arenas if they did not have a full-time music director. In fact, Jake suggested, various volunteers could take on various of Kayla's duties, one directing the children's choir, another directing the adult choir, etc. He even provided statistics to show that, typically, only much larger congregations employ full-time directors.

These other members took up the cause of dismissing the music director, and a meeting was called. Using his consensus skills, the congregation's president, Perry, chaired the meeting, at which a majority voted to retain Kayla. However, several people stopped showing up at services and other church events because they found the controversy distressing. Soon after the meeting, Perry was accused of misusing church funds. The treasurer checked and found no financial irregularities.

Suspicious of this sequence of events, minister Joan traced the rumor about Perry back to Jake. Joan applied her consensus skills, beginning with her interest in persuading Jake to change his destructive behavior and to find better ways to address his interests so that he could remain involved in the church in a positive manner. Joan thought she had made some headway with Jake, but now suspects that he has started criticizing her behind her back. Meanwhile, more people have stopped showing up.

It's time for Joan to re-develop her interest list. Changing Jake's behavior will no longer be paramount. Her former interest in keeping him involved in the church may have to be sacrificed in favor of more pressing interests—protecting the congregation and protecting herself from the results of Jake's destructive behavior.

When Giving Up Is Not Giving Up

When confronted with firmly fixed and harmful behavior, leaders should *consider the time, effort, and interim losses of continuing to deal with a determined troublemaker*: loss of other congregants or their good will; stress on one's own mental, physical or spiritual health; spending so much time trying to cure the one that she has to neglect the many. There is a duty, and therefore an interest, to protect the community from predatory behavior. The minister also has a legitimate and serious interest in protecting herself from defamation or other attacks, as in Joan's case just above.

She must *weigh these possible losses against a Plan B that no church leader finds attractive—asking the troublemaker to leave the congregation.* For some people, the very idea is shocking and extremely unpalatable in many ways. They may fear that other members will not support the decision.

They don't want themselves or others to think of their church as "the kind of place" where destructive behavior runs rampant, nor as a place where members get "fired."

In truth, a destructive person can appear in any group; it's not a function of the kind of congregation they are, but it may affect the kind of congregation they become. Yet, leaders know that others don't always bear this truth in mind.

Even closer to the heart, "firing" a congregant feels like giving up on the person, and giving up on someone can seem contrary to core values. Every fiber of a leader's heart and gut may recoil from this Plan B. *What good is a church if it's not open to all those imperfect souls who reach out for betterment?* she wonders. OK, maybe it's sometimes necessary to part ways, but surely none of *our* members is that impossible. A leader may *feel* that she failed if someone else has to leave, even though her rational mind tells her she can't "solve" the real human limitations of all concerned.

We can't help being moved by the circumstances that established this person's behavior. Perhaps the pattern developed from a childhood method of coping with adverse conditions such as abuse at home or rejection at school. The class nerd felt powerless to stand up for herself, so she learned to manipulate others into doing it for her. Triangulation did, in fact, work for her when nothing else would. Now, as an adult, she continues to triangulate.

Perhaps a parent modeled the pattern. Dad was verbally abusive, so that's what being a man feels like to the son who becomes an abuser in his own right. Some patterns, such as lying, develop as symptoms of alcoholism or drug addiction.

In any case, while our hearts go out to this person who had no better role model than an abuser, or who managed to survive an unhappy childhood, or who suffers from mental illness, we know that breaking the resulting habits is extremely difficult, and sometimes impossible, usually requiring long periods of hard work, at best. We also know that we can't do that work for the troublemaker. *We can't unilaterally fix her.* She has to want to change, and want it badly enough to do that hard work.

Nor is the desire to change enough to overcome the biological forces driving the dysfunctional behavior. *Just as alcoholism is biochemical, abusive behavior and other dysfunctions become wired into the brain.*

Imagine a young child whose first encounter with a dog terrifies her. She develops a phobia. All grown up now, she breaks into a panic every time she hears or sees a dog, even on leash or behind a tall fence. She can't think herself out of this because, of many possible neural paths in her brain, the dog stimulus got hooked up to the panic response. Brain scientists now know that we can't unhook that connection.

What we can do is establish a second connection so that the dog stimulus has options on which of two neural paths to follow. We can train our brains to take the second path more and more often, strengthening that path. A therapist may teach the phobic patient to enter a deep state of relaxation then view a small picture of a small dog, for example. When the patient can view the small dog while remaining relaxed, they graduate to a larger picture of a larger dog. Therapy progresses until she can relax in the presence of an actual dog at close range, perhaps even pet the dog.

Other behaviors become wired into the brain in much the same way. The grown child of an abusive parent may realize, on an intellectual level, that it is harmful and wrong to tell his own son he's no good. Yet, every time his son defies or frustrates him, some kind of put down escapes him. His emotionally abusive response may spill over to anyone who resists his control, including fellow congregants. Behind-the-back sabotage, lying, scapegoating, etc. can likewise become autopilot.

Most church leaders don't have the time, the training, or the malpractice insurance to facilitate progressive alternate brain wiring. Even if they do, they can't succeed without the subject's full cooperation. And again, they would have to weigh such a course against other losses to themselves and their congregations in the meanwhile.

Acknowledging the realities of such situations is not a minister's failure. If his church is located in a tropical or semi-tropical climate, and he wants to open the windows, he has to install screens over them. A congregation can't enter a spirit of worship or concentrate on a sermon when they're being eaten alive by mosquitoes. That's not the minister's failure. He is not giving up on the mosquitoes, who are God's creatures and strands of the interdependent web of which we all form a part. He is not trying to poison every mosquito within ten miles of the church. He is simply doing his job, just as the mosquitoes are doing theirs.

Sometimes, a parting of ways is best for all concerned, even the one who is asked to leave. Like an alcoholic, a person addicted to harmful behavior must sometimes "bottom out" to acquire the willingness to work at improving his brain wiring. Separation from the church could represent that bottom, or at least a step toward it.

It might also help to *think of this, not as giving up on the dysfunctional congregant, but as remaining true to and supportive of all the others*, while leaving the troublesome one no worse off (you couldn't "fix" him anyway) and possibly better (he may now bottom out and seek help).

When Making Someone Wrong Does Not Break the Silver Rule

We always practice consensus skills in the context of our ultimate objectives or interests. The Silver Rule—avoid or minimize wrong making—applies to situations in which you aim to bring about agreement or consensus between another person and yourself. Again, when you have tried your best, using all these skills, to persuade a destructive person to change his behavior pattern, but he persists, *your interests change from winning his whole-hearted agreement to establishing and maintaining a healthy environment*.

The Last Clear Chance

There are times when one person's behavior pattern is adversely affecting the community but does not yet seem to justify asking him to leave. It is unwise to wait for the situation to deteriorate until removing him becomes necessary. Yet skilled practice of consensus skills with the problem maker simply hasn't worked. *The risk to the group calls for us to clarify boundaries for all concerned, even if it means the problem maker will feel made wrong.* The interest in clarifying boundaries now takes priority over the interest in changing the troublemaker's behavior.

You may wish to give him one last clear chance to change his behavior before ejecting him from the congregation. You wish to state the matter in terms he is least likely to misunderstand. You also want the group as a whole to understand the boundaries so that they support, rather than thwart, this intervention.

269

Try offering a last clear chance only after realistically prioritizing and weighing the interests affected, respectively, by the last chance or the immediate departure. A leader responsible for handling this situation should also consider her *legitimate interest in protecting herself against possible attacks for "kicking him out unfairly."* If the value of stating the last clear chance outweighs the probable further harm if he remains awhile longer, it's time to *abandon tact for blunt speech that no one could reasonably claim they did not understand.* For example:

> Each of the three church committees you have joined have suffered because other members quit. All had the same reason—they felt bullied by you. In one incident, you shouted in a threatening manner when a majority voted against one of your suggestions. In another incident, you threatened to spread a story about the committee chair when she failed to support your view on an issue. In still another incident, you became so angry that you threw a heavy book across the room.
>
> We've discussed this before, but the complaints have continued. I must now ask you not to join any other committees or groups and that you refrain from bullying in any other place and time you encounter other church members. Never raise your voice, ever. If you are not sure whether or not a statement would be considered bullying, don't make the statement. If you can't think of any way to convey something without bullying, then keep silent, or come to me for advice on how to state the matter. Never throw, slam, kick or strike anything or anyone. This is your last chance. One more bullying incident, and we will have to ask you to leave the congregation.

Such a statement certainly makes the offending person wrong. It uses the form "You did…" rather than "I feel…." Its most likely effect is to alienate that person. But we have assumed you've already tried all the better ways of communicating and persuading. You are no longer aiming to persuade this person while retaining his enthusiasm and goodwill. Those things are gone anyway. Your goal now is to offer the chance that he might make the minimum acceptable change in response to a different type of communication, while protecting the community in the meanwhile.

The last clear chance is more likely to achieve the interests of protecting the group and its leaders than it is to change the behavior of the troublesome member. That is appropriate because the chances of changing his behavior are small in any event, and because the interests in protecting the others have assumed priority.

Be sure to *spell out*, in terms even someone without an ounce of empathy can understand, *precisely what behavior will and won't be tolerated*. If the person has shown (or claimed) he cannot accurately assess certain kinds of situations, take his judgment off the table by formulating a rule without exceptions, even if that rule goes too far for most people, "Never raise your voice, ever." Also, indicate the consequences for breaking that rule, "One more bullying incident, and we will have to ask you to leave the congregation."

Legitimate Self-Protection

Let's assume that, with or without a last clear chance, the person fails to change his behavior. He has to go; he's just too destructive. A second reason to make someone wrong deals with what has now become one of your legitimate primary interests, covering your back when you tell him that he must leave.

Right-making techniques are more effective in the vast majority of cases (though they haven't worked with this person). Yet, while usually effective, *they are also less direct*. A person who was disposed to make trouble to begin with, is disposed to blame you for not telling her what she was doing wrong, for not giving her a second chance, for kicking her out "for no reason," or the like.

She is more likely to feel vindictive, so she may voice this blame to whoever can hurt you most—people who are your biggest donors, people who aren't your biggest fans, naïve people who won't see through these accusations, perhaps your bishop or other judicatory official.

At this point, you may want to *go on record as having spelled out, in no uncertain terms*

- Exactly what behavior has caused harm
- What kind of harm the behavior caused

- The fact that you have tried other means to resolve the matter
- That the person's departure is the lesser evil compared with the harm
- That the person must leave

This statement should be delivered by the authority empowered to ask a member to leave—whether minister, president, governing board or other body—and should be made in front of a witness and/or confirmed in writing. The statement is part of your Plan B. Here's an example:

> You have engaged in a pattern of continually criticizing church projects and ministries behind the backs of the committee chairs in charge of them. You've declined to voice your complaints to the chairs, either privately or in open meetings, even though those chairs are the only people who could do anything about your complaints. In fact, you berate the chairs behind their backs as well. Sometimes, you didn't even attend those meetings when welcomed to do so.

> I have interviewed some of our members who have not come to church lately about their reasons. They tell me, and I have their permission to tell you, that the service may lift them up spiritually, but the unkindness and negativity of the after-service conversation drags them down even lower than they were to begin with. They say such negative conversations have become difficult to avoid.

> This is threatening the health of the entire congregation. We've tried every other way we know to help you toward more positive behavior. It doesn't make sense for us to neglect or lose a number of members in order to accommodate one individual who causes ongoing harm. With regrets, I must ask you to leave the congregation.

When you go on record with a wrong-making statement, be sure to make it clear whether you are giving the person one last chance or asking him to sever the relationship immediately.

Sometimes the biggest challenges arise, not from one difficult individual, but from the sheer number of people involved. The next chapter will introduce you to some of my favorite skills for helping groups reach agreements that actually work out in practice.

Key Points from Chapter 14

- When one person's behavior is harming the congregation as a whole, and all else has failed
    - o Leaders should re-assess their current interests
    - o If the harm being done to the congregation and/or oneself outweighs the loss of one member, it's time to part ways with the troublemaker
- Even the silver rule has exceptions
    - o While right-making dialogue is usually more effective, it is also less direct
    - o If the risk to the congregation is high enough to require setting boundaries, set them in unambiguous, albeit wrong-making, terms
    - o Make it clear whether you are offering the person one last chance to change, or are asking him to leave the congregation immediately

CHAPTER 15
THE MORE THE MESSIER

Meetings… are rather like cocktail parties. You don't want to go, but you're cross not to be asked.

- Jilly Cooper

We learn to walk before we run. We learn how to drive on a city street before we race on a track. And we should learn to build consensus between two people before advancing to larger groups such as committees, boards or entire congregations because the challenges increase with the number of people involved. The additional challenges of working with larger groups cannot be adequately addressed in one chapter. However, we will touch on these challenges, a few basic group skills, and their relation to our interest-based system.

Group agreements that work out in practice, that stand the test of time, and that build bridges between people evolve from processes in which as many as possible feel that their interests have been aired, understood and addressed. In short, they are built on the same foundations as successful one-on-one agreements.

Practices, like asking fanciful questions, that boost creativity between two people also boost creativity in groups. Communication skills, such as mirroring and asking open questions, likewise work well in groups.

When seeking consensus in a group, we don't set aside our two-party toolkit and pick up a different set of tools. We use our original kit. It might take a little longer, and we might add some additional tools to the mix, but everything you've learned in the preceding chapters will also serve you in groups.

The Challenges

There are many challenges to creating agreements in groups:

- The more people in the group, the more time and effort needed to plan the meeting process, inform the attendees, and get them all heard and involved in crafting the consensus. Yet, people sometimes seem less willing to spend time and effort on group decisions, as compared to two-party interactions.

- Those who don't participate—either don't attend meetings or don't speak up—can be the very ones to stir up trouble in subsequent parking lot conversations.

- If their interests, albeit unexpressed, aren't addressed, these people may become submarine saboteurs of an endeavor and/or of particular individuals whom they blame for their complaints.

- Some people may feel, for example, *I will not show my face at a meeting called for the purpose of trying to fire our music director. The very idea is odious to me. I won't be a party to it.* As a result, the anti-director minority represents a majority of those present at the meeting, creating a skewed impression of the views of the group as a whole. Like the child who fails to support a victim of bullying, absentees are presumed to be disinterested when, in fact, some of them strongly disagree with dismissing the music director.

- Even more often, those who do attend meetings and do contribute fail to express *all* their interests or to fully express the strength of their feelings, believing they must squelch themselves for the sake of "togetherness" or "being nice." Others exaggerate their feelings, and again, may create a false impression of the overall mood in the room.

The most common reasons people fail to participate adequately are:

1. They don't feel safe fully expressing all their interests, at least not in larger groups, and sometimes not at all.
2. They can't or won't take the time.
3. They know, or believe, their ideas are in the minority or contrary to those of the people in power, and therefore, see no use in trying to express them.

These are among the reasons I recommend participative consensus training for entire groups. Once people learn better ways to talk about difficult issues one-on-one, and actually experience success using their consensus practices in well-designed hypothetical exercises, they let go of the fears associated with expressing their interests—fear of confrontation, fear of making wrong and being made wrong, fear of being the one to hurt someone's feelings, etc. Knowing that many of the others in the group have learned the same practices further increases their confidence.

As for the time issue, training shows people how much time they save in the long run when they use effective consensus skills.

A common vocabulary also saves time and allays fears. For example, someone who has always had trouble speaking up for herself can now say, "I have some interests I'd like you all to know about," without fear of seeming too pushy, on the one hand, or being ignored, on the other. The others know what she means. They know their job is to hear and address her interests, and to express their own interests in turn.

That said, let's look at how some of the most effective group techniques build on what we've already learned.

Using the Brakes, Revisited

In Chapter 9, we saw the value of using the brakes on the communication car, taking time to listen well and think about others' statements before responding. We saw the benefits of both parties taking a think break before finalizing a decision. Yet, people often expect a large group to reach an important decision in a single meeting. They may feel frustrated, or even cheated, if this doesn't happen. And, even when they believe they have reached a sound agreement, a think break may reveal bugs that need to be worked out to finalize a feasible plan.

After a lively Solution Smorgasbord brainstorming period, it's easy to be swept along by the energy in the room to agree to a "final" plan. But if you want the benefit of everyone's best thinking, finalizing the plan should wait until those who think best alone have time to reflect on what they've heard. A second meeting, or even a third, is a small investment compared to regrouping after everyone has begun to act on a plan that won't work.

Every group has its own temptations to work fast rather than work smart. In smaller congregations with little or no staff, administrative functions fall to volunteers. They become accustomed to working as quickly as possible, and find it hard to turn off that mindset when careful reflection is needed. Larger congregations, on the other hand, have the luxury of a well-oiled administrative staff. Their challenge is recognizing when they need to take time to hear from their constituents.

Promoting Reasonable Expectations

I recommend that leaders plan for more than one meeting on issues that are important, complex or emotionally charged, and let the group know, up front, what to expect. Encourage participation at every turn. Educate people, in digestible bites, about these key points:

- Time invested at the front end pays for itself many times over by saving time, effort and false starts later on.
- The purpose of the initial meeting is to hear as many views as possible and give us things to think about without pressure to reach a final decision on the spot.
- It is important for *everyone* to weigh in. Even if they are undecided or neutral, they are encouraged to say so, and if possible, explain why.

Reinforce these messages through different means, especially if the group is not used to this new way of thinking—the meeting notice, statements made at the beginning and end of the meeting, etc.

In the congregation where some people have raised the issue of dismissing the music director, let's assume the leadership decides it would be best to hear from the congregation at large. They could use statements like these (not necessarily all at once):

1. The purpose of the meeting is to give everyone an opportunity to express initial views on possible budget reallocation between our music program and our outreach ministries.
2. We want everyone's input, and have designed a process for hearing everyone efficiently.
3. We learned a lesson last year when we had low turnout at our meeting to discuss the children's religious education program. We made the best decision we could with the information we had, but

later learned that some members' needs weren't met. Regrouping from this mistake required two additional congregational meetings of about three hours each, as well as hundreds of extra hours from our staff and volunteers. Still, some people were unhappy.

4. We want your input, and we want it sooner rather than later. If you can't attend, please contact Finance Committee Chair Emma Womack or Rev. Joan Black to make other arrangements for letting your voice be heard.

5. When people don't participate, others tend to make assumptions about their preferences. Such assumptions are often incorrect. If you are happy with the status quo, we need to know that, and why. If you would like a change, we need to know what change, and why.

6. We all have better ideas if we have time to think about a discussion before decisions are made. Therefore, we won't be making decisions at this initial meeting. You can relax and think out loud.

Notice how the above statements tie the multi-meeting format to the interests of the people. They assure people that the process has been designed for efficiency, provide a brief, real-life object lesson on the value of time investment, and frame the fact that no decision will be taken at the first meeting as an opportunity to relax and think out loud.

At the information-gathering meeting, let people know what to expect going forward. For example, "After today's meeting, our team will summarize issues and provide them to everyone before the follow up meeting in two weeks. At the second meeting, we will allow for further comments and begin discussing possible solutions. At the end of the second meeting, we'll assess together whether we have enough information and a strong enough consensus to propose a specific plan."

People are less likely to feel dissatisfied at the end of the meeting if a realistic goal was set at the beginning.

In the example, the congregation had its own cautionary tale to bring home the ultimate savings of investing time up front—last year's meeting on religious education. If you have no such tale, you can find others in *Facilitator's Guide to Participatory Decision-Making.*[43]

A few more tips on process timing:

- Beware of apparent agreements that seem to come too easily for the level of difficulty of the issue. Someone makes a suggestion. Two or three people reply, "Yeah," or nod, and the rest remain silent. Don't assume silence means consent. The silent majority may have reservations they have not mentioned. Some have not had time to get their minds around what's bothering them. Others might not feel comfortable expressing their concerns, especially if an authority figure made the suggestion. Take time to let these people think. Find ways, such as those described later in this chapter, to make them feel safe and to draw them out.

- After asking a question or introducing a topic for discussion, a good facilitator will allow ten to fifteen seconds of silent think time. When you're the one who asked the question, this seems much longer than it does to those who are considering the question. Don't push for answers. Relax and count off the seconds in your head, *one Mississippi, two Mississippi...* Face the group, but don't fix your eyes on any one person. Sometimes one member of the group feels particularly uncomfortable with these silences and rushes into the breach with frequent comments. Accept his comment graciously then encourage others by saying something like, "Can we hear from someone who hasn't spoken in awhile?"

  o Trying to cut the wordy member short can offend him and often takes more time than briefly acknowledging his point. Your call for others' input may actually relieve him from the pressure he's putting on himself to keep things moving at what seems, to him, like a normal pace.

  o Calling on a shy or reticent member by name puts her on the spot. Instead, make a general request for comments from additional attendees.

---

43 Sam Kaner et al (Jossey-Bass, 2007).

Drawing Out Interests in Group Meetings

The biggest challenge to healthy, sustainable agreements in larger groups is reluctance to candidly express interests, especially feeling interests. The larger the group, the more reticence prevails.

Of the many techniques in *Facilitator's Guide*, I find two particularly useful in drawing out the interests of those attending a meeting of an entire congregation or a large board, committee, or other sub-group.

Pause to Reflect and Write

A meeting facilitator or chair can help attendees get clear on their thoughts and feelings by asking them to spend a few minutes of meeting time writing, for their own eyes, about a relevant question. This technique also allows a large number of people to explore their interests without taking an inordinate amount of time, and it often boosts their confidence in expressing themselves when the meeting returns to open discussion.

The leader should specify the topic people are being asked to write about and how many minutes the group will spend on this segment of the meeting. Emphasize the fact that no one will be required to read aloud or turn in what they have written.

Here are a few examples of topics or questions that might be used for a writing segment of the music director meeting (use only one for a given writing segment of the meeting):

- What does everyone need to know to make a good decision?
- What will the way we allocate funds say about us as a congregation?
- What would losing our full-time music director mean to me?
- What would increased funding for the outreach ministries mean to me?
- How might our stated congregational goals help us decide this matter?

The leader can plan some questions in advance of the meeting. He can also suggest a writing segment anytime the group seems stuck or reticent or if there is unexplained tension in the room, crafting an appropriate question on the spot.

After writing, allow time for voluntary discussion of the question or issue. Thank those who volunteer and mirror their comments: paraphrase the repetitive; rephrase the unclear; reframe the tactless or inflammatory. After all volunteers have been heard, ask, "Would anyone we have not heard from like to speak?" Wait ten to fifteen seconds in silence before moving on.

Sometimes the meeting process itself, a process in which people were often encouraged, but never pressured, to express themselves, helps to discourage subsequent complaints from those who chose not to share.

When facilitating a meeting, I also like to use writing as a prelude to a more vocal activity, such as a structured brainstorm.

Breakouts

A more active way to help meeting attendees collect their thoughts and feel heard is to break them into pairs or small groups to discuss a relevant question such as those listed in the preceding section. Even the person whose knees quake at the thought of speaking before a group may find it hard to remain silent in the presence of only one individual who patiently waits for his input on an assigned topic or question.

After the breakout, the leader should direct the whole group into either an open discussion of their reflections or another activity, such as listing the interests served by the two programs (music and outreach, respectively) on a chart.

In addition to drawing people out, breakouts engage many attendees in a relatively small amount of time. They also maintain or recharge group energy.

Safety

As mentioned, it's unwise to assume that silence means consent. This error can be exacerbated by stating a proposal then asking, "Any objections?" That question tends to stifle, rather than encourage, comments, particularly when asked by an authority figure. When few people participate in discussion of an important topic, the others either haven't formed an opinion, or they don't feel safe expressing their opinions. The thing *not* to do at such a point is call for a vote

If reticence seems to be the problem, this is a good time for a private writing or breakout segment of the meeting, focused on a question such as:

- What isn't being said?
- What would it take for me to feel safe expressing my opinion?
- What would it take for others to feel safe expressing their opinions?

Diverse and Unrecognized Safety Concerns

Just as people resist the need for contingency plans, they sometimes resist the notion that some people don't feel safe expressing themselves freely in the group. Leaders may resist this notion all the more. They may even resent and misjudge reticent group members as unjustifiably anxious, uncooperative, or motivated by ill will or hidden agendas.

Some leaders are even naïve enough to believe that everyone will feel safe if they say something like: "I want everyone to feel safe expressing themselves during this meeting," or "To set a safe atmosphere for open exchange of all ideas, can we agree that nothing said now leaves this room?" or "Grounded in love and fellowship, we open our hearts and minds to free expression of all concerns."

Such preludes are no cure-alls for reticence. Nor should the leader take the existence of reticence personally. Concerns about speaking candidly, some legitimate, others not, can arise from many different circumstances, and they aren't all about the leaders or the character of the group. Consider just a few examples:

- The person is so shy, he never feels really safe expressing himself.
- He sees a pious hypocrite in the group. She makes a great impression on the leadership, but he has known her to insidiously injure those who disagree with her, behind the leaders' backs.
- He can't speak up because of possible legal ramifications.
- He has tried airing his present opinion to one or more other group members in the past, with disastrous results.

We can't always tell who's reluctant to speak candidly and when.
- Choir alto Alma may say nothing during the music director meeting because Sophie soprano is doing a fine job of expressing what Alma thinks.

- Baritone wannabe Barry may support a suggestion that the choir hold auditions open to any who wish to attend and listen in. He may even express an interest that would be addressed by open auditions, such as helping people who are trying to decide whether or not to audition. Because Barry spoke up, others at the meeting assume he felt safe and got all his interests out on the table. They may have no way of knowing that Barry didn't feel safe stating an even more important interest—he doesn't trust Kayla's objectivity.

- Ted the tenor comes across as very confident and assertive in general. Thus, no one dreams that he failed to air his views on the audition issue because it was especially touchy for him. He had a traumatic experience at an open audition as a child, and didn't want to relive it.

So don't try to guess whether people feel safe. Make a practice of using the techniques recommended in this chapter. They enhance safety. If everyone already feels safe to begin with, these measures do no harm, and they have other advantages such as stimulating thinking.

Then, even when you've taken all these measures, don't assume everyone was candid (sometimes people have legitimate reasons not to tell all), and don't judge those who weren't.

Gradient Voting

Yes-or-no votes mislead us because "yes" and "no" mean different things to different people under different circumstances. "No" can mean "Ho-hum. This idea isn't bad, it just isn't good enough," "I disagree," or "I refuse to participate in this hair-brained plan."

If, in a committee of ten, there are seven "yes" votes, and three "no" votes, that may seem like a fairly strong majority. But if only one of the "yes" votes means "I really like the idea," three mean "No objection," and three mean "I don't really like the idea, but I don't want to make an issue of it," there is not enough enthusiasm to sustain the decision.

Instead, specify five to seven voting choices such as:

- I love the idea
- Not perfect, but basically a good plan

- No opinion
- I don't agree, but will do my part if others like the idea
- I don't want to obstruct the group, but don't ask me to participate
- Strongly object

Lay out a separate line or column for each choice and tabulate the votes using tick marks. If you don't have a strong majority of ticks for the first two voting categories, there's not enough enthusiasm to carry out the plan. Go back and further develop your Solution Smorgasbord.

Gradient voting is also an excellent vehicle for weeding out those lukewarm compromises that offend no one, but excite no one.

Myths and Realities of Group Decision Dynamics

In *Facilitator's Guide*, the authors devote the entire first chapter to how groups actually make good decisions, decisions that work out in practice. I would add that these are the kinds of decisions that build bridges on which people come as close as possible to unanimous consensus. Rather than merely settling for a mediocre compromise that minimizes objections, they create an optimum plan that positively engages and energizes their members. Few people appreciate the process by which such decisions are reached, especially with difficult issues.

Examples of Decision Phases

People who start out with different views of a situation tend to assume that, if they do the dialogue "right," these views will move closer and closer until consensus somehow materializes. This only happens when a good solution is fairly obvious, in other words, in low stakes situations where no particular skill or creativity is needed to reach an acceptable decision. The sexton needs a new ladder. He found one for a good price and needs the grounds committee to approve the purchase.

In other words, we can reach good decisions on such issues without engaging in any significant process. Decision dynamics only come into play when a good solution is not obvious. Then, the process moves through several predictable phases.

Phase I: Diverging but Conventional Ideas

Surprisingly to many, *views actually tend to diverge, rather than converge, early in a discussion.* The walkway from the sanctuary to the classroom building is cracked and uneven. The sexton advises doing something about it before someone trips and gets hurt. He suggests removing the old concrete, leveling the path, then either repaving it with concrete or laying steppingstones.

The committee begins to discuss the relative merits of concrete versus steppingstones. Concrete would provide a smoother path, and would be less expensive, at least at first. But if we have another drought, and the underlying ground shifts again, the concrete will crack once more. But if steppingstones shift, we can more easily remove them, smooth the path, and re-use the same stones, saving money over time.

Then Arnie mentions that gravel might be better. Betty thinks gravel presents a fall risk, but favors wood chips. Chet points out how often a mulched path must be serviced. "What about some of that new stuff they use around pools?" asks Diane. Eloise says steppingstones are prettiest. Frank says you have to keep after the grass and weeds that grow up between steppingstones. Gabriella thought we had moved on from steppingstones; she can't follow this disjointed conversation. Harold knows either concrete or steppingstones would work fine and wishes they'd all stop wasting time.

Their instincts tell them that things are spinning out of control because they're now considering five options instead of two. *Can't we stick to the point? they think (or say), but everyone has a different idea of what "the point" is.* They may wish to pull others back on track, or to say, "It's six of one and a half-dozen of the other. Let's just pick something (or delegate someone to decide and handle it) and move on."

But if they buck this instinct and continue discussing the various conventional materials, they eventually reach a decision. It's a good decision precisely because they considered many options.

It's also a good decision because all committee members were allowed to air their different ideas and to think in the ways their respective personalities dictated. Even though Gabriella found others' thinking style disorganized, and Diane thought Gabriella rigid and unimaginative, they honored the diversity of styles and allowed things to play out. All members came to a decision in the way their respective minds needed to work. Diane waited for Gabriella to "catch up." Gabriella took note of disjointed remarks even though she couldn't yet see where they were leading. Consequently, all bought into the final decision.

Honoring this kind of diversity sometimes takes a little more time, but that's more efficient than making a decision that fails to address their interests well. How much time will they spend if the walkway needs replacing again a year later? How much goodwill do they lose if, when that happens, some members say, "I knew it. If only you had listened to me"?

Although views initially diverged, the choice of walkway could be resolved quite well by choosing from among various conventional materials. For this reason, the conversation was boring. No particularly creative thinking was required. Sometimes boring is okay. Trying to make ordinary decisions fun by adding activities, such as dot charts or structured brainstorms, really does waste time.

Phase II: Diverging Creative Ideas

When conventional wisdom will not serve, and creativity is needed, views continue to diverge even further. *People begin to toss out wild ideas* because none of the conventional approaches adequately address their interests. *They become playful*. The case of music director Kayla could produce such tongue-in-cheek statements as:

> We could pick a director of the week. No one would serve more than one week every few years, so no need to pay anybody.

> When it's my son's turn, he'll have a rap service.

> Better than my service. I'm tone deaf.

> Well, hey, if we have the worst music in town, and we drive all our people over to Fourth Street Church, maybe they would just split their income with us. We could spend all of ours on outreach ministries and forget about worship services.

Hey, this isn't boring, it's fun, people think. So they instinctively expect the fun to lead directly to that breakthrough solution. And, in fact, some progress in that direction might ensue:

> Seriously, perhaps we could do more outreach with less money if we joined forces with another congregation.

> But we should still consider whether we are spending too much on our music program. If we can cut costs there, we'd have even more to spend on outreach, whether we join forces with another congregation or not.

> We could do even more outreach if we fired our ministers and merged with Fourth Street Church. How far are we willing to take this? Dismissing Kayla is just as unkind and irresponsible as dismissing our ministers would be.

Playfulness ends. The fur begins to fly. People may panic unless they've been educated to the fact that they are moving into another natural step in the process of making a difficult decision.

Phase III: Hard Work that Pays Off

Playful divergence can be a sign that the matter will be difficult to resolve. *After the fun,* people still can't agree. ***They may become impatient and snappish.*** They feel they're at an impasse. While some dig in their heels, many others want to give up—either give up the effort, or give in to something they don't really agree with—just to relieve the discomfort of what *Facilitator's Guide* calls "the groan zone." Still others are tempted to call for an up or down vote, even though the majority is too small or too unenthusiastic to sustain the decision.

Their instincts say, "This is hopeless," when in reality, they are standing on the threshold of a breakthrough if only they stay the course. The kind of creativity that comes from deep mutual understanding of interests will be required. The work needed to acquire that understanding is challenging, but its rewards are spectacular.

Work is needed because people either have not adequately aired their own interests and/or don't yet fully appreciate the interests of others. It is challenging because, the deeper or more important the interest a person has been suppressing, the greater the chance that, when he finally reveals it, he blurts it out in a tactless manner. Conversely, the same depth of feeling squelches one's tolerance of others' tentative or clumsy efforts to get their interests out on top of the table. And even if everyone speaks clearly and tactfully, this phase is challenging because working to understand perspectives we don't agree with taxes our patience and discipline, our compassion, calmness and curiosity. We work hard to resist being sucked into a spiral of wrong making.

No wonder so many groups make premature decisions, decisions that don't work out in practice, in order to avoid this difficult phase of the process. Members of congregations are especially prone to such avoidance and its unfortunate results. Laboring under the delusion that "good" people simply don't engage in unpleasant discussions, some clam up, some walk out, some give in, and some resent and harshly judge those who have the courage to say things that are difficult, but necessary, to hear.

What makes a situation tricky enough to warrant a trip through this difficult phase? Many factors can play a part.

- Large numbers of people, and their respective interests
- High emotional content, as in the dispute over the music director
- Situations where it's hard to see past an either-or point of view— either make everyone pay for any damage they cause or forgive all accidental damage
- High stakes. In the music director controversy, both Kayla's job and funding of outreach ministries are at stake
- Multiple and/or complex issues, as is often the case in legal matters

At the end of day, however, *you know that an issue needs the Kaner "Groan Zone"* when you find yourself in that zone—when no conventional approach satisfies a strong majority, when even playful creativity fails, when people begin to get testy, and most importantly, *when you feel like you're at an impasse.*

The best thing a neutral facilitator can do to support people faced with a tricky decision is *help them to understand that this is a natural and necessary part of the process and to encourage them to keep working through that phase.* But you don't have to be a professional facilitator, or even the group leader, to explain the dynamic and encourage the group to stay the course. Any member of the group who understands what's happening can speak up.

This works best if, in the absence of a neutral facilitator, the person who explains the dynamic and encourages the others is as close to neutrality as possible, one who has the least personal interest in the outcome and is least emotionally invested in the issue. In the music director situation, this might be someone who is not good friends with Kayla, who is not in the choir and has no relatives in the choir. He doesn't feel strongly about how much, or what kind of, music and outreach programs they have, as long as there is music and outreach.

This nearly neutral person does, however, hold a strong interest in the integrity and health of the congregation and the relationships between its members. Most importantly, he understands that a "good relationship" does not mean avoiding difficult discussions. Rather, a good relationship is one in which people feel empowered to engage in those discussions.

Any such person(s) present might be the only one who can muster the calmness and discipline to craft incisive open questions, to paraphrase the statements of the more invested individuals so as to help them gain mutual understanding, to reframe inflammatory remarks so that they neither escalate nor get dismissed because of the manner in which they were stated, to rephrase rambling or confusing statements, to encourage pauses and breaks while also insisting on resuming talks after those breaks, etc.

For Kayla's congregation, a successful Phase III would mean that members who have felt they or their children were slighted by Kayla acknowledge those feelings, at least to themselves and possibly to all. Likewise, Kayla's friends, those whom she recruited into the church and choir, soloists and parents of soloists, acknowledge the interests those circumstances create.

Kayla herself may have the strongest feelings of all, and she certainly has the biggest financial and professional interest in the outcome. Yet she might have the most difficulty airing her interests. Many people, in her position, would feel that everyone must know how wrong making this controversy feels to her. Everyone must know it would be a hardship to lose one's position.

She's hurt and humiliated by the suggestion that she be fired, so the prospect of talking about that hurt only looks like further humiliation. She might well assume that she could never again be happy in a congregation where some members have "attacked" her. She might decide to resign and try to move on without trying to participate in a resolution.

But when everyone hangs in till they all fully appreciate one another's interests—even though they may not agree with them, when they under-stand the strength of others' feelings, and when they have a working knowl-edge of the impact various options would have on others, they are most likely to find a mutually acceptable, or even optimal, solution.

Phase IV: Coming to Consensus

Once people gain deep mutual understanding, they are equipped for the kind of decision that will stand the test of time. A true consensus then results, *often more quickly than we expect.* Even if a vote must be taken, that vote will be heavily weighted toward the "love it" end of the voting gradient.

Kayla's congregation might generate a Solution Smorgasbord including such items as:

- "Behind-a-screen" auditions for soloists judged by a panel of people with no personal interest in the choir, perhaps outsiders to the congregation
- Open auditions anyone can attend and observe
- Musical performances incorporated into outreach ministries
- A volunteer takes over the children's choir; Kayla continues choosing music for services and working with the adult choir; relieved from her children's choir duties, Kayla takes on other church administration functions without cut in working hours or pay
- Join forces with Fourth Street Church on some outreach programs
- Join forces with Fourth Street Church on music, for example: joint choir that performs at each church on alternate weekends; congregation without choir on a given weekend has piano music with congregational singing
- Outreach programs that generate income, such as educational programs, concerts, inspirational plays or movies

- Outreach ministry, such as prison ministry, that could form the basis for a research grant to a cooperating local university
- Two separate choirs: the first, by audition and directed by Kayla, performs on Sunday mornings; the second, open to all and member directed, performs at informal evening services on Wednesday or Saturday evenings
- A healing service to help everyone strengthen bonds and relationships

Any number of final agreements might be developed by picking and choosing from this list, embellishing and modifying the points.

Notice that many of the items on the above Smorgasbord menu address interests in objectivity in the selection of choir members and/or soloists and interests in fairness and appreciation toward Kayla. These matters previously fell into the category of stealth interests. They had not been discussed openly. Other reasons had been given in support of people's positions: "If we get rid of the music director, we can do more outreach"; "Our music program draws visitors and new members." These statements may be true, but they were not the real interests driving some people's positions.

By taking the time to work through the Kaner Groan Zone, this group uncovered all the real driving interests so they could develop a Smorgasbord menu with potential to inspire a sustainable decision. If only the original arguments for and against the music director had been addressed, those with interests in objectivity in choir and solo selections and those with interests in decent treatment of Kayla would not have been satisfied, and their interests would have continued to spawn other problems.

One caveat about this consensus phase of the process: As people move quickly to agreement on a basic plan, they feel relieved and proud of a creative result that satisfies the interests of two factions that formerly seemed at an impasse. This *relief, pride and the quick pace can cause a group to overlook details* needed to flesh out the basic points of agreement into an efficient, fully workable plan. This is the time for the quick and creative to honor the diverse thinking styles of the reflective forward planners, of the introverts whose circuits are so overloaded that they need time to unpack what happened at the meetings, and of the detail-oriented implementers. A draft plan might be laid out at this phase, but finalizing that plan should be left to a future meeting so that it may incorporate the best thinking of everyone involved.

In achieving such decisions, people see and feel the benefits of working through Phase III in a way that no words on a page can convey. They become willing to take on that work again whenever difficult issues arise.

Our next, and final, chapter shifts from the hardest situations to the easiest. You'll see the beauty of our consensus system at its best.

Key Points from Chapter 15

- Challenges increase with the size of the group seeking consensus
- Prepare the group to invest time at the front end
  - o Tie the investment in the process to their interests
  - o Set realistic goals from the outset
- Plan ways to draw out interests during group meetings
  - o Allow meeting time for private writing on a relevant question
  - o Break out into pairs or small groups to discuss a relevant question
- Make the meeting environment as safe as possible
  - o But never assume everyone has spoken candidly
  - o And don't judge those who may have held back
- Replace yes-or-no votes with gradients of enthusiasm
- Educate attendees to the realities of sustainable group decision process
  - o Expect initial divergence
  - o What seems like an impasse is the threshold of creative thinking; encourage them to keep working
  - o After an apparent consensus, take time to flush out bugs and flesh out details

PART V: WHERE IT ALL COMES TOGETHER

CHAPTER 16
PULLING THINGS TOGETHER AND
MOVING FORWARD

Dreamers and doers,
Mystics and prophets,
Wonderfully we gather together:
Each of us unique,
All of us together.

- Rev. Bruce Southworth, adapted

Throughout this book, we've seen a number of sample dialogues in which one person consciously used consensus skills and the other did not. Now let's see how easily things can work out when both consciously use the skills.

The Beauty of Mutual Skill

We begin with a simple example.

Dialogue 16: Mike and Laurel both use the skills

Dialogue:	Characters' Views:
M: Hi, Laurel. Got a minute?	
L: Sure.	
M: I heard you broke a window a few weeks ago.	Introduces the issue without pre-judging or making Laurel wrong.
L: That's right.	
M: I was wondering what approach the church took about the cost of repair.	Uses an open question to get his facts straight before discussing his interest.

L: It happened while babysitting. I told Abby [chair of the Child Care Committee] I was willing to pay for the window. She said she'd check it out. Never heard anything more. Why do you ask?

Laurel doesn't get defensive. She answers the question candidly. Then, sensing Mike has something on his mind, she asks the first magic question, "Why?" to encourage him to discuss his interests.

M: Well, I accidentally backed over a sign a few weeks ago. They were Johnny-on-the-Spot to send me a bill. So I guess I have a feeling interest about this—concerning consistency.

Since they both know the skill set and vocabulary, he can efficiently get to the point using the term, "feeling interest," that lets Laurel know he wants consensus, not argument.

L: You want everyone treated fairly, right?

Paraphrases and checks for accuracy. Also takes a manageable step toward discussing a mutual interest in fairness before judging what is fair in their specific cases.

M: Yes.

L: I want that too. I can think of several possible reasons why I haven't heard. Maybe they forgot or were busy with other things. Or it might be the way my accident happened.

Validates Mike by confirming mutual interest in fairness. She knows Mike knows "reasons why" relate to the church leadership's interests. Then she takes a step toward airing other interests revolving around her accident circumstances.

M:	How was that?	Open question encourages elaboration.
L:	I saw a little girl running with a sharp pair of scissors. When I rushed to grab her, I accidentally knocked a big desk chair against the window.	Explains her interests at the time of the accident.
M:	Are you thinking maybe they forgave the accident because you were doing volunteer work for the church when it happened?	Uses a closed question to see whether he understands how she thinks the circumstances of her accident relate to the decision about payment.
L:	That's possible, too. My own idea was that Abby knew I broke the window while preventing a worse accident—the child getting hurt.	Mike's closed question does it's job. Laurel corrects him by giving more detail on her original train of thought, after first validating his idea.
M:	So you're saying they considered your actions reasonable under the circumstances, right?	Again, Mike paraphrases and seeks confirmation.
L:	Yes, like I did what I had to do. But I'm speculating. Who sent you the bill for the sign?	
M:	Wendy	

L: Why don't we speak to Wendy together. All three of us are interested in fairness.

         Laurel suggests the next step forward in the context of a three-way mutual interest.

M: OK.

Doubts?

That last dialogue was almost incredibly short and sweet, wasn't it? An individual who has not yet assimilated consensus skills, much less had the opportunity to use them with an equally skilled partner, might have doubts about it. Those doubts range across a wide spectrum.

"Isn't This Only Natural?"

With hindsight, many readers may find the above dialogue natural and simple. We might think, *That's just the way any two sensible people would have this conversation.* If you had read it in Chapter 1, you might have thought, *I would have spoken just that way. Who needs skill to do this?* Yet earlier examples with a less pleasant Mike also seemed realistic, perhaps more so. Here, a big part of each person's ease arose from the other person's use of consensus skills. When both practice their skills, the ease of reaching a mutually beneficial decision increases exponentially.

"Is This Really Plausible?"

Other readers, at first blush, may consider the last dialogue a little too pat, not very likely to occur in real life. Remember, however, that we are assuming that both Mike and Laurel did more than just read about the skills. They bought into the skills, assimilated them through practice, and remembered to use them in this conversation.

I've seen it over and over again in my students and clients, when two people develop consensus skills and both use them in a challenging conversation, they are often astounded at how quickly and easily they reach agreement, and at the satisfying nature of that agreement.

But even if you doubt that some of the members of your congregation can or will really assimilate these skills, you've seen in the foregoing chapters how your using them can help you both, even if the person you're talking to doesn't know them at all.

So assimilate and use them yourself, and prepare to be pleasantly surprised, regardless of the skill level of others.

"Will We Feel Like We're Manipulating Each Other?"

Still others may worry that people who know the skills, and recognize when we're using them, might feel manipulated. Mike might have wondered, *If I ask Laurel the open question, "What approach did they take in the case of your accident?" will she know I'm trying to persuade her of something? If so, will she resist or resent me?*

But if Laurel understands the skill set, she knows that Mike has learned the best way to get what he wants is to learn about her interests and try to address them. The skills only work for him when he makes them work for her. Would a skilled Laurel prefer that Mike simply demand what he wants without regard to her interests? Would she prefer that he make assumptions about her ideas rather than asking the open question? Would she like him to argue with her and make her wrong? Not if she understands these skills.

Speaking for myself, if everyone I had to deal with used the skills I teach, I'd think life was easy as pie and just as sweet.

"Will Common Vocabulary Put People Off?"

What about using buzz words and phrases like "feeling interest" or "Magic Questions"? If Mike and Laurel use such terms with a third party who has not had their training, that person might feel left out. But this need not be a problem.

If Mike and Laurel are working with Holly, who has not had their skills training, they don't need to use buzz words. They can proceed as in preceding chapters, where there was always one party to a dialogue who did not know the skills.

Or they can offer to share with Holly: "I'd like to show you something we learned. It's called a Solution Smorgasbord. Here's how it works."

"What If I Can't Do It All?"

The skill demonstrated in the last dialogue may come easily, even naturally, to some people, some of the time. Many others find it more challenging, especially when confronted by that less pleasant Mike. But anyone can improve their individual skill level with knowledge, training and practice. Those who are naturally gifted can codify what has worked for them before, so that they replicate past successes more often and more easily. They can also add additional refinements to their skill set. Those who find such conversations more challenging can practice and assimilate the skills one manageable step at a time.

Don't worry if you find some of the skills more difficult than others. In the vast majority of cases, using any of the skills will serve you better than using none at all. If, for example, you are great at interest talk, but forget to paraphrase, you are better off than if you used no consensus practices whatsoever. If you forget and ask a closed question when an open question would have been preferable, you are better off than if you only stated your own perspective, but never asked questions at all. You'll find, however, that if you gradually assimilate the entire system, you'll build consensus even easier, faster and better.

A More Challenging Example

Notice how short the above dialogue is, compared to those in preceding chapters. The time spent learning consensus skills pays off handsomely in efficiency as well as effectiveness

Now let's look at another, more challenging, example, once again with both parties consciously using their consensus skills, albeit imperfectly.

Dialogue 17: Yolanda and Fran both use the skills

Dialogue:	Characters' Views:
Y: Fran, do you have time for a cup of coffee with me?	Yolanda uses the brakes. Sitting down and taking some time over this conversation will pay off in the long run.

F: Sure.

Y: How is your work on the fundraiser coming along?

Neutral open question introduces the general topic Yolanda wants to discuss. The answer may tell her something useful about Fran's interests regarding the fundraiser.

F: I've discovered some good speaker candidates. Now the hardest part—getting all the volunteers signed up and organized.

Now Yolanda knows that Fran is enthusiastic about potential speaker(s), so her feeling interests might make her sensitive on this subject.

Y: I'd like to hear about those speaker candidates and why they excite you.

Implied open question. Yolanda needs to know more about Fran's interests before deciding how to introduce her own concern.

F: One is a professor of religious studies on what early followers of Jesus actually did in their congregations. It's based on surprises in recently-discovered Roman documents. Another is a head docent from the Natural History Museum who can show some fascinating slides.

Y:	What if we could have the fundraiser at the Museum and include a tour?	Ties one of Fran's interests, the docent, to her own interest in a more active program.
F:	What attracts you to that idea?	Fran envisions problems with a tour. She asks "Why?" (in different words). If she can identify some underlying interests, she might be able to address them without taking on the problems of a museum tour.
Y:	I'm interested in making sure the program engages the young adults. We can't always afford to spend a lot at the auction. The program is the more likely draw for us, but sometimes we find it challenging to sit and listen for an hour or more.	Discusses underlying interests rather than suggesting additional solutions too quickly.
F:	I see. (Takes a sip of coffee.) So your suggestion about touring a museum hall is to get people up and moving, right?	Although Yolanda has not used the word "boring," Fran gets the idea and feels a little hurt. She gives herself a break to recover by sipping coffee, then paraphrasing and confirming Yolanda's last comment.
Y:	Right.	

F: I think they'd charge a lot to let us have the whole fund-raiser at the museum, and we'd lose the opportunity to show off our church to visitors. Plus we'd need to have multiple tours, or make it self-guided, which further complicates the planning and execution.

Fran tells some of her concerns (interests) about Yolanda's suggestion.

Y: It's only one idea. Why don't we try to think of several ideas, then go back and evaluate them?

Leads Fran toward the idea of suspending judgment while creating a Solution Smorgasbord.

F: Give me a minute to think.

Fran feels offended. It seems Yolanda presumes "we" are going to decide on Fran's program. Yolanda's trying to dive in and re-think all Fran's hard work. Fran wants to apply her brakes so she doesn't blurt out something ill-considered. She simply asks for a break.

Y: Sure.

Understanding the need for breaks after new, and possibly unsettling, ideas are introduced, Yolanda encourages Fran.

F: I share your interest in engaging the younger adults. I also want to be sure we hang on to the middle-aged and older people who prefer a more sedentary program.

Fran validates a shared interest before adding an interest of her own that might not be served by some types of programs that Yolanda would like.

Y: What, if anything, can I do to help at this point?

A variation on "What would help?" Yolanda senses that her suggestions might have seemed officious. She implicitly offers to either back off and leave Fran to consider the younger and older members' respective programming interests, or to continue trying to help.

F: I'd like to get more information before answering that.

Y: Sure.

F: How many people do you think would like more activity?

Open question.

Y: There are about six of us twenty-somethings who attend services regularly. I don't know how many share my preference, nor how many young visitors an active program might attract.

F: And, if I've got this straight, you six would like to feel you're contributing something, but the auction items are generally too pricey, correct?

Paraphrases and seeks confirmation.

Y: Yes.

F: OK. So a start on a Solution Smorgasbord includes my two potential speakers, and a museum tour. I'd like to add some more ideas. I could easily use six kitchen and serving volunteers; that would be a way your friends could contribute. I also think that younger adults can offer fixed-price auction items, like game nights in their homes. Those are inexpensive to host because you don't have to put on a big meal, and they're also inexpensive to buy.

Uses their common consensus vocabulary. Suggests ways to address Yolanda's interests consistent with the interests of older people.

Y: Those are interesting ideas. What would you like from me at this point?

Another "What would help?"

F:	I want to speak to the museum docent. Maybe she can bring actual show-and-tell objects here. People could walk around and view, or maybe even handle, them. I also want to speak with some other people about their program preferences. Once I have more information, we can talk again about how you might help.	Fran has now settled down enough that she wants to keep the door open to Yolanda's help. Asks for a longer break to work on a mutually beneficial solution.
Y:	Thanks, Fran.	Shows appreciation.

In this dialogue, neither woman used the consensus skills perfectly. *There is no perfect dialogue*; one can always look back and see things they could have done even better. *The point is that this mutually-skilled dialogue went better and faster* than it would have if only one of them had used their skills, and much better than if neither had used them.

Fran was still offended, despite Yolanda's best efforts. If Yolanda had a transcript of this conversation, she could improve on some of her statements and questions. But her skill use minimized the offense, so Fran remained engaged in working toward consensus.

Fran may have been a little too fast to point out problems with Yolanda's suggestion of holding the event at a museum, and a little slow to welcome the idea of Yolanda's contributions to a Solution Smorgasbord. She, too, could look back and see room for improvement. But she expressed her concerns about Yolanda's suggestion in the form of interest talk, rather than a yes-or-no judgment, so Yolanda remained engaged in working toward consensus.

Though each woman could look back and see room for improvement, this was an excellent conversation. By calmly persisting in practicing their skills as well as they could, even when they sensed those less-than-perfect moments, they developed mutual interests and laid the groundwork for future cooperation on a better fundraiser. They built a bridge between them, rather than burning one.

From Knowledge to Skill

How did Mike, Laurel, Yolanda and Fran achieve this level of skill? They did it through knowledge, training and practice. They did it with compassion, with calmness and with curiosity. They persevered, and the more they learned, the more their compassion, calmness and curiosity grew, spiraling upward.

Occasionally, I meet someone who has read one of the books I've referred to in previous chapters, usually *Getting to Yes* or one of Dr. Tannen's works on inter-gender communication. Invariably, the person will remember that they thought the book was good. But they only retained one or two, maybe three, points, and haven't assimilated even those few points into their lives.

My hope for this book is that it inspires people to actually acquire and use a full complement of consensus skills. Congregations do good work. They can do it better and faster with consensus skills. They can prevent disagreements from impeding, or even arresting, their progress. Beyond their own organizations, they can build bridges with those of other faiths at a time when increasing religious polarization too often erects barriers. They can use consensus skills to make this world a better place. Which brings us back to our original analogy—learning to drive a car. You can't acquire skill without practice.

Theoretically, some of us could figure out how to drive a car, and become skilled at doing so, given a driving book, a practice car (or maybe several cars in case we wrecked the first one or two), and a safe place to practice (such as an unused airport with empty tarmacs and taxiways). For a few people—naturally physically adept and mechanically apt—the process might even be fairly easy. Most of us, however, would experience a long, slow, discouraging ordeal. Driving lessons could save a lot of time, effort, and maybe a few of those expendable practice cars. But we could learn the basics of driving on our own if we had the perseverance to stick with it.

However, we couldn't learn to drive if we tried to practice the entire skill set at once. Imagine the first time you get into the driver's seat. You've never even started a car. Now you must not only start the car, you must merge onto a freeway, stay within lanes, at fifty-five miles per hour, signal for all your lane changes, make some quick stops, and oh, by the way, it's dark and sleeting.

Well-designed training starts with the most basic skills, gives the trainee opportunities to practice the basics without distraction by more advanced skill requirements, and then adds more skills when the trainee is ready. Such training also builds in just enough challenge plus enough early success and fun to inspire the perseverance that leads to true proficiency.

When you begin to practice consensus skills, whether or not this book leads you to a training course, *begin with one skill at a time and practice each skill first in low stakes situations*. You need not wait for these situations to arise in your congregational life. Consensus skills apply in every setting.

Let's say you begin by getting comfortable with airing the interests behind your requests of others. Start with stating an interest behind a request that is likely to be granted, "I had spicy food for lunch. May I have a drink of water?" Do this in various low-stakes situations until you feel comfortable.

Then build up to a relatively small request that someone might resist. Your wife is watching her favorite TV show. She has the volume up high and it's aggravating your headache. You add a skill, asking about her interest, "Why is the volume so high?" She replies, "I'm having a hard time following that character's accent." Now you state your interest and offer two options for addressing your interest as well as hers. "My head is splitting. Would you mind watching in another room or recording the show for later?"

You can practice some skills even when you don't want a thing from the other person. You can practice paraphrasing and seeking confirmation, for example, or asking open questions, over a friendly meal. However you go about it, *low stakes practice is essential to your ability to call up your consensus skills under the stress of strong resistance to something that is very important to you*.

Lenses Revisited

Sometimes a high skill level can make a person impatient with others. In Dialogue 17, Yolanda might have thought, *Fran should know better than to shoot down my idea of a museum tour. She should get into Solution Smorgasbord mode.* But Yolanda's compassion for others' imperfections and her sense of communication diversity stood her in good stead. The suspended judgment of a Smorgasbord process comes easier to some personality types. Conversely, a trouble-spotting frame of mind comes easier to others. Yolanda recognized that both types of thinking are important to a good final decision. Wisely, she continued to use her skills (including avoidance of wrong making) even if she thought Fran had forgotten her skills.

Fran, in her turn, might have thought it presumptuous of Yolanda to suggest changes to her plans. *Yolanda should have explored my interests and made sure I welcomed suggestions before diving in. She should have known that her approach would make me feel made wrong.* But Fran, too, continued to use her own consensus skills even when she thought Yolanda had forgotten hers.

Anyone can intuitively respond to a suggestion by pointing out its disadvantages, as Fran did. Yolanda saw this as poor timing because she thought they were, or should have been, in a Solution Smorgasbord frame of mind at that point. In other words, her assessment, while inspired by her consensus skills, was subjective. Anyone can exuberantly blurt out a suggestion, as Yolanda did. Fran saw this as poor timing because she knew she had feeling interests Yolanda hadn't recognized. Her assessment, too, was subjective.

Temperamental, cultural and gender differences in communication style can exaggerate these subjective judgments, and at the same time, can make them seem objective to the judger. Leaders and congregants alike can be quite liberal minded when it comes to religious dogma, yet amazingly dogmatic when it comes to their concepts of "the right way" to deal with one another.

The person who naturally speaks bluntly, and finds subtlety more challenging, may be quick to declare that we should be "direct" and equally quick to pin the label "manipulator" on the one who indirectly leads the conversation to a desired point without overtly stating her own opinion. Yet, her indirect approach avoids wrong making and often works better, for both parties to a conversation, as shown by many of the above sample dialogues, such as Dialogue 6.

Conversely, it is possible for a particularly sensitive person, or one who has been raised (as many women are) to believe that she should "be nice" and "not make waves" to label clear, direct expression of interests as "self-centered," "pushy," or even "aggressive." Yet, we've seen that airing our interests helps us build consensus.

We all have our temperamental, cultural and gender prejudices about polite, respectful speech. I encourage people, rather than assuming ill will, to learn to recognize these differences. We should also realize that we can never catch them all. But we can still build consensus if we persist in using our skills even when it seems to us that another has abandoned his.

Most of the sample dialogues in this book portray one of the characters as unaware of such skills. Yet the other character succeeded in steering him toward consensus. How much greater is your success when both try to use their skills, even though neither gets it all perfect.

Always use your own skills, and have compassion for those who don't. The PBS mini-series, "This Emotional Life," points out the contagious nature of happiness, citing studies indicating that, when we do something to make one person happy, he passes it on, and this extends to several degrees of separation, possibly affecting dozens of others. I believe the same is true of other types of feelings. When our skills help others feel heard and validated, calm and satisfied, we truly spread good will more widely than we might imagine.

In summary, educate yourself, practice often, and persist in using your skills, no matter what the other person does. You will find yourself getting more of what you need from others, while building bridges, not burning them.

APPENDIX A:
SAMPLE PREPARATION NOTES

Here is a fully fleshed-out example of *one way* Spencer might develop notes on his interests and Fran's interests in preparation for a meeting with her. The format is one I find helpful. Each time I ask another "Why?" I indent the answer so that I can observe the different threads or chains of answers. The format resembles an outline, except that the broadest interests are indented farthest. Those interests Spencer decides to concentrate on are underlined.

My Interests:
First Magic Question—Why do I want the following?

1. I want Fran to consider games instead of speaker—*Why?*
   - More young people attend fundraiser—*Why do I want that?*
     o Maximize attendance—*Why?*
       ▪ <u>Maximize fundraiser income</u>
       ▪ Maximize member involvement—*Why?*
         • <u>High energy level of congregation as a whole</u>
   - Reduce overhead for fundraiser—*Why?*
     o <u>Maximize fundraiser income</u>
2. I want to keep Fran happy—*Why?*
   - It's the kindly thing to do—*Why be kind?*
     o It's the right thing to do
     o It makes me <u>feel good</u>
     o As a representative of the church, I should model kindness—*Why?*
       ▪ So others will be kind—*Why?*
         • <u>World runs better</u>
   - Keep her actively involved in church leadership—*Why?*
     o She generally leads toward goals I like—*Why do I like those goals?*

- They promote overall health of congregation—*Why?*
  - Consistent with <u>our values</u>
  - Consistent with <u>our mission</u>
- Loss of her contributions could provoke a crisis—*Why?*
  - <u>Fran's large pledge</u>
  - Extensive experience on fundraiser
  - Direct or indirect influence on her friends' involvement and contributions—*Why?*
    - <u>Older founding members pledge and volunteer a lot</u>
    - <u>Overall energy of congregation</u>
- Reap benefits of her knowledge & skill—*Why?*
  - <u>Optimize current fundraiser</u>
  - Pass on knowledge and skill to others—*Why?*
    - <u>Back-ups</u>
    - <u>Smooth future transitions in leadership</u>
- Recently laid off, Fran benefits from the sense of identity and purpose—*Why do I want that?*
  - Pastoral care—*Why?*
    - <u>Duty</u>
    - <u>I care about Fran's welfare</u>
- So Fran does her best work on the fundraiser—*Why?*
  - So she will <u>feel good</u> about it
  - So her <u>enthusiasm</u> will spread to others
  - So fundraiser will be a success—*Why?*
    - <u>Maximize net fundraiser income</u>
- Fran may be typical of older members—*Why do I care about that?*
  - Also wish older members to keep attending fundraiser—*Why?*
    - <u>Maximize net fundraiser income</u>
    - <u>Maximize member involvement</u>

Second Magic Question—What else do I want?
3. Relief from overwork—*Why?*
   - Leisure time—*Why?*
     - <u>Enjoyment</u>
     - <u>Health & well-being</u>

- Better organized work life—*Why?*
  - More effective—*Why?*
    - Spend time <u>doing things only I can do</u>
    - Bring my <u>best gifts</u> to congregation
4. Everyone personally fulfilled in their work—*Why?*
   - Everyone bringing their best gifts—*Why?*
     - <u>Health & well-being of individuals</u>
     - Enthusiasm—*Why?*
       - <u>Health & well-being of congregation</u>

Third Magic Question—How do I want to feel?

5. <u>Calm</u>, that things are under control
6. <u>Objective</u> in my assessment of program
7. <u>Compassionate</u>
8. <u>Curious</u>

Fran's Interests

First Magic Question—Why might Fran want the following?

1. ? Keep running the fundraiser—*Why?*
   - Fun
   - Social contacts
   - ? Business contacts
   - Feels good to contribute
   - Outlet for her unique personal gifts—getting excellent speakers at low cost & organizing a major event with many facets—*Why does she care about unique gifts?*
     - <u>Values and utilizes what makes her who she is</u>
     - Validates <u>pride in herself and her accomplishments</u>
     - Encourages her to <u>work zealously and joyfully</u>
2. ? Have speaker/not games—*Why?*
   - Personally enjoys speakers (? and/or doesn't enjoy games)
   - ? Easier to do what she's done before
   - Wants to feel she's still with it (not a has been)—*Why?*
     - <u>Values who she is</u>
   - Enjoys engaging and working with prestigious speakers—*Why?*
     - ? Business reasons
     - Intellectual stimulation

      o   ? Expand circle of acquaintances

      o   ? Interacting with important people makes her feel important

- Switching to games seems to devalue her past work and <u>who she is</u> (gifts)

Second Magic Question—What else might Fran want?

3. ? New, different volunteer role—*Why?*

- ? Getting bored
- ? Learn something new

Third Magic Question—How might Fran want to feel?

4. Feel <u>valued</u> for who she is (gifts)

5. <u>Assured of a fulfilling role</u>

APPENDIX B:
SAMPLE RESPONSES TO "TRY-THIS" SEGMENTS

Most Try-This segments have more than one possible solution. In fact, some have an infinite number. *The following are examples only.*

For some segments, based on one's personal experience, no solutions are given.

Recognizing Resistance, p. 41

While I was checking out at the grocery store, the sacker plopped some apples into the bag so that they banged hard against the underlying counter. I took the apples out of the bag and observed that they were bruised. I gave the apples to the checker, told her I didn't want the bruised fruit, and asked her to subtract them from my tab.

The sacker said, "Well! It's not like I was playing baseball with them."

My rejection of the bruised fruit made the sacker wrong since he had caused the damage.

His reaction included elements of both rationalization and projection. He implied a rationale, albeit faulty, that anything less than playing ball with the apples was OK. While he did not project onto another person as having behaved worse than he did, he did project another scenario, playing ball with the apples, that made his dropping them seem trivial by comparison.

Asking Yourself Why, p. 59

Why do I want Mike to stop making snide remarks?

- It's unpleasant—*Why do I care about that?*
  - Detracts from the spiritual benefits I get from attending church
  - Puts me in a bad mood—*Why do I care about that?*
    - I don't enjoy the rest of the day
    - I pass the bad mood along to others

- It's frustrating because I don't know why he's picking on me—*Why frustrating?*
  - ○ I want to know what, if anything, I did to inspire these remarks—*Why?*
    - If I did something wrong, I would like to put it right
    - If I didn't do anything wrong, I can stop fretting about it
- I don't want others to hear Mike's remarks—*Why?*
  - ○ It could influence the way they think of me
  - ○ It could influence the way they think of Mike—*Why do I care about that?*
    - It could be heard as saying something negative and inaccurate about the character of this congregation as a whole
  - ○ People who hear the remarks could be visitors who would be put off our congregation

These answers inspired me with some interest talk I might use with Mike if I were in Laurel's shoes. One way: "I don't understand why you said that, but I'd like to. Can you help me understand?"

Another possibility: "If I've done something to offend or anger you, I'd like to know what it was so I can try to put it right. On the other hand, if it was a misunderstanding, I'd like to clear it up so we can both enjoy church more."

Appreciating Time Investment, p. 61

Answering my whys for the preceding Try-This Segment took about ten minutes. Because I knew they would appear in this book, I later spent some time polishing them. However, for purposes of talking to Mike, I felt I had done enough with the Why tool after ten minutes.

If I were Laurel, I would prefer to have spent those ten minutes asking and answering the questions. I now have some ideas about how to speak to Mike when I see him. Having a plan helps me calm down and stop stewing about it in the meanwhile. My calmness, in turn, will increase my chances of success with Mike.

Asking How I Want to Feel, p. 66

As Laurel, I feel:

- Upset
- Angry
- Made wrong

I want to feel:

- Calm
- Happy
- Right

Converting to Interest Talk, p. 76

1. Molly to Brandon: "My grandfather made the dollhouse, so it's precious to me and irreplaceable. I don't feel I can take any risks with it."
2. Brandon to Molly: "Can you help me think of a way for the children to do a program featuring a dollhouse?"
3. Mike to Laurel: "I'm concerned that our leadership doesn't take an even-handed approach to accidental damage."
4. Fran to Spencer: "I'd like to share my experience on why speakers work so well."

Asking about Feelings, p. 85

- Brandon might ask for an analogy, "Can you think of another time when you've felt the same way you now feel about lending the dollhouse?"
- Laurel could guess and verify, "You seem aggravated. Are you?"

Converting Statements to Open Questions, p. 165

1. How did you feel the last time you brought me flowers?
2. If you got a fridge for your room, where would you put it? What would you move to make room for it?
3. How can I get some help with cleaning up after coffee hour?
4. How can I come to feel I'm heard and fully understood?

Paraphrasing, p. 173

1. So, the dollhouse is irreplaceable. Have I got that right?
2. I'd like to be sure I'm following your train of thought. You feel there's a certain risk involved in experimenting with games. Correct?
3. The accident happened for the greater good. Correct?
4. You believe dismissing Kayla is contrary to our congregation's values. Is that what you mean?

Plan B, p. 206

Brandon's Interests:

1. Obtain a dollhouse—*Why?*
   - To use in children's program—*Why?*
     - o Program is already planned—*Why do I care about that?*
       - ▪ Re-planning will take time and trouble
       - ▪ <u>Do the program in time for the holiday season</u>
       - ▪ <u>Avoid disappointment</u>
2. Keep my promise to the children—*Why?*
   - Keep them happy—*Why?*
     - o Time with them will be more pleasant for all
   - Keep their parents happy—*Why?*
     - o So I can <u>continue as teacher</u>—*Why?*
       - ▪ <u>I enjoy it</u>
   - My <u>reputation and standing</u> in the congregation
3. Avoid trouble with Molly—*Why?*
   - <u>Pleasant experience at church</u>
4. <u>Feel competent</u>
5. <u>Feel reliable</u>
6. <u>Feel like I've got things under control</u>

Possible Walk-Away Alternatives, with a Plan B underlined:

- Have children build their own dollhouse
  - o Display this and tell about it as their holiday presentation for the adults, and reserve the program planned around the dollhouse for next year

- Use an enlarged picture of a dollhouse on the stage instead of a real dollhouse
    - On a backdrop for the scene
        - Children can make the backdrop
    - Supported on a table as a prop for the scene
    - Find a small picture for them to copy
- Enlist help re-planning the program
- <u>Organize an alternate holiday activity that doesn't take so much planning</u>
    - Field trip
    - <u>Social action</u> such as visiting a nursing home
    - Instead of program, <u>children can present a report</u> on the activity for the congregation
        - <u>With pictures</u> taken during the activity
    - Get the <u>children to help decide on and plan</u> activity to inspire enthusiasm and quell disappointment
    - <u>Talk up the activity</u> to inspire enthusiasm

Reframing Hostile Remarks, p. 250

- Spencer: I, too, want you to be in a place where you feel your talents and contributions are appreciated.
- Fran: I do have a head for business.
- Molly: Neither of us wants to be blamed for disappointing the children any more than we'd like facing each other if something happened to the dollhouse

If You'd Like More Help...

Anderson Persuasion Training offers the following services, customized for congregations and other non-profits:

Training Programs
- **Essential Consensus Skills**
  Master basic consensus-building skills through lively interactive exercises that make learning fun and make it stick.
- **Communication Styles—from Babel to Brilliance**
  Take the "You Can't Lose" quiz (with no wrong answers) and meet humorous characters to learn more about personality, cultural and gender differences and how they affect our communication.
- **Group Decision Making**
  Actually experience the process of building a sustainable group decision and practice skills for working through the various stages of that process. Expert demonstrations and real life success stories make knowledge come alive.
- **Consensus Plus**
  Our most comprehensive course includes Essential Consensus Skills, plus introductions to Communication Styles and Group Decision Making, as well as extra skills practice.

Custom Training
If none of our regular curricula precisely meet your needs, we'll design one that does.

Private Consulting and Coaching
Group training is fun and a cost-effective way to learn skills you can apply to many different situations. But what do you do if a situation arises before you can complete a course? What if your issues are unique and complex? What

if there are questions you can't ask in a group? Private one-on-one consulting or coaching is the answer.

Clergy and other leaders especially value the ability to address urgent matters in a timely manner, at their convenience, and with all the privacy and confidentiality they desire.

Meeting Facilitation

When the number attending a meeting is large, or the issues are complex or hotly contested, properly managing the meeting processes and communication quality requires full-time attention. Yet the group deserves its clergy's and lay leaders' full focus on the issues at hand. A neutral facilitator can help you reach more satisfying and sustainable decisions.

Conflict Management

An experienced dispute resolution professional, with special training in church mediations, Margaret Anderson can mediate resolution of disagreements before they grow. She can also design, teach, and help implement a customized protocol for resolving future disagreements with a minimum of outside assistance.

For more information, please visit www.persuasioncoach.com/nonprofit

ABOUT THE AUTHOR

Margaret Anderson brings to the table decades of actual use of the consensus skills she teaches, as well as many years of teaching her own curricula in consensus building and related communication skills.

A Harvard-trained negotiator, Margaret is also trained in general and church mediation. She designs and regularly teaches interpersonal persuasion courses for Rice University's Glasscock School of Continuing Studies. She has also designed and taught meeting facilitation for Glasscock and has lectured for the University of Houston and for Texas State University. Some of her classes have been taped and broadcast as part of the University of Houston's distance learning program.

Prior to launching her training and consulting business, Margaret gained experience in international and domestic business and was instrumental in resolving a number of business disputes. Her training and consulting clients include religious congregations, corporations, professional organizations, and individual leaders and professionals.

Margaret is a Unitarian Universalist residing in Houston, Texas.

Made in the USA
Charleston, SC
24 June 2011

Other Books by George Sanderlin

ST. JEROME AND THE BIBLE

FIRST AROUND THE WORLD:
A Journal of Magellan's Voyage

EASTWARD TO INDIA:
Vasco da Gama's Voyage

ACROSS THE OCEAN SEA:
A Journal of Columbus's Voyage

1776: *Journals of American Independence*